EUROPE:
a brief history

VOLUME TWO

W9-DHW-357

EUROPE:
a brief history

**Revised and Expanded
Second Edition**

VOLUME TWO

Renaissance to the Present

GEORGE A. ROTHROCK

University of Alberta

TOM B. JONES

University of Minnesota

 RAND MᶜNALLY COLLEGE PUBLISHING COMPANY / Chicago

RAND M^CNALLY HISTORY SERIES

Fred Harvey Harrington, *Advisory Editor*

Copyright © 1975, 1971 by Rand McNally College Publishing Company
All Rights Reserved
Printed in U.S.A.
Library of Congress Catalog Card Number 74–27273

Preface

Confronted with the rich mosaic of national societies that comprise the world of the twentieth century, universities now are offering studies of the histories of many peoples and areas. Despite this wholly commendable trend, however, European history and its antecedents always must occupy a special place for the western student, for it is the background and foundation of his own past. It can claim consideration from non-western peoples, too, for many of the ideas and attitudes deeply affecting non-western societies in the modern world are products of western culture, from Christianity to communism. Thus, the broader range of historical studies now available may be expected to complement and enrich rather than displace European history.

There are several texts on the market that present the course of European history or western civilization in one form or another, and it may be useful to suggest why the authors were moved to write yet another. In general, the nature of introductory history courses has changed rather markedly in the last decade or two and textbooks have failed to keep pace with the change; perhaps a fondness for traditional patterns is the occupational hazard of the historian. We are persuaded that the courses now being presented to beginning students are much more sophisticated than was the case not very long ago. We think this development stems partly from the fact that our students are more sophisticated today and partly from two innovations: discussion groups and supplementary readings. In the recent past, reliance upon insufficient staff time resulted in courses depending almost wholly upon lectures, for few graduate students were available to cope with quantities of junior students in small groups; and supplementary readings usually entailed a chapter here and there from books placed on reserve shelves in the library, a system unsatisfactory to all concerned but unavoidable because of the cost of books. In recent years, however, the expansion of graduate study and the growth of the paperback book market have made both discussion groups and supplemental book purchase almost standard for introductory courses.

Despite these changes, textbooks today are little different in concept from those written long ago. There are undeniable improvements, such as broadened perspectives, which include social and economic history, and interpretive rather than purely factual approaches; but almost without exception texts still assume that a student's whole course must be subsumed between two covers, and that the instructor will lecture and examine from the text. This assumption and the attempt to bring a more sophisticated distillation of recent scholarly erudition to the beginning student result in rather formidable bulk and cost; a discouraging consequence is that an instructor must limit severely the number of paperback supplements that he can ask a student to buy and use if he has any regard for the limitations of the student's time and money.

In an attempt to avoid these frustrations, from time to time some of us have tried to run a course without a text, using a list of paperbacks instead, but the results have not been very satisfactory. The student emerges with several bits of fragmentary expertise and weak perspectives. There seems still to be a consensus among instructors of history that a summary text is highly desirable, and it was with this idea that the present book was conceived.

Another consideration that has influenced the writing of this book is our impression that the role as well as the level of sophistication of introductory history courses has changed rather radically since World War II. It once was fair to assume that most liberal arts students would take several history courses and that few other students would take any. Both of these assumptions now are open to serious challenge. On the one hand, the growth of new approaches to the study of human experience—in sociology, psychology and anthropology, for example—has provided meaningful competition to historical study, and working within systems of "options," many students now take only one or two history courses and sometimes none. On the other hand, more and more students from other degree programs are turning up in history courses. Some rather haphazard surveys made in several universities during recent years, have shown that over half the enrollment in introductory history courses came from outside the arts faculty. In part this trend is attributable to the shift in emphasis from method to content study in education faculties; in part it reflects a developing pattern of increased study of humanities and social sciences on the part of science students. Whatever the reasons, many students will take only one history course, and they will come from a variety of areas of study, facts that should make us pause to reflect upon what the course should accomplish.

In one way historians are singularly fortunate. A teaching department must provide its students with both scope and depth, broad views and methodological precision. In contrast to the student in the sciences, who must learn methodology and laboratory technique before proceeding, the history student can begin his study with either aspect of his discipline, scope or depth, so long as he learns both synthesis and criticism in the course of his total program. Future history majors do not suffer by beginning with a broad view which they will fill in with more intensive studies of particular periods and societies, acquiring research methodology as they proceed.

An introductory history course can—and these days must—serve many roles. For the history major it must provide a broad overview that will allow him to make meaningful choices of the areas in which he wishes to concentrate and it must give perspective to his later studies. For other students in the humanities and social sciences it should offer a frame of reference that will add depth and understanding to studies of literature or economics or art. For the non-arts student it should provide a background that can aid his comprehension of his own world and at the same time can challenge his ethnocentrism by showing the validity of other societies based upon values quite different from his own. And for the undecided student, who might contemplate further historical studies, it should show how the historian works, his tools and methods and material, so the student may judge realistically whether this is the sort of endeavor that he would wish to pursue.

A course conscientiously structured achieves success in most of these roles, however, if sufficient flexibility can be maintained, and flexibility and variety are achieved best through the use of several different kinds of paperbacks. Paperback supplements can provide documentary collections to be analyzed, monographic studies to illustrate the complexity of the past, biographies to lend human perspective and "problems" books to show how interpretive theories vary. A prime goal of this book is to provide some perspectives on the European background in sufficiently small bulk and cost as to allow great flexibility in the assignment of paperbacks.

This approach offers several advantages. It should increase the utility of discussion groups, since assignments in the text will be sufficiently brief to permit the assignment of supplementary readings as the basis for group discussion. The use of several outside readings instead of just a few will make it possible to avoid overemphasizing the easy generalizations that are part of any text and to demonstrate how sharply historians disagree on the meaning of the past.

And such an approach should increase the instructor's freedom to determine the nature of the course, for the text presents only general perspectives, and areas of emphasis will depend upon the supplements selected. In Volume I, for instance, when a class comes to discuss Chapter 11, which deals with the period of the Viking depredations, it might go in any of a number of directions. Instructors who consider the Vikings interesting only for their effects upon the more southerly regions of Europe may find the material presented here quite enough about the raiders themselves, but others might wish to assign a supplemental book on the Vikings. Those whose major interests lie in the British Isles may find the sketch of developments on the European continent sufficient and want to add a book on Anglo-Saxon England. Someone else may feel that western Europe is overemphasized and add readings on Kiev Rus, while yet another instructor might prefer a book on the Carolingian Empire. By the same token, in connection with Chapter 15, which concerns itself with tensions and conflicts in medieval society, choices might range widely over heresy, economic development, the apogee of the papacy or the court of Frederick II.

Thus, a course can be shaped around those elements of our ancient and European past that particular instructors find most interesting or most important, and the student can be exposed to the viewpoints of several authors. We hope this book provides the basic background while allowing whatever national or period or topical emphasis an instructor may wish to use. To this end, we have included some rather brief "suggestions for further reading." To discover which of these selections are available in any given year reference should be made to the full listings of *Paperbacks in Print* (dealing with the offerings of American publishers) and *Paperbound Books in Print* (British publishers). Fuller critical lists also can be found in Lyon, Rowen and Hamerow, A *History of the Western World* (Rand McNally, 2nd ed., 1974).

GEORGE A. ROTHROCK
TOM B. JONES

Contents

Introduction   *xv*

1. The Renaissance   *1*

2. Religious Reaction and Reform   *15*

3. Habsburg Hegemony   *33*

4. The Scientific Revolution   *45*

5. The Rise of the National State   *60*

6. The Birth of the Balance of Power   *74*

7. Man, God, and Reason   *88*

8. A Harvest of Violence   *101*

9. Restoration and Reaction   *117*

10. Industrialization and its Consequences   *130*

11. The Nation Deified   *143*

12. The New Europe   *160*

13. Competition and Collapse   *176*

14. The Retreat of Liberal Democracy   *190*

15. The End of European Hegemony   *205*

Epilogue: Brave New Worlds   *220*

Suggestions for Further Reading   *231*

Index   *241*

Maps

Europe in the Mid-fifteenth Century *xxi*

Italy in the Late Fifteenth Century *xxii*

The Empire of Charles V 28

Established Churches and Religious Minorities about 1600 58

Europe in 1810 *115*

Europe in 1815 *116*

Unification of Italy (1815–1870) *156*

Unification of Germany (Bismarck's Empire, 1866–1871) *157*

Ethnic Groups of Austria-Hungary *158*

Alliances, 1871–1890 *159*

Alliances, 1890–1914 *159*

Africa in 1914 *174*

Balkan Peninsula to 1914 *175*

Central and Eastern Europe in 1947 *219*

Dissolution of European Colonial Empires
 after World War II *229-230*

Charts

The House of Habsburg   29

The House of Valois   29

The House of Tudor   30

The House of Stuart   30

The Austrian Habsburgs   31

The Spanish Habsburgs   31

The House of Bourbon   59

The House of Romanov   59

Rulers Since 1815   218

Introduction

The beginning student often is tempted to assume that history is a dead record of the past, and unfortunately a great deal of traditional instruction—emphasizing names and dates and battles and treaties—has tended to confirm that view. But new historical works continue to pour from the presses, and historians argue among themselves constantly. There is a dynamic, a process of continuous change in the understanding of the meaning of events.

No wholly satisfactory definition of history ever has been recorded. Descriptions have ranged all the way from Lord Acton's optimistic opinion that "history is the progress of liberty" to Henry Ford's observation that "history is bunk." Whatever else it might be, however, history is not a dead record but a living tradition, a collective memory offering some roots and a sense of continuity to men and women in any age, people who must confront the challenges and choices of their own times.

Several sorts of variables operate more or less constantly in historical scholarship. First, we continue to learn about what actually happened in the past, and new data often force changes of interpretation. For instance, the discovery and study of the famous Dead Sea Scrolls in the middle of this century have expanded greatly our understanding of life and customs and beliefs in early Palestine, with important consequences for Biblical history. The deciphering of an early Greek script some years ago added new perspectives to the study of early eastern Mediterranean societies.

Moreover, other sources of knowledge have been added to the traditional basis of written records. The excavations undertaken by archeologists and the resultant analysis of physical artifacts—tools, weapons, ornaments and buildings—give us information about preliterate peoples for whom we have no written records and reinforce our studies of other peoples for whom the written record is meager. Related to these studies is the development of technical tools of great advantage; for instance, the carbon 14 dating process and other newer but similar approaches can be immeasurably valuable in helping to confirm estimates of dates on ancient sites. By no means do we know all that we would like to know about what happened in the past, and new knowledge may confirm or may invalidate what we long have thought we knew.

But more significant to the dynamics of historical interpretation is the transformation of our understanding of what events mean, changes that occur for a great variety of reasons. One obvious influence upon historical interpretation has been the development, during the last hundred years, of new techniques of analysis. In the late nineteenth century, Marxism, with its emphasis upon economic causation, produced more than political controversy; it forced historians to a more minute and more sophisticated analysis of the impact of economic factors upon social and political development. The psychological studies of Sigmund Freud early in this century have added enormous depth to our understanding of the complexities of personality and character, so that today one finds little of the "heroes and villains" interpretation that runs through a great deal of older work. New scholarly dimensions have been added by the work of anthropologists in comparative cultures and of sociologists in statistical analysis. So changes in historical interpretations sometimes are motivated by perspectives developed by scholars in related fields of study.

Perhaps the greatest stimulus to changing historical interpretation is the fact that we continually ask different questions of our past. It is remarked sometimes that every generation rewrites history for itself, and the remark carries a subtle implication that because history can be used to prove anything, it really proves nothing. Yet without the cynicism, the observation is valid. To a certain extent every generation *must* rewrite history, because every generation seeks perspective upon its own problems and, therefore, wants to know different things about its past. Certainly circumstances never repeat themselves sufficiently for one to be able to find in the past a definitive prescription for the ills of the present; but categories of problems recur, and at the lowest level of commonality all problems in history are problems of men in conflict with their environment and/or their fellow men. In the process of attempting to choose between competing courses of action—say between concession and repression in the face of political violence—the experience of our predecessors may aid us in making decisions.

The easiest illustration of this phenomenon is a theme that became extremely prominent in historical writing during the last two generations, the multinational approach. It is no coincidence that many-volume integrated studies of European and world history were launched in three languages and in three different countries at roughly the same time—the years between the first and second world wars. Most histories written during the nineteenth and early twentieth centuries tended to have a distinctly national orientation, reflecting the great strength of nationalism in most European countries at that time. While conceding certain commonalities of a classical and Christian background and of modern alliances and trade, historians tended to stress the individuality and uniqueness of their own nations and to write histories of the development of national institutions and national cultures that helped to explain this individuality and uniqueness. Then the cataclysm of the Great War demonstrated irrefutably the close interconnection of the several national societies of Europe, showing clearly that whatever their differences of organization and aspiration their fates were interwoven inextricably. The need to understand better the development of Europe as a whole, the relationships among its various components, produced three new historical series: in France, *Peuples et Civilizations,* in Germany, *Propylaen Weltgeschichte,* and in the United States, *The Rise of Modern Europe.* All of these turned back to material often studied before, but they asked different questions of the material, and consequently they were able to offer new and different understandings of modern European history.

Another question that one must confront in any study of mankind, historical or contemporary, is the problem of free will and determinism. The problem is particularly acute when dealing with prominent or great men and women. Do individuals change the direction of their society and impose their will upon it, or are they but products of inexorable processes, puppets of economic, political and social forces? The ancients believed in the unreasoning vagaries of the gods and the fates, granting one man happiness and condemning another to tragedy quite haphazardly. Early Christians had to confront the problem too, for if they asserted the existence of an all-powerful God, how could they maintain that man had free will and, hence, the responsibility of choosing good instead of evil? (In general terms the rather complicated solution was to assert that God refrained from exercising his potentially all-determining power so as to leave mankind choice, offering the strength to choose goodness to all who sought it sincerely.) To the later medieval world the problem appeared in yet another guise. Astrology, a belief that the future could be read in the stars, was largely an import from the Near East and won wide support in Europe. The implications of determinism, and hence of lack of responsibility, were dangerous, but the church found a compromise, conceding that events in the physical world might be determined and their pattern revealed by God in the heavens, but asserting that man remained responsible for his moral and spiritual choices.

In more recent times determinist arguments have arisen most often from the development of the social sciences. A number of relatively recent approaches to the study of man have been quite disturbing to the supporters of free will. Psychology has demonstrated, for instance, that some human behavior is conditioned by sexual attitudes, parental relationships, and early experiences. And sociologists have been able to establish fairly accurate estimates of crowd behavior, suggesting that when a group of certain composition is confronted with a particular situation, given percentages will react in predictable ways. The proponents of free will reply, however, that psychology can predict only how an individual *is likely to* behave in certain categories of situations and cannot predict how a person *will* behave in every particular situation. By the same token, sociology can predict patterns of crowd behavior, but it cannot predict how particular individuals will behave.

Most modern students of human behavior tend to compromise between the extremes of absolute free will and complete determinism, asserting that man exercises free will within generally definable limits. In this context the social sciences may be regarded as helping to define the limits of the range of choice. Thus one might suggest that on the eve of the French Revolution the king could not have chosen to study and estimate popular discontent by holding a plebiscite and tabulating the results. This idea was wholly foreign to the structure of his society and the tools required to implement such an idea did not exist. On the other hand, he did have to make significant choices—absolute repression, some combination of resistance and concession, sweeping reform. Or one may observe that in struggles for equal rights, where prejudice operates against blacks or Asians or Jews or Catholics, only some men can choose consciously to reject their prejudices as a result of rational persuasion, while others cannot make that choice because years of conditioning or deep-rooted psychological compulsions persuade them unshakably that the objects of their prejudice are inferior or evil or whatever.

Among these many problems and pitfalls the historian must walk cautiously. Probably it is impossible to avoid bias and preconception entirely, but we must at least try to be aware of them. Probably there will always be exaggerated enthusiasm for "new insights" and "revisionist" interpretation, but we must not allow a disdain for fads to render historical methodology inflexible. In any case, among so many variables and challenges history cannot be a "dead record."

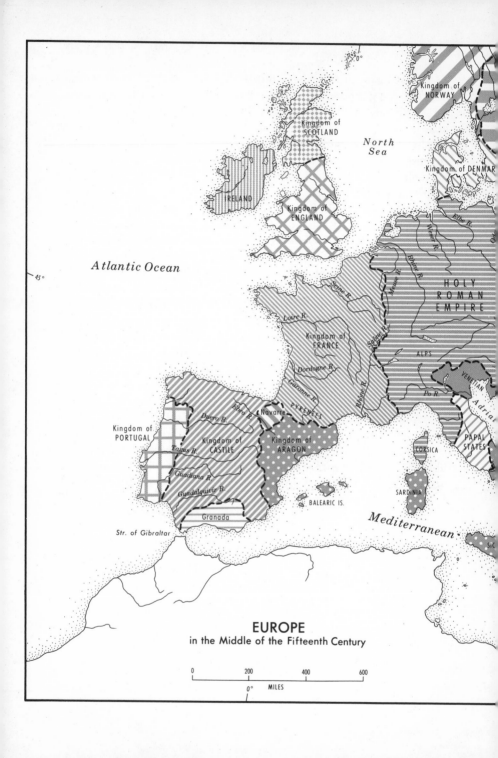

EUROPE
in the Middle of the Fifteenth Century

| 0 | 200 | 400 | 600 |

MILES

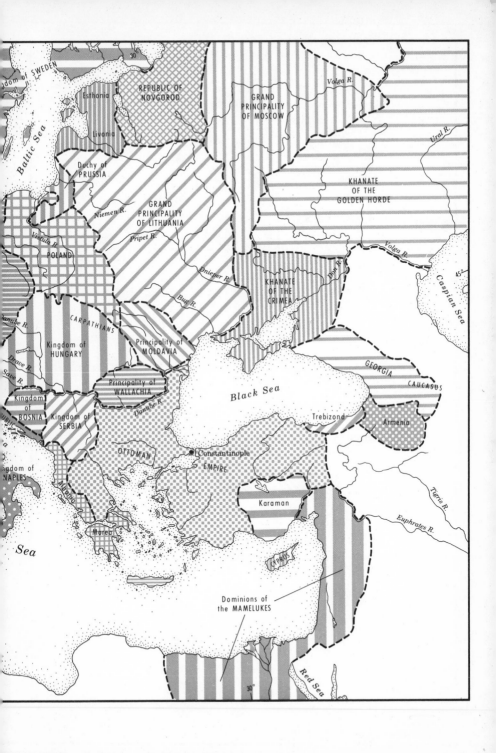

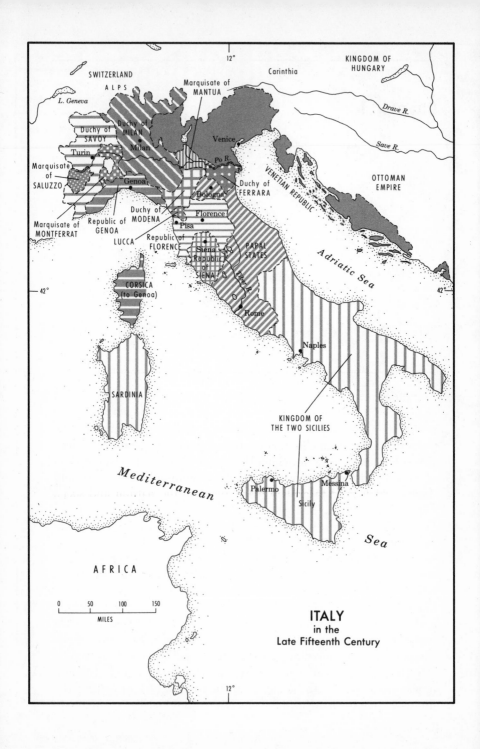

ITALY
in the
Late Fifteenth Century

Chapter 1

The Renaissance

Any survey of the development of Europe must take note of cultural changes, and it should be noted, too, that to a large extent the nature of the cultural product of any given period is determined by the interests of the social elite that controls the society's resources. Thus, Greco-Roman culture, in which the social elite was a leisured class of worldly aristocrats, consisted largely of philosophy, literature, and drama which tried to explain man's place in the natural and social world and of plastic arts which idealized the human form and embellished daily life; this culture disintegrated before the impact of economic decline, civil war and barbarian invasions.

The society that emerged after the decline of Rome had to struggle at first for bare subsistence, and the new elite consisted largely of illiterate soldiers. Artistic product seems to have been limited to a few articles of daily life, such as ornaments for clothing and tableware of precious metals, and to finely worked hafts for weapons and accouterments for horses; items of this sort, which survive today as museum pieces, suggest highly skilled craftsmanship, but the scope of such artistry was very limited, and of course it was accomplished by almost no literary product in a primarily illiterate society. Some of the more Romanized Germanic kings supported a weak revival of Latin pagan literature, but with few exceptions it was the church that could provide literate and reflective individuals and only the church that had the resources and willingness to support them. Thus, it is not surprising that Europe's outstanding writers between about A.D. 400 and A.D. 800 were two bishops and a monk: St. Augustine (*Confessions* and *The City of God*), Gregory of Tours (*The History of the Franks*) and Bede (*The Ecclesiastical History of the English People*). This sort of cultural development reached a peak in the Carolingian renaissance and then suffered another decline under the impact of the Magyar and Viking invasions.

During the rapid development of medieval society between the eleventh and thirteenth centuries, a period that produced the monastic and cathedral schools and then the universities, there was a corresponding cultural revival, but again it was largely in the service of the church. One must not ignore the impressive military architecture of medieval castles, the beautifully carved furniture and finely woven tapestry that embellished later medieval households or the intricately developed epics and poems recited and sung for the entertainment of the nobility; but the finest products of medieval culture were the great cathedrals with their rich decoration and the scholastic works of theology and Christian philosophy, all produced under the patronage of the church. Despite contact with highly sophisticated Islamic thought and the recovery of important parts of the classical heritage, medieval culture subsumed all to the Christian interests of its patrons. Thus, though the idea may be repugnant to modern artists and intellectuals, the direction of European cultural development depended upon the interests of the elite that commanded sufficient wealth to support that culture; in medieval Europe the elite meant primarily churchmen, though noble patronage produced a minor counterpoint to the dominant religious culture.

While the Hundred Years War was being fought in western Europe, a cultural revolution was developing in Italy that was to inspire a whole series of transformations of European society. This movement, called the Italian renaissance, began in the fourteenth century, and in the fifteenth century it swept through northern and central Italy. The culture that grew out of the Renaissance differed from medieval culture in that its chief interests were in political and social life, with stress upon the human individual, rather than in religion and eternity with stress upon God. This secular emphasis reflected a new sort of patronage, town governments and wealthy businessmen instead of the church and wealthy ecclesiastics.

Ever since they had attained virtual independence under the Hohenstaufen emperors in the twelfth and thirteenth centuries, the towns of northern and north central Italy had been developing rapidly, both economically and politically, and rivalries among them were fierce. One of the most prominent was Florence, in Tuscany; its industry and commerce grew so successfully that in the mid-thirteenth century it reestablished gold coinage, the florin, and its money quickly was accepted all over Europe. Florence fought wars with its neighbors, especially Pisa and Siena, and its internal politics hardly were less violent, with twenty-one guilds struggling for control of the city government, but despite these vicissitudes the city continued to increase in wealth and strength, and in the fourteenth century it became the cradle of the Italian renaissance.

The Renaissance appeared first as a new human element within the general Christian context of medieval Italian culture. This new interest showed itself in two ways, a greater concern with man and the world he lived in and a growth of a literature in the vernacular, the language of the people, instead of Latin. In the arts it appeared in the form of more realism, especially in the treatment of human subjects. In the birth of this new literature and painting, two Florentines were prominent, Dante (1265–1321) and Giotto (1276–1337).

Dante worked with a Christian subject, but he treated his material in ways that differed from his predecessors. His *Divine Comedy*, still one of the great works of European literature, illustrates well the tentative beginnings of Italian humanism. Presented as a journey through Hell, Purgatory and Paradise, the *Divine Comedy* is fundamentally a synthesis of medieval Christian thought, but in a series of imaginary conversations with and about great historical figures, Dante makes it clear that his judgments are based less on what people believed in hair-splitting theological arguments than on how they behaved toward their fellow man and what they contributed to humanity. Thus, though religious in content, its goals were ethical rather than theological, and the author showed great sympathy for pre-Christian pagans who had contributed humane philosophical ideas to the world. Finally, Dante composed his work, in verse, in the Tuscan vernacular rather than in Latin, making it accessible to educated laymen. In summation, through its concern with human behavior, its sympathetic interest in classical authors and its appeal to a lay audience, the *Divine Comedy* showed in primitive form the most important of the humanist elements that were to dominate early renaissance literature.

In painting Giotto illustrated the same sort of early humanist tendencies shown by Dante in literature. Probably his most famous work is the series of allegorical panels honoring St. Francis, which he painted in the late thirteenth century for the church of the Franciscan Order at Assisi. Again the theme was totally Christian, the life of a simple and pious saint, but Giotto's treatment of it made his work a new departure in painting. Early Christians had turned away from Greco-Roman realism in art in favor of a slightly abstract primitivism which allowed the treatment of spiritual subjects without the appearance of glorification of the flesh; this style had continued to dominate medieval Christian art, offering little differentiation of human figures, so individuals had come to be identified by spiritual symbols associated with them—keys for St. Peter (the keeper of the keys), a gridiron for St. Lawrence and arrow wounds for St. Sebastian (the instruments of their martyrdoms), etc. By contrast, Giotto painted St. Francis as a real person and portrayed incidents in his life which illustrated his piety, his humility and his simple faith; he made his subject a man with whom anyone could identify and explained his life pictorially so that all could understand. Then, in the first years of the fourteenth century, he gave even fuller scope to his new humanist treatment in a beautiful series of frescoes he painted for the arena chapel in Padua, which turned around scenes from the life of Christ.

Another development in early fourteenth-century Florence that was to prove important to the development of the Renaissance was the beginning of large-scale public works. To a considerable extent this reflected another aspect of the competition among Italian towns; the city fathers determined to beautify Florence beyond anything that neighboring towns could rival, and for a first project they decided to build a new cathedral. Again the theme was Christian, but the treatment was new. That the cathedral of Florence would be an episcopal center and a house of worship were secondary considerations; primarily it was to be a monument to the wealth and glory of the city. Moreover, the construction of the cathedral and its ancillary structures, a bell tower and a baptistry, lasted all through the fourteenth century and well into the fifteenth century and provided commissions for many important Renaissance artists.

The enthusiastic reception of vernacular literature and artistic realism and the undertaking of public works all reflected the growth of the Florentine bourgeoisie, worldly men of wealth who had leisure and wished to fill it with interesting and beautiful things. They were Christians, but they were businessmen, not churchmen, and they did not find theological debates or edifying accounts of saints either entertaining or interesting. They were building large comfortable houses, and medieval Christian art did not provide the warmth, the gaiety or the sense of luxury that they sought in the decoration of their new homes. Urban politics, business rivalries and warfare with other towns posed problems for which they found no guides in medieval literature. And their wealth, leisure and local power gave them an enjoyment of daily life for which there was little justification in medieval tradition. This class comprised potential patrons of enormous resources, and scholars and artists soon began producing for it in quantity.

Classical authors had concerned themselves with many of the interests reborn in the Italian cities, and through the fourteenth and fifteenth centuries masses of manuscripts—mostly Roman and some Greek—were unearthed in old libraries, recopied and circulated widely. Here were poems and essays extolling the intrinsic value of man and the joy of life, treatises expounding the purposes and methods of government, speeches and letters on the subject of patriotism, scandalous biographies and racy stories simply for entertainment, a whole literature concerned with man and his place in the world. In addition, the physical remains of classical civilization—triumphal arches, amphitheaters, aqueducts, temples, villas and public baths—provided models of monumental construction for city councils seeking to embellish their towns and for wealthy merchants and princes desirous of building impressive palaces; the larger remains were excavated, measured and studied, while smaller artifacts such as statuary were sought eagerly for private collections.

So vast and exciting was the human content of the classical heritage, that soon *studia humanitatis* came to refer to the study and imitation of classical culture, and both the literary and the artistic remains of classical civilization soon were being emulated.

A generation after Dante and Giotto, Florence produced two more eminent writers important to the development of the Renaissance, Petrarch (1304–1374) and Boccaccio (1313–1375). The revival of interest in Roman literature led to the study of classical Latin, which differed considerably from the Latin commonly used in the fourteenth century, and Petrarch became famous as an outstanding classical Latinist. He also wrote beautiful lyric poetry which contributed to the growing appreciation of man and nature. His friend Boccaccio was a many-faceted scholar and writer, one of the first Italians to read ancient Greek fluently, a collector of classical manuscripts, a lecturer on Dante and the author of the first prose work in Italian, the *Decameron*. In the *Decameron* Boccaccio took as his setting a group of wealthy young men and women who had shut themselves away in a country house to escape the Black Death which was raging in Florence; to pass the time they told one another stories, a schema which allowed the author scope for the use of different styles and for the presentation of themes ranging from social criticism to sexual satire. Not only does the gentle humor of the *Decameron* still make delightful reading, but subsequently its literary device of isolating a group of people and having them recount stories was used frequently; probably the most famous example is the work of Boccaccio's near contemporary, Geoffrey Chaucer, whose *Canterbury Tales* is one of the seminal works in English literature, but the device is timeless and still is used.

During the fifteenth and early sixteenth centuries the Italian renaissance developed rapidly, and Florence remained its center. Under the patronage of the Medici family, especially Cosimo and Lorenzo the Magnificent, the city produced distinguished artists in every field: the painters Fra Angelico and Botticelli, the architects Brunelleschi and Alberti, the sculptors Ghiberti and Donatello, and those two universal artists who defy categories, Leonardo da Vinci and Michelangelo. Humanist scholarship also flourished as Cosimo di Medici founded the Library of San Marco, the Medici

Library and the Platonic Academy for Greek studies, and in the early sixteenth century Florence produced the brilliant and controversial historian and political theorist, Machiavelli.

In the middle of the fifteenth century the Renaissance spread to Rome, Milan and several other Italian cities. Pope Nicolas V (1447–1455) had been a librarian for Cosimo di Medici before his election to the papal throne, and as pope he continued his interest in humanism and the collection of manuscripts by founding the Vatican Library and supporting scholars and artists. His immediate successor opposed the new culture; but most of the late fifteenth century popes supported the Renaissance with varying degrees of enthusiasm. In the early sixteenth century popes of the Borgia, della Rovere and Medici families made the papacy famous for artistic patronage, political intrigue and immorality at the price of religious leadership. In Milan the Renaissance was associated chiefly with the rule of the Sforza family and reached its peak under the patronage of Ludovico "the Moor" (1479–1500). The Sforzas undertook large public works in the city, bringing in Florentine architects and painters, including Leonardo da Vinci, until Milan was established as a cultural center in its own right. Though the Milanese renaissance was short-lived, the city was beautified greatly. By contrast, Venice with her strong eastern orientation toward Constantinople, long remained outside the mainstream of the Renaissance, and older Byzantine and Gothic influences continued dominant. Ironically, the high quality of Venice's printing industry from the late fifteenth century onwards resulted in much of the Renaissance literature of other Italian cities being transmitted through the Venetian presses, but except for the painting of the Bellini family in the second half of the fifteenth century, there was little sign of a Venetian renaissance until after 1500. Then the city suddenly exploded into prominence by producing two of Italy's best Renaissance painters, Tintoretto and Titian.

In the course of the fifteenth and early sixteenth centuries the Italian renaissance developed a philosophical basis that moved far beyond the simple humanism of its early writers and artists. Christian thematic material was used less and less, and admiration of the classical Greeks and Romans grew into adulation, so that the Renaissance became a pagan cultural movement. The Italians conceived a new ideal to replace the medieval Christian, the *uomo universale*, the universal man who did everything well with no apparent effort. This Renaissance individualism was only for the elite, of course, for it assumed wealth and leisure, but it became the goal of many wealthy fifteenth and sixteenth century Italians. They not only patronized artists and scholars but also painted and composed Latin songs and verses themselves, designed new palaces and public buildings, laid out gardens and developed elegant and witty society. This adulation of man was reflected in the art works of the period. Portraiture became a major subject in painting as merchants and princes sought a secular immortality; palaces, city halls and gardens replaced cathedrals as the chief subjects of architects; and authors concerned themselves primarily with man and his works as exemplified in Castiglione's *Book of the Courtier* (a handbook of elegant behavior in everything from table manners to seductions), Guicciardini's *History of Italy* and Ariosto's epic poetry.

Perhaps the work that best sums up the purely secular, pragmatic and somewhat cynical intellectual climate of Italy toward the end of the Renaissance, however, is *The Prince*, published in 1514 by Niccolo Machiavelli. Not only was this book one of the last great literary works of the Italian renaissance, it was also one of the most controversial books ever written and may be considered the first step in the establishment of political science as an empirical study rather than as an exercise in moral philosophy. Almost without exception, classical and medieval writers on government had concerned themselves with political theory, reflecting upon the goals that government should seek to attain, the forms of political organization that would assure the fullest social development, the governing apparatus that best would provide justice, or the underlying principles that could legitimatize some men's power over others. Machiavelli cast all of this aside. He had been involved personally in the political life of Florence, and when his party was ousted he was forced to retire to a country house, where he passed his time reflecting upon and writing about politics. All around him he saw strong states swallowing weaker ones, *condottiere* captains of mercenary bands of soldiers seizing control of states they were supposed to serve, political rivals using torture and assassination to defeat each other. He had seen Caesar Borgia, a pope's son, subject most of central Italy to papal rule, using every means no matter how unscrupulous. Thus, the major influence upon Machiavelli's thought was experience of turbulent Renaissance politics. Abandoning moral judgments and philosophical commitments, he attempted in *The Prince* to present a rational and dispassionate analysis of the political process that he had observed. It was largely this amoral position that his critics found scandalous.

In Machiavelli's analysis, politics is the means whereby some men acquire and attempt to retain authority over others. Thus, it has no goal, no moral purpose; it is a mechanism for the exercise of power. Starting from such a postulate, Machiavelli necessarily concluded that the important questions for anyone interested in politics are: what succeeds? what fails? The observations he presented in trying to answer these questions revealed a view of man and society that moralists found as shocking as his basic amorality. He stated that a prince could sustain himself and command respect through fear; if laws were enforced harshly and consistently most people would prefer to avoid trouble and would render obedience. He stated that a prince ought not to be impeded by the moral precepts of religion or philosophy where his self-interest was concerned; if it were advantageous to break his word or violate a treaty, he ought to do so. Implicitly he justified the use of bribery, torture and assassination if they would strengthen a prince against his enemies. Perhaps the most cynical aspect of *The Prince* is the author's judgment of public opinion: however moral and just a ruler might be, he observed, if he be overthrown he soon will be despised and forgotten by the public; but a ruler who succeeds in maintaining himself securely, even if cruel and unjust, will be acclaimed, and his worst deeds will be forgiven, for the public admires nothing so much as success and will judge that the ends have justified the means.

About the beginning of the sixteenth century the influence of the Renaissance began to spread significantly, northward to France and England and westward to Spain, largely as a result of foreign military involvement in Italy. There were five major states in the peninsula at this time: Milan, Venice, Florence, the Papal States, and the kingdom of Naples; they competed viciously with one another in a web of shifting alliances, and at the end of the fifteenth century they began invoking foreign aid. Both the French and the Spanish crowns had some claims in Italy, and the Holy Roman Emperor still possessed at least theoretical rights, so there was no lack of pretext for intervention. The French came first, in 1494, at the invitation of the Sforza ruler of Milan, and by 1500 German and Spanish forces were involved. For the next three and a half centuries Italy was to be a battleground for Europe's great powers, but the most important immediate effects were to expose large numbers of influential foreigners to the culture of the Renaissance and then, through the devastation consequent upon the wars, largely to put an end to the growth of that culture in Italy.

The cultural ferment of the Renaissance already had had some effect outside Italy even before 1500, chiefly in the field of scholarship. News of the study of ancient languages and the recovery of classical manuscripts had attracted students from other countries to northern Italy, and by the middle of the fifteenth century they were there in some numbers. Through their efforts, northern scholars developed a considerable acquaintance with the classics, and studies in Latin, Greek and Hebrew were established firmly, but prior to the great invasions of Italy the impact of the Renaissance upon the north was limited almost wholly to literary activity carried on in scholarly circles. The invasions exposed princes and wealthy noblemen to the opulence of Italian art and architecture and to the elegance of Italian social life, opening the way for the expansion of the Renaissance on a much broader basis.

As it spread outside Italy, Renaissance culture changed considerably, adapting to very different social and political circumstances. In France, Spain and England, for instance, the existence of strong royal governments tended to make Renaissance artists depend primarily upon monarchical patronage, and the courts of the kings became the focal points of the new culture. Moreover, Gothic traditions in art and architecture were much stronger beyond the Alps than in Italy, where the Gothic style never had displaced Byzantine and Romanesque forms; one result was that Renaissance styles were used at first simply as decorative motifs in the north, producing unlikely combinations of columned porticoes, arcaded facades and sweeping staircases on basically Gothic buildings.

Perhaps the most notable adaptation consequent upon the expansion of the Renaissance was the transformation of humanist thought. Lacking the strong pagan backgrounds of Italy, French and English intellectuals tended to be more religious than their Italian counterparts, and the universities with which they often were associated generally were more conservative, more closely linked with church and monarchy. Consequently, while they adopted with enthusiasm the Italian passion for collecting old manuscripts and studying ancient languages, they balanced classical interests with studies of early Christian sources; and while they concerned themselves with man in his world, it was primarily Christian man in a Christian world that they considered. In Spain seven hundred years of war against the Moslems had produced a fervent Christianity that had no tolerance for the pagan elements of Italian humanism, and in consequence the Renaissance was more influential in changing artistic styles than in effecting any basic intellectual re-orientations. Thus, though northern and western Renaissance writers produced secular and satirical literature, as exemplified by the works of Shakespeare, Rabelais and Cervantes, the intellectual climate generally remained less frankly pagan, and Christianity retained a far more important role in scholarly endeavor.

The German experience of the early sixteenth century differed so greatly from that of the rest of Europe that there is a real question whether there are grounds to justify speaking of a German renaissance, though on a scholarly level the impact of humanism was felt strongly. About the middle of the fifteenth century the new learning, particularly ancient languages, began to take root in the universities, largely through the influence of German scholars who had studied in Italy, and these studies evoked enough enthusiasm that some of the German princes founded new universities. In the sixteenth century some Italian art was imported and even copied to a limited extent. But the new learning and the new styles failed to arouse deep interest throughout German society, and the best artists and most able scholars of the Holy Roman Empire tended to come from Flanders, the Netherlands and the Rhineland, where the flourishing culture of the late medieval Burgundian court had established a solid foundation. German intellectual interests remained more religiously oriented than those of either Italy or other northern areas.

No doubt the deep-rooted pietism for which German Christianity was known had some effect; and perhaps some influence may be attributed to the fact that the beginnings of German civilization east of the Rhine went back to Christian missionary work rather than to Roman experience, with the result that a search for origins led through the medieval church to early Christianity rather than through a Roman conquest to classical culture. In any case, though German humanist scholars were no less able or less learned than the Italians, their interests were very different and their religious commitments far more profound, while Renaissance influence upon German art and architecture remained slight until the seventeenth century, when it penetrated Germany from France.

Outside of Italy the Renaissance made its strongest impact in France. Direct contact between France and Italy was frequent and profound for a quarter of a century after the first Italian expedition of Charles VIII in the mid-1490s, and it continued on a reduced scale throughout the sixteenth century. Generous patronage by Kings Francis I (1515–1547) and Henry II (1547–1559) established Renaissance artistic influence firmly, first as decoration added to older French forms and then as a vigorous new French style, exemplified by the sixteenth century portions of the Louvre in Paris and by the splendid chateaux of the Loire Valley. Secular humanism found expression in the works of Rabelais, Ronsard and Montaigne, while distinguished religious scholarship developed in a Paris group, of which the most famous members were Lefebvre d'Etaples and John Calvin.

In sum, the Renaissance, which was born in and first flourished in Italy, stimulated a comparable movement in France and to a lesser degree in Spain and England, and while it may be debated whether one can speak of a German renaissance, there is no doubt that there were important specific influences in Germany. Everywhere it spread, the movement released great creative energies, resulting in impressive scholarly achievements and vigorous artistic development which changed profoundly both the content and the style of European culture. The classical and early Christian heritage of Europe was reestablished. Princely residences were transformed from gloomy uncomfortable fortresses into graceful pleasure houses. The entourages of kings developed from bands of crude soldiers into royal courts with highly formalized etiquette, peopled with courtiers who sought to practice elegance and wit.

The creative impulse of the Renaissance continued much modified on into the seventeenth century, when far-reaching religious and political developments demanded symbolic expression. One result of the Reformation was to accentuate the dramatic elements of Christian conceptions of the power of God and of the struggle between good and evil, while at the same time the kings of France developed power undreamed of by their predecessors and indulged in policies that threw all of Europe into turmoil. In an attempt to give expression to these dramatic new developments, Europe's architects and artists combined elements of Renaissance styles in new ways, abandoning earlier commitments to static forms and introducing instead a new plasticity and dynamic line. Drawing upon tentative experiments of Palladio and Michelangelo in mid-sixteenth century Italy, they began designing buildings so that the play of light and shadow upon colonnades and windows would give a sense of movement, and they began incorporating spatial masses in their designs, tying courtyards and gardens to facades by paths and balustrades. Sculptors moved away from figures in repose to subjects in tension, caught in the midst of action, and painters oriented entire canvasses around a single dramatic focal point. The new style, which was called baroque, was well adapted to express the evangelical vigor of seventeenth century Christianity and the aggressive ambition of seventeenth century monarchy, and it flourished, further illustrating the impressive adaptability of the artistic creativity unleashed by the Renaissance.

The considerable cultural development consequent upon the Renaissance ought not to be allowed to obscure the movement's negative aspects, however, for a number of adverse effects upon European society can be identified. The Renaissance certainly was not consciously progressive, and there were some humanists who damned the printing press because they feared it would cheapen knowledge and open the scholar's preserve to a large literate public. The enthusiasm for the classics led to an attempt to purify Latin by reestablishing the language of Cicero and Livy, deleting all the changes of vocabulary and grammar that had developed through fifteen hundred years; the result was that Latin was destroyed as a vibrant living tongue and became a dead language, more and more restricted to the formalities of legal and governmental usage as time passed, and Europe slowly lost the linguistic unity that had characterized its cultural development since the Roman Empire. The adulation of classical authors also had an adverse effect upon natural studies. While the medieval intellectual climate was not conducive to any considerable scientific advances, there had been some progress in the later Middle Ages, exemplified most notably by Friar Roger Bacon, but the great admiration of Greek scientific writers, such as Aristotle and Ptolemy, largely destroyed confidence in modern data and set European science back to the level of the ancient Greeks; for instance, European maps continued for years to show features derived from Ptolemy despite the fact that modern voyages showed some of them to be erroneous, and medical schools continued to teach Greek anatomy although it was contradicted by modern dissections.

Finally, it seems likely that the amorality, the ostentatious luxury and the hostility to religion that were intrinsic to so much of Renaissance culture aggravated the social and political problems that already were assuming serious proportions in fifteenth and sixteenth century Europe, further alienating an elite that accepted these values from a population still largely committed to the medieval ideals of piety, charity and stability. In its negative as well as its positive influences, the Renaissance had far-reaching effects upon Europe.

Chapter 2

Religious Reaction and Reform

The medieval church had experienced many movements of reform, and in fact its history almost could be written in terms of cycles of deformation and reformation. Anticlericalism, heresy and schism had been confronted many times, and national churches were clearly identifiable within the broad framework of medieval European Catholicism. Thus, the real problem in attempting an estimate of the reformation of the sixteenth century is to try to determine what was different in the mixture of problems so that the church was unable to contain the movement within itself.

The woeful condition of the early sixteenth century church inspired frequent criticism of two sorts. There were those who sought to reform and purify the church by improving those who served it, accepting its doctrines and structure; and there were those who believed that not only the clergy but also the doctrine of the church had become corrupt and had to be reformed. The two positions were exemplified best by Erasmus and Luther.

Erasmus has been accused of lacking courage, by comparison with Luther, but such a judgment is unfair, for his purposes were different. As a Christian humanist he was scandalized by the condition of the clergy and wrote biting satires designed to shame the corrupt and provoke a reform of morals, but he never doubted the fundamental truth of the church's doctrines. Confident that God's love and mercy, aided by the sacraments, would bring salvation, his concern was with the Christian life—how laymen might live in greater love and charity and clerics might fulfil their offices in God's church more worthily. If Erasmus' criticisms contributed to Luther's movement, the contribution certainly was inadvertent; he never would have agreed that the corruption of men justified the destruction of the unity of God's church.

By contrast Luther's major concerns were very different. While he certainly shared the horror of clerical abuses and was deeply concerned that the clergy should fulfil a pastoral role in guiding their flocks to a better Christian life, these things were for him secondary considerations. What mattered above all else, the heart and essential core of Christianity, was the fulfilment of Christ's promise of salvation, and it was in this fundamental matter that Luther lost confidence in the church. Like many Christians he found several grounds on which to base criticism, but his intransigence, his refusal of all compromise, is explicable only on the issue of salvation. To imagine that Luther was willing to overturn the traditional church because of the human frailties of some of its clergy is to underestimate him. Rather, he became convinced that the church's teachings regarding the means to salvation were wrong and that, in consequence, many laymen risked damnation. As a responsible priest and theologian he could not compromise on that issue.

Probably too much has been made of the matter of indulgences, but because they are widely supposed to have been at the root of Luther's protest, they must be considered. In fact, they were more a catalyst than a cause. The concept of indulgences is rooted in rather complex doctrines developed by medieval theologians, doctrines which made a clear distinction between the guilt of sin and the penalties of sin. No one ever claimed that any man could forgive sin, wipe away its guilt, for that power belonged only to God, Who presumably would grant forgiveness to those who prayed for it with sincerity and true repentence. God's forgiveness would assure ultimate salvation, but only after the penalties had been paid. Since most men were assumed to accumulate more penalties than could be expiated by good works during a lifetime, the theologians posited the existence of purgatory, a condition between the heaven of the saved and the hell of the damned. In purgatory the soul continued its expiation through suffering, until the penalties had been fulfilled and it was released to heaven. On the basis of the power of the keys, the power of loosing and binding, the pope was asserted to have control over these penalties for sin in the same way that modern civil authorities can grant pardons, which do not eradicate the guilt of an act but do excuse the offender from the fulfilment of the usual penalties. An indulgence was this alleviation of penalties, granted for good cause.

In the medieval period indulgences first were granted for extraordinary personal effort, such as going crusading, which involved enormous cost and risk in the service of the faith. Then they were granted for money payments so that those who were old or crippled could participate in the good work and the benefits of it even if they could not serve personally. Given the financial strains of the early sixteenth century and the corruption of the clergy, probably it was inevitable that indulgences were exploited as a source of revenue, sold at varying prices for different periods of alleviated penalties. The papal agents who handled transactions in indulgences often added poor taste to what was already poor practice and became, in effect, hucksters. One of the worst of these was the monk Tetzel, who was operating in Germany in the early sixteenth century. An evangelistic preacher who painted horrifying word pictures of the torments of purgatory, Tetzel was notably successful as a salesman, but his crass merchandizing of ecclesiastical benefits offended many, including Luther, to whom the whole process was simply blatant extortion and financial exploitation of the faith of simple Christians. It was the indulgence issue that persuaded Luther to pose his first overt challenge to papal authority, but the challenge was the result of years of patient reflection and meditation upon the problem of salvation.

In essence Luther had become convinced that salvation was attainable only through faith, through a personal commitment of love and belief in man's worthlessness and God's mercy. Holding this conviction he could not believe in the efficacy of priests or saints as intermediaries between the individual and God, he could not accept the role of the sacraments as steps to salvation, and he could not accept the formalized role of papal powers in distributing God's mercies to men. In many ways Luther was the revivalist voice of medieval pietism hurled against worldliness and formality, the voice of St. Bernard reborn, protesting both the pagan corruption of the clergy and the genial tolerance of Erasmus' Christian humanism. If in any way Luther represented the Renaissance spirit in religion as often is asserted, it was in the individualism of his belief, his conviction that a man must stand naked and alone before his God, without intermediaries and with nothing but his faith to justify him.

Moved to action by Tetzel's scandalous behavior, Luther offered his first overt challenge in October of 1517 by posting his Ninety-five Theses on the doors of the church in Wittenburg, where he was professor of theology. It was a very modest revolt; the theses were simply theological positions relative to indulgences which he wished to debate, and traditionally the churches were the centers of their towns and their doors the bulletin boards. The posting of the theses was simply an attempt to stimulate interest among other theologians in the hope that ripples would spread with beneficial effect. The rapid and explosive effects of the theses must have astonished their author.

The church's reaction to Luther's challenge followed normal practice, for he was simply another dissenting priest. In 1518 he was summoned before Cardinal Cajetan, the papal legate in Germany, and ordered to retract his statements, but he refused. Then in 1519 a theologian of some eminence, Dr. Eck, undertook to debate with him, and almost immediately the situation took a more serious turn. An experienced debater, Eck maneuvered Luther into extremist positions—denial of the divine right of the papacy, assertion of the supremacy of Scripture, doubt of the authority of councils and defense of some Hussite propositions that had been condemned as heresy. Luther's excommunication followed naturally, in 1520, and in an act of defiance he publicly burned the papal document of excommunication (called a bull from the Latin *bulla,* for the great seal on it). Since heresy was considered a serious offense by civil as well as religious authorities, carrying the penalty of outlawry, the case was reviewed by the emperor at the Diet of Worms in 1521; there Luther maintained the positions he had adopted and consequently the emperor outlawed him. At this point Luther might have been executed, as had happened to Hus, but the emperor honored his safe-conduct and allowed him to go in peace. As he had become a controversial figure, his life was in real danger, but his immediate overlord, the elector of Saxony, soon took him into protective custody, and his movement continued to grow.

Thus far Luther's protest had revealed nothing that the European church had not experienced many times, and the question as to why it succeeded while earlier efforts failed becomes more and more complicated. One new factor which probably was important was the recent invention of reasonably cheap printing. This fifteenth century invention, usually attributed to Johannes Gutenberg, made possible the wide distribution of Luther's statements, first his theses and later the eloquent pamphlets in which he explained and developed his positions. The printing press made available to him a larger audience than earlier preachers of reform had been able to reach, and while recognizing the limitations posed by widespread illiteracy, one must regard the press as important in the rapid and extensive communication of Luther's ideas.

In the successful establishment and expansion of the Lutheran movement, however, as distinct from its origins in Luther's own agony of conscience, the most important factor was its relationship to the secular power structure. In the early 1520s the political and social situation in north Germany was singularly receptive to the sort of movement that Luther launched. Agrarian depression, the decline of the once-prosperous Hanseatic league of trading towns, increased exactions by manorial lords to meet their own rising costs— all of these factors brought hardship to those who were economically vulnerable; among commoners this meant chiefly peasants and urban workmen, while among the nobility it meant that turbulent group known as the free imperial knights, a group of petty lords who were for all practical purposes independent of any higher authority. Luther's teaching that all men were equal before God appealed greatly to these groups, and they extended this spiritual equality to speculation upon social and economic equality. Moreover, Luther's ideas were capable of stimulating greed, for he said that the church was too much drawn into worldly affairs because it was a great landowner; his church, he said, would be maintained by the contributions of believers. The prospect of large tracts of church land available for seizure was attractive even to great princes of the empire.

Luther's movement was launched at a time when many of the German princes were resisting seriously the authority of the church and of the emperor. Many of them were attempting to consolidate territorial states based on Roman and Renaissance concepts of the sovereignty of the prince, and the loose medieval suzerainty claimed by the emperor and supported by the church was international in character and obstructive to this development. Emperor Charles V's position was vulnerable, for not only was he Holy Roman Emperor; he also was king of Spain and its growing colonial dominions and ruler of various Italian and Netherlands territories, and in the Danube valley he was beset by ferocious Turkish attacks which broke the kingdom of Hungary in 1529 and besieged Vienna. In these circumstances the princes sought to increase their power at the emperor's expense, and support of Lutheranism would help finance the effort with confiscated church lands, would eliminate the generally pro-imperial influence of Catholic clergy, and would offer a religious issue on which to rally the populace. German princes began to convert rapidly and to encourage Lutheran preachers. By the mid-1520s most of north Germany down to the Main River was Lutheran.

The spread of German Lutheranism stopped almost as suddenly as it began, however. In 1522 there was a revolt of imperial knights, and in 1524–25 there was a costly and destructive peasant revolt. Both groups claimed inspiration from Lutheranism, and though Luther disclaimed them, the revolts intimidated the princes by suggesting that Lutheranism carried the seeds of social revolution. Princely conversions stopped, and a few princes who had declared for Lutheranism even returned to Catholicism. The revolts were crushed, but Germany was left with a religious division, a Lutheran north and a Catholic south, each group eager to destroy the other in the name of the true faith.

The emperor, who was a dedicated Catholic, sincerely sought compromise. He recognized the validity of much of the criticism levied against the Catholic Church and wanted the pope to convene a council to reform the church and heal the rift, but the pope feared the anti-papal conciliar movement which had survived from the previous century, and he refused. Within the empire, Charles V convened a diet at Speyer in 1526 to try to find a compromise. When this produced no result, a second was called in 1529. The second Diet of Speyer was dominated by Catholics and it resolved that the empire's laws against heresy should be enforced. This meant civil war.

The Lutherans withdrew to Augsburg, where they drew up a confession (basic creed) of their faith and a protest, whence the term Protestant. In their own defense they also formed a military alliance known as the Schmalkaldic League, while their opponents formed a Catholic Union. The Lutherans soon got aid from France, which was willing to help any enemy of the emperor, while Catholic forces were supported by the emperor's Spanish resources. For the next quarter century Germany was torn by religious war that ended only in 1555 with the Peace of Augsburg. Religiously the wars changed little; for the north remained Lutheran and the south Catholic. Politically they had important results, however, for the Peace of Augsburg allowed every prince to choose between Lutheranism and Catholicism for his state, although the ecclesiastical reservation forbade further secularization of church lands; this meant legality for Lutheranism where the prince supported it, and also it meant the transfer of an important area of decision from the emperor to the princes.

Implicit in the German religious wars and the Peace of Augsburg was a general principle: religious protest movements could succeed where they had the support of important elements of the political establishment, but without that support they failed. This general principle also was supported by the experience of Lutheranism outside of Germany. Henry VIII of England opposed religious innovation and wrote a pamphlet attacking the Lutherans (which, ironically, won the papal title "Defender of the Faith" for the man who later was to launch the Reformation in England), while the king of France actually persecuted and burned any Lutherans he caught; in neither England nor France did Lutheranism make significant progress. In fact, after the mid-1520s the only area of notable Lutheran expansion was Scandinavia, and there the religious reformers had political support; in Sweden a new monarchy in revolt against Danish domination supported Lutheranism as an element of national consolidation, and a bit later the Danish crown did the same thing to rally the populace against the Catholic nobility.

Another dissident religious movement of wide influence was launched by John Calvin. At the same time that Luther was taking the first steps toward founding his church in Germany, there was emerging in Paris a reformist group of which the most prominent member was LeFebvre d'Etaples. Calvin, a brilliant young man educated in both theology and law, was influenced strongly by this group and undertook extensive study of early Christian writing, particularly the work of St. Augustine; in 1536, at the age of twenty-nine, he published the first edition of his *Institutes of the Christian Religion*. This highly sophisticated theological tract, which Calvin continued to develop and expand through subsequent editions, became the foundation of a new church. Calvin's doctrines differed radically from both Catholicism and Lutheranism, for Calvin believed that there was nothing an individual could do that would help him to achieve salvation. Both Lutheranism and Catholicism maintained that though man was too degraded by sin to merit salvation through his own efforts, if the efforts were sincere, God's mercy would extend the necessary grace. Calvin argued that if God were all-knowing and all-powerful, as was necessary by definition of God, then He must have known from the day of creation who would be saved and who would be damned, and, moreover, men were saved or damned because God willed it. This doctrine, known as predestination, divided humanity into two groups: those whom God intended to save, called the Elect, and those whom God intended to damn. Instead of evoking fatalism and resignation, as might seem likely, this doctrine proved very dynamic. Though a man could do nothing to improve his chances of salvation, he could seek signs that he was chosen for the Elect. He could never really *know*, but since everything in the world happened by God's will, the individual might hope that if his affairs prospered, it was a sign of God's blessing upon one of His chosen. Thus the followers of Calvin were motivated to live frugally and work hard, not for their own prosperity or comfort but to demonstrate through their activities the power of God's blessing and to find in their success some encouragement for their hopes of salvation.

King Francis I enjoyed good relations with the Catholic Church, and by agreement with the papacy (the Concordat of Boulogne, 1516) he had important patronage powers controlling most high appointments in the French church. Consequently he was hostile to religious innovation, particularly after seeing and encouraging the division and violence it brought to Germany. He launched persecutions which broke up the Paris group and forced Calvin to flee abroad. The brilliant eighteenth century writer Voltaire later observed cynically that Francis I was a good king, burning heretics at home while subsidizing them in Germany, both for the greater glory of France.

After some wanderings, Calvin went to Geneva, in Switzerland, where he had been invited by a group that was attempting a two-fold change in the city: religious reform and overthrow of the authority of the bishop who was the city's overlord. Calvin soon was accepted as the leader of this group, and it was in Geneva that he established the theocratic government that became the model Calvinist community. The city and the church were run by the same people, the laws of the civil government enforced the rules of the church, and church and state together supported an extremely puritanical moral code that sought to force Genevans to be godly.

Because Calvinism was dynamic and sympathetic to worldly success, it appealed strongly, though not exclusively, to middle-class people. Its spread from Geneva can be traced along the trade routes: down the Rhine to the Netherlands, down the Rhone and thence along the great highways of southern France. In neither France nor the Netherlands did it become an important social force, however, until the latter half of the sixteenth century when political circumstances became favorable. In France King Henry II was killed in a sporting accident in 1559, leaving a minor heir, and confronting a weakened royal government Calvinism spread rapidly; in the Netherlands a great revolt broke out in the 1560s against the king of Spain who ruled the area, and Calvinism soon became the unifying force of the revolutionaries. Both of these processes will be considered in more detail later.

Generally it was in the towns that the new church found support at first, though it soon began to recruit noblemen. In fact, one of its greatest successes—Scotland—depended upon the support of nobles. The Reformation in Scotland was enmeshed so deeply with political revolution that it is difficult to separate religious and political motivation. In the middle of the sixteenth century the Scottish crown was held by Mary, Queen of Scots, a woman reared in France and very French in outlook. A Scot, John Knox, was Calvin's most dedicated disciple in Geneva, and when Knox returned to Scotland the new faith he brought soon became the rallying issue for a consolidated aristocratic opposition to the crown which, in 1568, drove Queen Mary to seek refuge in England. The uncompromising new faith found wide support among the Scots, and Scotland soon was predominately Calvinist except for the highlands, which remained Catholic until the mid-eighteenth century.

Luther and Calvin were not alone in launching religious dissidence, however, for there were other important movements. In

Switzerland an independent protest movement was started in 1518 by a priest named Zwingli; though differing from Luther on important doctrinal points, the Zwinglians also insisted upon the unique importance of personal faith and the inefficacy of the clergy as intermediaries. Their movement spread importantly through some of the northern Swiss cantons, but after Zwingli's death it was absorbed by Lutheranism and Calvinism. And much more radical than Lutherans, Calvinists, or Zwinglians were the Anabaptists. These were people who sought to re-create primitive communal Christianity. It is difficult to generalize about them, for they never established any formalized organization. Though their name implies opposition to baptism, what they were against was infant baptism, maintaining that such an initiation into the Christian community should be an adult decision. Some were pacifists who "turned the other cheek" while others had the reputation of fighting like lions. What they shared was a primitive and simple faith in Christ the Redeemer and in the Bible as God's word. They were persecuted by both Catholics and Lutherans and never became a very influential movement, surviving in modern times as Mennonite and Amish communities.

A unique reformation occurred in England, where the movement was directed by the crown and in its origins was clearly political. Henry VIII was only one generation removed from the devastating Wars of the Roses, which had been based chiefly on the lack of a clear line of succession to the throne. Thus the king was terribly aware of the succession issue and was disturbed deeply that in twenty years of marriage the queen had produced only one child, a girl, Mary. Henry desperately desired a male heir to ensure his family's succession, and in 1527 he sought a papal annulment of his first marriage so that he might remarry. There were grounds, and such annulments often were granted to royal families, but in this case the pope was reluctant. In 1527 Rome had been occupied and sacked by the armies of Emperor Charles V; Queen Catherine, whom Henry was seeking to divorce, was Charles' aunt, and the pope feared to give offense in that family. He tried to procrastinate, hoping to find a solution, but Henry became impatient, for his mistress was pregnant and he wanted to marry her before the birth so the child would be legitimate. He used his considerable power over the English church to confiscate church lands, cut papal revenues from England and intimidate the English clergy, and when these attempts at pressure proved unavailing, he had his annulment pronounced by the archbishop of Canterbury. Undaunted by papal excommunication in 1534, the king passed an Act of Supremacy through the English Parliament, cutting off the English Church from Rome and making himself "Supreme Head of the Church of England." Additional benefits of these actions were increased control over the church and increased support for his government from those to whom he had distributed the confiscated church lands.

Henry VIII was a religious conservative, however; in his lifetime few doctrinal changes were made in the English Church, and he resisted the efforts of reformers of Lutheran or Calvinist inclinations, maintaining a sort of Catholic Church that denied the authority of the pope. Henry's bold action had secured him greatly increased political and economic power as well as matrimonial freedom, but England was to suffer religious struggles despite his efforts to control religious change.

Despite several marriages, at his death Henry left only three children: Mary, Elizabeth and Edward. The male took precedence over his older half-sisters and succeeded to the throne as Edward VI (1547–1553), a sickly boy. His government was run by a regency council sympathetic to religious reform, and a number of changes were made in the English Church, moving it far in the direction of Calvinism. But after only six years, young Edward died and was succeeded by his half-sister Mary (1553–1558), an ardent Catholic who was married to Philip II of Spain, the European champion of Catholicism. Persecutions and violence followed as Mary attempted to return England to Roman obedience, and then she too died and was succeeded by her half-sister Elizabeth.

It was during the reign of Queen Elizabeth I (1558–1603) that the English Church was stabilized as a moderate and national reformed church. The queen had no sympathy for extreme Calvinism, and she could not support Catholicism for Catholics considered her illegitimate and hence ineligible for the crown. She chose a middle course, continuing to deny papal authority in England but otherwise adopting deliberately vague positions and avoiding enforcement of laws that required membership in the Church of England, so as to give offense to as few people as possible. The enormous personal prestige she developed in defending England against Spanish aggression combined with her moderation to create a situation most unusual in late sixteenth century Europe—a strong and popular monarchy supported by a stable church.

Finally, the mid-sixteenth century witnessed another important reform movement, the Catholic reformation. Pious and responsible popes rebuilt the dignity and spiritual responsibility of papal government and then led a reform movement within the church along rather Erasmian lines. The chief instrument of this reform was the Council of Trent, which met in three sessions in the middle 1540s, the early 1550s and the early 1560s. The church made no doctrinal compromises with Protestantism, to the great disappointment of the emperor, who long had pressed for this solution, but it achieved a considerable reform program for morals and practices. After confirming the authority of the pope and traditional Catholic doctrine, it forbade financial abuses, plurality of offices and non-residence of clergy; and it provided for the foundation of new seminaries to produce better-educated priests. It took a long time for some of the council's proposals to be effective, and some never were, but the council marked the beginning of an important rejuvenation of the Catholic clergy.

As well as internal reform, the reinvigorated papacy also began a counter-attack upon Protestantism, for which two new instruments were the Roman Inquisition (not to be confused with the corrupt Spanish Inquisition) and the Index of Banned Books. The Roman Inquisition was a special court with jurisdiction over the whole church; it heard questions of faith and tried to establish a little clarity in the sixteenth century confusion of argument and counter-argument. Unfortunately it proved a very conservative body, and in the early seventeenth century, in the Galileo case, it put itself in the ludicrous position of condemning as heresy a scientific hypothesis. The famous Index was an attempt to limit the spread of Protestantism by establishing a list of persuasive but heretical books forbidden to Catholics. In the long run neither of these efforts was very effective.

Without a doubt, the most successful Catholic response to the challenge of Protestantism was the foundation of the Society of Jesus or Jesuits. Authorized by the pope in 1543 the society was the creation of a former Spanish soldier, St. Ignatius Loyola. Setting a very high educational standard for its members, the society dedicated itself especially to preaching, teaching and instructing the conscience in the confessional. By the end of the sixteenth century Jesuit colleges, such as the University of Ingolstadt on the Danube, had won the reputation of being among the best and most progressive schools in Europe. Jesuit scholars had achieved considerable fame as controversialists defending the validity of Catholicism, and the society was developing rapidly the missionary work that with expanding European colonialism was to carry its priests as far as China and the Philippines.

By about the middle of the sixteenth century the first phase of the Reformation had ended. New churches had been founded and the old unity of western Christendom, often more apparent than real, had disappeared. Lutheranism had run its course and dominated Scandinavia and north Germany. The Church of England had left the Roman fold, and though it was still incompletely developed at Elizabeth's accession, it was established solidly as another variety of Protestantism. Calvinism, the dynamic new force in the mid-sixteenth century, had a secure base in Geneva and was reaching out to the south of France, the Netherlands and Scotland. And a reform movement had been launched within Catholicism. The latter half of the sixteenth century witnessed another phase in which the lines of controversy were drawn more sharply as Protestant Europe was put on the defensive by the ambitions and might of King Philip II of Spain.

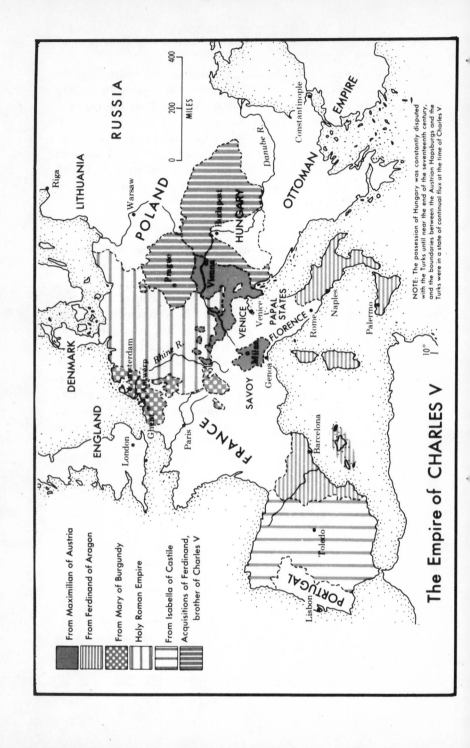

The Empire of CHARLES V

Legend:
- From Maximilian of Austria
- From Ferdinand of Aragon
- From Mary of Burgundy
- Holy Roman Empire
- From Isabella of Castile
- Acquisitions of Ferdinand, brother of Charles V

NOTE: The possession of Hungary was constantly disputed with the Turks until near the end of the seventeenth century, and the boundaries between the Austrian Hapsburgs and the Turks were in a state of continual flux at the time of Charles V.

MILES
0   200   400

10°

RUSSIA

LITHUANIA

Riga

Warsaw

POLAND

DENMARK

ENGLAND

London

Amsterdam

Antwerp

Ghent

Rhine R.

Paris

FRANCE

SAVOY

Genoa

Milan

VENICE

Venice

Prague

Vienna

HUNGARY

Budapest

Danube R.

Constantinople

OTTOMAN EMPIRE

PAPAL STATES

FLORENCE

Rome

Naples

Palermo

Barcelona

Toledo

PORTUGAL

Lisbon

THE HOUSE OF HABSBURG

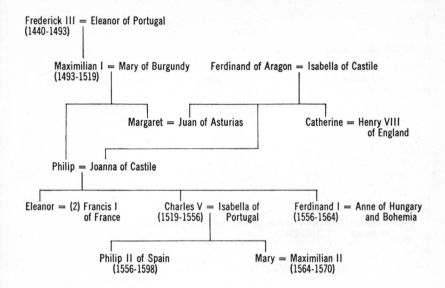

Frederick III = Eleanor of Portugal
(1440-1493)

Maximilian I = Mary of Burgundy   Ferdinand of Aragon = Isabella of Castile
(1493-1519)

Margaret = Juan of Asturias   Catherine = Henry VIII
                                                      of England

Philip = Joanna of Castile

Eleanor = (2) Francis I   Charles V = Isabella of   Ferdinand I = Anne of Hungary
          of France   (1519-1556) Portugal   (1556-1564)   and Bohemia

Philip II of Spain   Mary = Maximilian II
(1556-1598)   (1564-1570)

THE HOUSE OF VALOIS

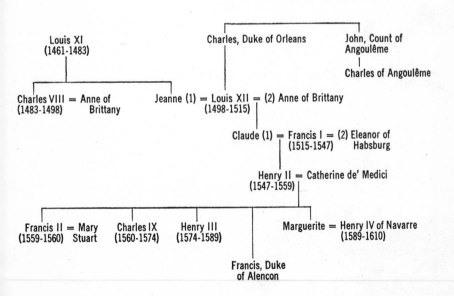

Louis XI   Charles, Duke of Orleans   John, Count of
(1461-1483)   Angoulême

                                                            Charles of Angoulême

Charles VIII = Anne of   Jeanne (1) = Louis XII = (2) Anne of Brittany
(1483-1498)   Brittany   (1498-1515)

                              Claude (1) = Francis I = (2) Eleanor of
                                           (1515-1547)   Habsburg

                              Henry II = Catherine de' Medici
                              (1547-1559)

Francis II = Mary   Charles IX   Henry III   Marguerite = Henry IV of Navarre
(1559-1560) Stuart (1560-1574)   (1574-1589)   (1589-1610)

                              Francis, Duke
                              of Alencon

THE HOUSE OF TUDOR

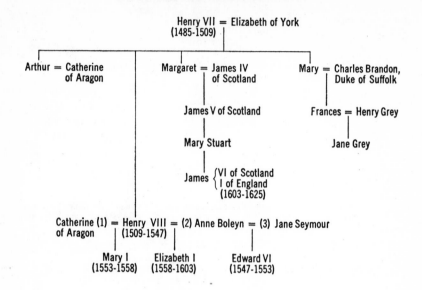

Henry VII = Elizabeth of York
(1485-1509)

Arthur = Catherine of Aragon

Margaret = James IV of Scotland

James V of Scotland

Mary Stuart

James { VI of Scotland / I of England / (1603-1625)

Mary = Charles Brandon, Duke of Suffolk

Frances = Henry Grey

Jane Grey

Catherine (1) = Henry VIII = (2) Anne Boleyn = (3) Jane Seymour
of Aragon   (1509-1547)

Mary I
(1553-1558)

Elizabeth I
(1558-1603)

Edward VI
(1547-1553)

THE HOUSE OF STUART

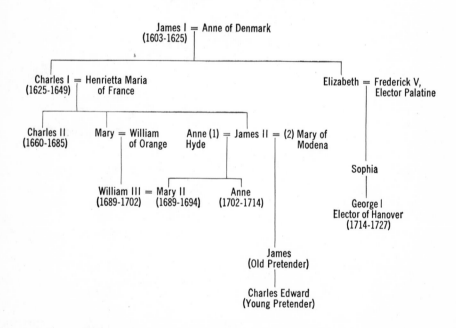

James I = Anne of Denmark
(1603-1625)

Charles I = Henrietta Maria
(1625-1649)   of France

Elizabeth = Frederick V, Elector Palatine

Charles II
(1660-1685)

Mary = William of Orange

Anne (1) = James II = (2) Mary of Modena
Hyde

William III = Mary II
(1689-1702)   (1689-1694)

Anne
(1702-1714)

Sophia

George I
Elector of Hanover
(1714-1727)

James
(Old Pretender)

Charles Edward
(Young Pretender)

THE AUSTRIAN HABSBURGS

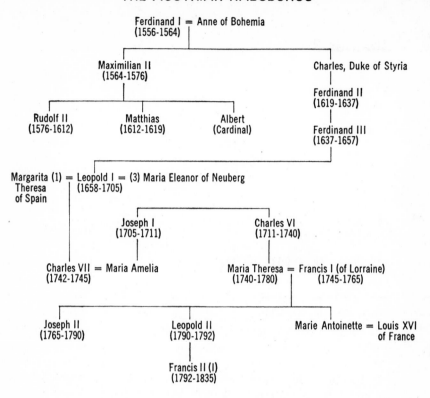

Ferdinand I = Anne of Bohemia
(1556-1564)

Maximilian II
(1564-1576)

Charles, Duke of Styria

Ferdinand II
(1619-1637)

Rudolf II
(1576-1612)

Matthias
(1612-1619)

Albert
(Cardinal)

Ferdinand III
(1637-1657)

Margarita (1) = Leopold I = (3) Maria Eleanor of Neuberg
Theresa   (1658-1705)
of Spain

Joseph I
(1705-1711)

Charles VI
(1711-1740)

Charles VII = Maria Amelia
(1742-1745)

Maria Theresa = Francis I (of Lorraine)
(1740-1780)   (1745-1765)

Joseph II
(1765-1790)

Leopold II
(1790-1792)

Marie Antoinette = Louis XVI
of France

Francis II (I)
(1792-1835)

THE SPANISH HABSBURGS

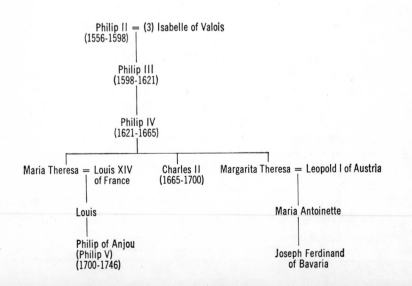

Philip II = (3) Isabelle of Valois
(1556-1598)

Philip III
(1598-1621)

Philip IV
(1621-1665)

Maria Theresa = Louis XIV
of France

Charles II
(1665-1700)

Margarita Theresa = Leopold I of Austria

Louis

Maria Antoinette

Philip of Anjou
(Philip V)
(1700-1746)

Joseph Ferdinand
of Bavaria

Chapter 3

Habsburg Hegemony

When Charles V abdicated his many titles in the mid-1550s, he divided his vast holdings between his brother and his son. To his brother, Ferdinand, who already was king of Bohemia and Hungary, he left his central European domains; to his son, Philip II, he left the Spanish crown with its New World dependencies, the Netherlands, the Franche-Comté and the Italian territories of Naples and Milan. Thus the old emperor tried to rationalize somewhat the crushing burdens of governing the far-flung Habsburg lands.

The troubles in Germany had abated after the Peace of Augsburg; if its recognition of Lutheranism was distasteful to the pious emperor and its transfer of religious decisions to the German princes marked some further diminution of imperial authority, at least the settlement brought an end to much of the exhausting military conflict and weakened the excuse for French intervention. In the Danube Valley the Turkish wars had settled to a series of sieges and sporadic peace treaties. Internally and on both the eastern and western borders, German conflicts were dying down, while Spain, with a rapidly expanding colonial empire, seemed to be developing rapidly.

The new Habsburg rulers appeared to be men of great promise. Ferdinand was a central European in his attitudes; his experiences in Bohemia and Hungary involved him in a point of view wholly congenial to the Holy Roman Empire, and as Charles V's deputy for German affairs since 1522 he appeared to have won wide respect among the German princes. Young Philip had been reared mostly in Spain, spoke the tongue naturally, and had the piety and austerity of the Castilian; his obvious intelligence, his capacity for hard work and his serious demeanor all promised well for a man who was by birth one of Christendom's most important princes. Both branches of the house of Habsburg seemed to be in good hands, and at the same time there were possibilities for a further growth of Habsburg influence. In England, there appeared hope for a stronger Spanish alliance and perhaps even for England's return to Catholicism, for Mary Tudor—Catherine of Aragon's daughter— married Philip of Spain in 1554, and England was drawn into Spain's war with France in 1557; even after Mary's death in 1558 the situation was far from irretrievable, for her half-sister and heir, Elizabeth, held forth hope of Catholic conversion and Spanish marriage.

But behind this optimistic facade stirred many troubles. The religious peace in Germany reflected exhaustion more than agreement. The settlement merely extended to Lutherans (if their prince so decided) the position formerly enjoyed only by Catholics; it made no provision for the various groups of Anabaptists nor for the aggressive new Calvinist cult. It accepted things as they were, but it sought to impede further change, and the religious protest movements had not exhausted their dynamics yet. Despite the ecclesiastical reservation of the Peace of Augsburg, church lands continued to be secularized, and Calvinism—quite without legal recognition—became the established faith of the Rhineland state of the Palatinate.

The Spanish branch of the family also ruled over undercurrents of potential trouble. Castile and Aragon were staunchly particularistic, and amalgamation had made little progress under Charles V. The Moorish south was still restive under Spanish Catholic rule, breaking into revolt in 1569. The New World provided some treasure, but its importunities were many, and the sea routes were dangerous. The Netherlands were prosperous but also very particularistic, and the Spanish Philip, so very different from his cosmopolitan father, soon was to fan fires of rebellion with an attempt to impose outside authority. Italy seemed firmly in the Habsburg grip, but the Republic of Venice was hostile, and the papacy never had countenanced quietly a dominating secular power. The Turks, relatively quiet on the Danube, still controlled the Mediterranean and threatened Christian shipping. And no one could guess how long France would be willing to accept a secondary role, ringed in by Habsburg power. The potential of conflict lay on all sides.

Philip II of Spain (1556–1598) long has been the subject of characterizations ranging from fanaticism and bureaucratic rigidity to saintly devotion and impractical idealism. During the nineteenth century he was portrayed often as a king who had sacrificed the national resources of Spain to a religious crusade, much to the disgust of nationalist historians. But modern study has delineated a man of much more persuasive character—pious, austere and unbending but intelligent and hard-working and quite as devoted to the secular ambitions of his dynasty as to religious goals. It was easy for generations of historians still fascinated by the internal divisions of the Christian faith and still reacting to the universal pretensions of Roman Catholicism to portray King Philip as a Catholic crusader; yet, while such an interpretation can be defended, modern research has added broader perspectives, and historians now believe that the king's religious goal should be considered as one among many motivations of his policy. Certainly Philip II saw himself as the champion of the counter-reformation; as the strongest Catholic king in Europe, he felt God had laid upon him a special obligation to defend the church. But this aspect of his character should not be allowed to obscure his other important motives.

Moslem naval power constituted an old threat to European shipping on the Mediterranean, and in fact Moslem raiding of the south coasts of Europe continued into the seventeenth century, but Spain's vigorous efforts under King Philip made European commerce a bit more secure. In 1571, with support from the papacy and Venice, Spain mounted a strong naval expedition led by the king's half-brother, Don Juan, and struck at the main Turkish flotilla. The two fleets, totalling nearly four hundred and fifty galleys, came together off the coast of Greece, and the ensuing engagement took its name from the nearby town of Lepanto. The fighting was bloody, and both sides sustained heavy losses, but in the end the Turkish fleet was destroyed, and though the Turks rebuilt, they remained somewhat weakened in waters west of Sicily. It would be an exaggeration to suggest that the western Mediterranean became safe, for piracy was rife, and expeditions from north Africa still descended upon the European coast to carry off plunder and slaves; but there was a difference between such irregular activity and the constant threat of regular battle squadrons.

King Philip had a long-standing interest in England, and although religion undeniably was a motive, there were important commercial and political considerations, too. He and Mary Tudor had tried to restore English Catholicism, and as the champion of the counter-reformation, Philip hoped to see his task completed. But there also was the fact that England's seamen proved an expensive nuisance and a potential danger to Spain's colonial empire; the great days of the Elizabethan sea-dogs were just beginning, but there was enough harassment to make the Spanish government eager to control English activity at sea. And finally, there were political issues. After 1567 King Philip faced insurrection in the Netherlands, armed resistance to what he believed to be his just authority; England was aiding the rebels, and Philip felt that if he could neutralize England he would be able more easily to pacify the Netherlands. Thus, an important element of Spanish policy all through Philip II's reign was an attempt to dominate England.

Philip began peacefully enough with proposals for a marriage alliance with Elizabeth, but when these efforts met no result he sought alternatives. It was an age when some men still took their religion more seriously than their country, so of course the king of Spain had supporters among English Catholics; intercepted correspondence and often-exaggerated rumors of plots and conspiracies escalated the tension between the two governments, and growing popular animosities resulted from increased English raiding of Spanish colonial interests—activities at which Queen Elizabeth connived, often providing part of the capitalization of such expeditions. A crisis developed only in the 1580s, and by that time religious, commercial and political interests were intertwined thoroughly. The focus of the crisis was the exiled queen of Scotland, Mary Stuart.

In the third quarter of the sixteenth century Scotland underwent a violent religious and political transformation. It was the misfortune of the house of Stuart that the crown became the object of religious and political opposition at the same time. Mary Stuart had succeeded her father while still an infant, had been reared in France and when grown was married to the French King Francis II (1559–1560). During her minority and her absence abroad, her mother, a French princess, ruled as regent of Scotland, and French influence was strong at the Scottish court. But French governmental concepts of monarchs who ruled as well as reigned grated hard upon the stubborn independence of the Scots nobility, and there was trouble even before the frivolous and head-strong Mary Stuart returned from France in 1561 to begin her personal reign; her autocratic views worsened the situation. At this inopportune time John Knox returned to his native Scotland to preach the Calvinist gospel; his detestation of the Stuarts and their French adherents was exceeded only by his hatred for the Church of Rome. Knox's preaching won wide support, and soon the religious and political protests fused. Queen Mary antagonized the nobility by her autocratic behavior and all of her Calvinist subjects by her frivolity, her lovers and her gay court. Knox's fiery attacks upon the queen rallied popular support to the aristocratic opposition, and civil war broke out. Mary was forced to abdicate in favor of her son James in 1567, and the next year she fled to England to seek refuge, despite the fact that Elizabeth had been helping the Scots rebels.

In England Mary Stuart constituted a political danger to Elizabeth. Anne Boleyn's daughter had been born while Henry VIII's first wife, Catherine of Aragon, still lived; she was considered illegitimate by English Catholics who did not recognize Henry's divorce, and they denied her right to the throne. By an unhappy coincidence, if Elizabeth's claims were disallowed, the next heir to the crown of England was Mary Stuart. She was, therefore, the natural rallying point for Catholic opposition in England.

Mary did nothing to make Elizabeth's problems easier, for she intrigued constantly to usurp the throne of her protectress. Legend to the contrary, Elizabeth's treatment of Mary was not ungenerous. She was provided with a residence, and though her movements were restricted, close confinement came only when her subversive activities made it a political necessity. Still she dabbled at conspiracy, attempting to bribe one of the servants whom Elizabeth had assigned to her; but that individual delivered her secret correspondence straight to a member of the royal council. Despite massive provocation, Elizabeth tolerated this sort of behavior for more than eighteen years. If not moved by sympathy, at least she had no desire to continue the unhappy precedent of shedding royal blood.

Meanwhile, Philip of Spain had grown weary of the cat and mouse game that Elizabeth had been playing with him. In 1577 she had made an alliance with the rebels in the Netherlands, and in 1585 she sent troops to their aid; English depredations upon Spanish shipping had grown worse; England was a bastion of heresy and a haven of pirates. Philip conceived a grand plan to make an end to England. In 1580 he had added Portugal to his domains by a combination of inheritance and military force, and in the port of Lisbon, one of the finest in Europe, he began to assemble a great fleet, the proud Armada. It was to sail north, embark the Spanish troops in the Netherlands, then cross the Channel and invade England. Simultaneously, English Catholics were to rise in rebellion, rally to Mary Stuart, and overthrow Elizabeth. The joint operation was to culminate in a Spanish marriage for Mary and reimposition of Spanish influence and Catholicism in England. Probably the English government, which was informed of all these projects, exaggerated the danger of a great Catholic rising, but undeniably Mary had become a serious political threat. Reluctantly, Elizabeth ordered her execution in February of 1587.

In the summer of 1587 Sir Francis Drake struck another damaging blow against Philip's plans. Off the south coast of Spain he caught and burned ships carrying hardwood to make the Armada's water casks; replacement was difficult, and England gained a year. More bad news came; Philip's brilliant commander in the Netherlands, the duke of Parma, insisted that the rebels were so strong in the shallow coastal waters off the Low Countries that the Armada would be unable to embark the troops. Philip prayed, hoped and decided to gamble. The Armada sailed anyway; somehow it would have to manage. Then disasters succeeded one another.

England did not flame with rebellion. English ships harried the Armada, rearming and reprovisioning from English ports while the Spanish ships were far from a friendly base. The Armada was forced into the lee of the European coast, and incompetent command and unfavorable winds wrecked many ships. A storm drove the rest of the fleet north; there was no hope of embarking troops, and the Spanish were without charts for these waters. They tried to round the British Isles to return to Spain, but bad weather continued, supplies ran low, and wrecks multiplied. Only a third of them got home, and England was saved.

Philip took the disaster bravely and decided that God was punishing him for his sins. Begging God not to punish all of Spain for her king's misdeeds, he sent other fleets to comparable fates during the remaining decade of his life, but the defeat of the Great Armada of 1588 had ruined his English policy. England preyed more vigorously upon Spain's shipping, continued to help the Netherlands and opposed Spanish interests in France. It should be obvious from this that a second important pivot of Philip II's policy was his quarrel with his subjects in the Netherlands. The civil war which resulted was carried on by his successors and lasted but for one brief interlude until the middle of the seventeenth century. Religion was only one of many issues, and at the outset it was not even the most important. Rather, the roots of the revolt in the Netherlands lay in the traditions and complex organization of that area.

The Netherlands were part of the old Burgundian inheritance, a loose association of seventeen separate provinces with many differences among them. Particularist traditions were strong, for the fishing and farming population of the north long had been secure behind the marshy barriers of what was almost a wasteland, and the wealth of the great textile cities of the south had made them proudly independent. When the area passed to the Habsburgs, both Maximilian I and Charles V humored local particularism. They used deputy governors in the Netherlands, maintaining a sort of autonomy from other Habsburg holdings, and they recognized the traditional right of local estates to determine grants of taxes and troops, thus allowing a large role to aristocratic and bourgeois interests. Not until 1548 did Charles V formally annex the Netherlands to the empire, and even then he created a Burgundian Circle (military district) which preserved much of the old autonomy. On the whole Charles and the Netherlanders got on well.

Within a decade of Philip II's accession, however, trouble broke out. At first two issues were involved, political authority and religion, but soon an economic consideration complicated matters further. Philip had introduced a Spanish garrison and Spanish clerics to the Netherlands, and religion became a sensitive issue as

Calvinism spread through the poor and restive lower classes of the southern cities, resulting in desecration of some Catholic churches and occasional riots. The government's heavy-handed endeavors to enforce religious uniformity no doubt reflected Philip's sincere convictions, but harsh penal edicts against heretics, the threat of the use of Spanish troops and a rumor that the dreaded Spanish Inquisition would be introduced seemed to violate the Netherlands' jealously guarded autonomy. There were sporadic outbreaks of popular violence, but the first organized resistance came not from a popular religious movement but from a league of three hundred nobles who protested the imposition of foreign authority.

Philip reacted with even harsher repression, sending from Spain the duke of Alva with twenty thousand troops. Alva created a special tribunal, soon called the Council of Blood for the many executions it prescribed, and prominent local aristocrats as well as many humbler folk were sent to their deaths.

Thus far the resistance to Philip had come chiefly from two sources: popular religious protest and aristocratic political protest. The persecutions gave rise to a much more general resentment, however, and Alva added a third force to his opposition, the urban oligarchies, those proud merchants and manufacturers who formed the wealthy backbone of the Netherlands' economy. The policies that Alva was attempting to implement were both unpopular and costly, and, certain that the estates would not support him, he sought financial independence by imposing a sales tax of ten percent on all transactions. Such an imposition would have ended all local restraint upon government and probably would have meant ruin to the area's important commerce. There was a new revolt. Alva had drawn into alliance against himself and his master the most disparate elements—urban magnates and their workmen, who usually detested one another, and the old nobility, who generally scorned both. Religious, political and economic issues melted together, inflaming the entire population to armed resistance. His policy a failure, Alva was recalled in 1573 at his own request.

Thereafter command changed rapidly: Requesen from 1573 to his death in 1576; Don Juan of Austria (the victor of Lepanto) from 1576 to his death in 1578. Neither could suppress the revolt, but the ferocity of the Spanish armies led in 1576 to the short-lived Pacification of Ghent, a compact wherein the seventeen provinces agreed to overlook their own rivalries and to unite to drive out the Spaniards. Philip II had achieved the greatest unity the Netherlands had ever known, but it was unity in opposition to him rather than in the service of his crown.

At the end of the 1570s the war settled into the patterns that were to mark its course until 1648, with the seven northern provinces in revolt and the ten southern provinces loyal to Spain. The catalyst of this change was the appointment of a new Spanish commander, Alexander Farnese, duke of Parma. A man as able in negotiations as he was brilliant in command of armies, Parma quickly exploited the conflicting interests that divided his opponents. The great bourgeoisie of the southern cities was Catholic in faith and conservative in politics; the merchants and manufacturers found the Calvinism and social radicalism of the urban lower classes frightening, and they resisted Philip chiefly in defense of traditional privileges and through fear of the sort of taxation that Alva had attempted. Parma persuaded King Philip to allow him to compromise. He confirmed ancient privileges, especially with regard to taxation, and he had the troops to guarantee social stability; the southern oligarchies agreed to return to obedience, to enforce religious conformity and to provide financial support for Parma's forces. At the price of some sacrifice of his personal political authority, Philip achieved his religious goals in half of the Netherlands and secured for his forces a base of operations against those who remained rebellious.

The seven northern provinces were a different matter. In contrast to the urbanized and industrialized south, this was a land of small towns, farms and fishing villages, a population of stubborn peasant stock. At first Calvinism had grown slowly in this conservative peasant society, but once it became the rallying standard of the revolt, it had spread rapidly. The northern provinces had offered refuge and men to aristocratic resistance leaders such as William of Nassau-Orange, called the Silent, and their men had gained some of the first victories over the Spaniards when their light fishing craft were armed to harass Spanish ships and raid Spanish positions. In the course of the war some of the northern towns, especially Amsterdam, grew in importance and wealth as they became centers of rebel shipping and the bases from which the Dutch raided Spanish commerce. After 1580, when Portugal became part of Philip's domains and hence fair game, Portuguese shipping began to suffer, and at the end of the sixteenth century a Dutch fleet sailed to the East Indies and cracked the Portuguese monopoly of the affluent eastern trade.

These stubborn northerners did not abate their resistance in the slightest when the southerners made their peace with Spain. In 1579 they bound themselves into the Union of Utrecht, and in 1581 they declared their total independence. It seemed a futile if brave gesture, for Parma appeared unbeatable, and in 1584 he captured the port of Antwerp, the last of the great cities that had not made terms with Philip. But the English sent aid in 1585, and Philip's attempt to bring the war to a quick conclusion ended with the disastrous loss of the Armada in 1588. Then in 1592 Parma died from an infected wound, and thereafter the fighting was intermittent and inconclusive. To the year of his death in 1598, Philip never abandoned hope of crushing the rebels, and his successor Philip III was equally determined to make no peace recognizing independence. Sheer exhaustion finally produced a twelve years' truce in 1609, and when hostilities were resumed early in the 1620s the Dutch war was subsumed in the larger struggle known as the Thirty Years War. Peace did not come to the Netherlands until 1648.

In all fairness to Philip II it should be noted that he attempted little that was not being done by his contemporaries. Toleration was foreign to the thought and spirit of the sixteenth century, and most governments sought religious uniformity; most governments also were trying to increase taxation sharply, for rising prices and increasing military costs made more money essential. But it is particularly ironic that Philip should be damned for his efforts to suppress particularism in the Netherlands, for similar efforts in the next century by the French government of Louis XIII and Richelieu, by the Prussian Hohenzollerns and by the Swedish Vasas are praised, and nationalist historians long have lamented the failure of Germany to achieve such a result until the late nineteenth century. Much of Philip II's policy in the Netherlands was a failure, but there was nothing unique or particularly wicked about his efforts, and in the south he managed to hold a strategically and economically important area for his crown and his church.

One other great effort was important to Philip II's reign, his attempt to establish dominant Spanish influence in France and perhaps even to secure the French crown for his family after disaster struck France in the middle of the sixteenth century. The Peace of Cateau-Cambrésis, which brought peace between the Valois and the Habsburgs in 1559, was the occasion of celebrations. One of the events was the old noble sport of jousting, and through a freak accident King Henry II was killed when a lance broke, and a splinter passed through his visor and penetrated his eye. Henry's oldest son, the sickly young Francis II (husband of Mary, queen of Scots), succeeded to the throne until his death in 1560; then he was succeeded by Henry's second son, Charles IX (1560–1574), who was only ten years old. The deaths of two kings and the succession of a minor removed the stabilizing influence of royal authority, and France was thrown into turmoil.

France had escaped serious religious trouble during the first half of the sixteenth century, for the French Church was largely in the king's hands, and no strong secular power was ready to offer the sort of support that the princes had given Lutheranism in Germany. But Calvinism won some adherents toward the middle of the century, and by then the political climate was more congenial to religious dissent. The long wars which France fought against Charles V largely had pauperized the lesser nobles, and they had tended to seek the support and patronage of a few wealthy aristocratic houses, creating a client system often called bastard feudalism. By the middle of the century, four great cliques existed: the royal house of Valois; the house of Bourbon, related by blood to the Valois; the house of Guise, a French branch of the important imperial house of Lorraine, related by marriage to the Valois; and the house of Montmorency, a proud old family with vast lands and great wealth. Until Henry II's death the Valois had maintained control, and the conservative Montmorencys usually had supported the crown, while the Guises and Bourbons had fought and quarreled for offices and patronage. But upon the death of Henry II the fortunes of the royal family passed into the hands of his widow, Catherine de Medici, and though clever and unscrupulous, she faced a difficult task in the scramble for power that marked the last half of the sixteenth century.

The succession of Francis II gave great influence to his uncles by marriage, the Guises. The Bourbons opposed this favor, and soon the Montmorencys also went into opposition. Younger members of both houses espoused Calvinism, and religious dissent took on strong political overtones. Under persecution French Calvinists took up arms and formed a political organization, and soon the cult had grown to impressive proportions. Called Huguenots (probably from a German word meaning "covenanters"), the French Calvinists at their peak claimed something near to half of the French nobility as well as many townsmen in the south and west, Montmorency and Bourbon territory; few peasants were attracted to the movement, however, and generally the north and northeast were little penetrated by the new doctrines. For both religious and political reasons the government tried to suppress the Huguenots, and fighting broke out which was to continue sporadically until the mid-1590s. Generally the Huguenot cavalry (drawn from the ranks of the nobility) was the best on the field, while royal armies fielded better infantry (peasants) and had the financial resources to support more artillery. The wars were savage.

In 1574 Charles IX was succeeded by his brother Henry III (1574–1589), a well-meaning but weak and vacillating man who sought peace with the Huguenots. To oppose Henry III's attempt at compromise, the fanatical Guises formed a Catholic League in 1576 and sought help from Philip of Spain, who thus was drawn into the French civil wars. Then France's troubles were aggravated further as a succession crisis loomed. Two of Henry II's sons had sat upon the throne and died childless. The third, who then reigned, was childless and was expected to remain so as he appears to have been homosexual. A fourth brother, known as the duke of Anjou, was the dynasty's last hope, but he died—also childless—in 1584. Under the old Salic Law, which governed the French succession according to male blood lines only, the next heir to the throne was Henry of Bourbon; but he was a heretic, the leader of the Huguenots and unacceptable to French Catholics. The Guises hoped to set aside the Salic Law and probably aspired to the throne themselves, arguing with some justice that the religious requirement of Catholicism went back to Clovis and was as old as the principle of heredity by male blood lines. Philip II of Spain hoped to have the Salic Law set aside in favor of his daughter, who was a granddaughter of Henry II.

When Henry III was murdered in 1589, the fighting became even more intense, and the pattern of the struggle clarified. Bourbon claimed the crown with the support of his Huguenots and of some Catholics called *politiques*, who set civil peace above religious uniformity; he was opposed by the Catholic League, which had the support of Philip of Spain. In the early 1590s, Bourbon managed to conquer most of France, but Paris was too strong for him to take, and after long negotiations he was persuaded that most of France would accept him if he were Catholic while Paris would accept him on no other terms. With many reassurances to his Huguenot supporters, he converted to Catholicism in 1593 and reunited the country as King Henry IV (by royalist tradition reigning from Henry III's death in 1589 until his own assassination in 1610). Everywhere opposition collapsed, and another of Philip II's policies was bankrupt.

In 1598 Henry IV fulfilled his pledges to his former coreligionists with the proclamation of the Edict of Nantes. By this edict he guaranteed freedom of conscience to all Frenchmen, extensive freedom of public and private worship to the Calvinist minority, equal access to governmental offices to people of both faiths and special mixed courts to avoid religious prejudice in judicial processes. In addition, he granted the Huguenots the right to fortify a number of cities for protection against the Catholic majority, and he agreed to help defray the costs of their fortifications and their garrisons. Thus France achieved internal peace again, and during the remainder of Henry's reign the country recuperated rapidly from the ravages of the civil wars. Despite Philip II's efforts, France—like the Dutch Netherlands—survived to become a major opponent of the Habsburgs in the seventeenth century.

Chapter 4

The Scientific Revolution

About the middle of the sixteenth century western man's traditional assumptions about his physical environment were challenged seriously by the growth of a critical movement usually called the scientific revolution. In the course of approximately two hundred years, from the mid-sixteenth century to the mid-eighteenth century, basically modern conceptions of astronomy, mechanics and anatomy were established, and perhaps most important of all this period saw the development of that critical and quantitative approach to natural studies which is called the scientific method.

To understand the problems and the achievements of the scientific revolution, it is necessary first to consider the broad framework of scientific theories that constituted earlier accepted opinion. These theories were outlined under the title of natural philosophy by the Greek thinker Aristotle in the fourth century B.C., for which reason this older body of thought is termed Aristotelianism. Though modern science has discredited most of Aristotle's ideas, he should not be underestimated. His brilliant mind conceived theories that integrated all branches of natural studies into a coherent whole, explaining persuasively the varied natural phenomena of man's environment.

Though Aristotelian natural philosophy was extremely complex, it rested upon a few relatively simple assumptions. Aristotle assumed, with many of his contemporaries, that there were four basic elements in the universe—earth, air, fire and water—and that each of these elements had inherent properties such as warmth or cold-ness, wetness or dryness. Since all material objects comprised some combination of these elements, physical differences could be ex-plained.

The four elements also had natural positions in the universe, places where they would come to rest were they not prevented from doing so by mixture with other elements. Freed from constraint, the elements had a natural motion toward their places of rest. The nat-ural position of earth, the heaviest of the elements, was at the center of the universe; water, the next heaviest element, found its place around the earth; and two successive layers formed the blankets of air and fire. Thus Aristotelians conceived of the terrestrial environ-ment as a series of concentric spheres and believed that only a for-tunate imbalance allowed some earth to stand above the level of the waters, forming a home for mankind. (One interesting result of this idea was the theory almost two thousand years before Columbus' voyage that another continent must exist on the other side of the world, the antipodes or counterbalance of the Eurasian land mass.)

The concept of natural position and its related theory of natural motion permitted a whole system of mechanics. An object was heavy, and fell when dropped, because its major element was earth, which sought to move to the center of the universe. Flames leaped upward because burning something released the fire that was en-trapped, and, freed from restraint, the fire sought its position farthest from the center of the universe. Unnatural motion could be imparted to an object, but it required the application of an outside force, and such motion stopped when the force wore out. Hence an arrow, with a large proportion of earth in it, could be made to fly perpendicular to the direction of its natural motion by the force the bow imparted to it; but as the external force was used up, natural motion would re-assert itself, and the arrow would fall.

A theory of astronomy was made possible by the addition of the assumption that natural motion could be inherent to form as well as to matter, particularly that it was a natural motion for a sphere to ro-tate. Aristotle theorized that beyond the terrestrial environment lay concentric spheres of heavenly crystal—a substance that was color-less, weightless and frictionless by definition. These spheres rotated because it was natural for them to do so, and planets imbedded in their walls were carried around with them. Separately these notions might appear superficial and even amusing to the modern student, but if one remembers that Aristotle was forced to depend only upon naked eye observation and his power of reason, his achievement is impressive. His system could explain coherently the appearance and behavior of the everyday phenomena of life.

Over years and centuries fundamental Aristotelian ideas were elaborated in detail. A basically physical theory of the human body developed in which health was dependent upon a happy balance of four humors—blood, phlegm, yellow bile and black bile; these humors were various combinations of the four basic elements. For instance, blood was the hot humor because it contained a large proportion of the element fire. Hence, fever was diagnosed as an excess of blood, and the standard remedy was bleeding. (It should be recognized that this theory appeared sound; bleeding lowers blood pressure and temporarily reduces fever. This was, of course, treatment of symptoms rather than of causes, but it had some temporary effectiveness.)

The growth of Christianity reinforced Aristotelian thought. Aristotle's science placed the earth in the center of the universe. Christians assumed that the universe existed only as a stage-set for the drama of the struggle for man's salvation, and naturally they expected to find the drama set center-stage. Moreover, popular preachers could derive many useful analogies from the Aristotelian universe. The outer sphere, nearest to the purity of God's heaven, held the fixed stars, which sparkled with the white of purity; the planets, closer to the corruption of earth, shone in softer colors; and of course poor dross earth, corrupted by man's sin, did not shine at all. Thus, on both theoretical and practical levels Christianity found Aristotelianism congenial, and with appropriate modifications to make room for God's creation and God's will as a motive force the medieval church adopted the Aristotelian world view. In consequence of this adoption, Aristotelianism remained the basis of "establishment" opinion for over fourteen hundred years.

One of the fascinating questions posed by the scientific revolution of the early modern period is why it succeeded with relative rapidity after so many centuries of Aristotelian predominance. An attempt to answer this question must consider several different subjects: the accumulation of challenges, the development of better mathematical tools, the invention of instruments and the growth of improved communications. The combination of these developments rather than any one of them ultimately overturned Aristotle.

Challenges to Aristotelian science had existed from the beginning—some sound and some foolish. There were some who maintained that the world was flat, not round. (This idea has been exaggerated greatly in popular lore; anyone who lived by the sea saw the curve of the horizon, and those who watched a ship disappear into the distance—hull down, then sail down, then masthead down— could not doubt the curvature of the earth.) Others asserted that the sun, not the earth, was the center of the universe. But generally these challenges posed too many problems. For instance, if one displaced the earth from the center of the universe, the whole structure of physics would collapse. Why would heavy objects fall if the element earth were not seeking its natural position at the center of the universe? Why would flames leap if the element fire were not seeking to move to the outer ring? An old Greek experiment had attempted to determine whether the earth moved by measuring angles to fixed stars at different times. The experiment was well-conceived, but it failed to produce valid results, for the Greeks vastly underestimated the distance to the stars, and their instruments were too primitive to detect the differentials of angle that such a measurement produces. They concluded that the earth did not move.

Yet by the later middle ages serious criticisms had accumulated, particularly in the areas of astronomy and medicine. The great vogue for astrology which entered Europe from the Arab world stimulated astronomical observation considerably. The scientific studies of the Franciscans, of whom Roger Bacon probably was the most notable, raised problems. And Renaissance experiments in medicine, clandestine dissections and attempts to treat illnesses with herbs and minerals, refuted some traditional medical views.

The greatest interpreter of Aristotelian astronomy was the Alexandrian geographer Ptolemy. In the second century A.D. he had translated complex Aristotelian natural philosophy into astronomical charts on plane surfaces, showing planets revolving around the earth in concentric orbits. Even Aristotle had recognized, however, that planetary orbits were not perfect circles around the earth, and he had theorized that the spheres which carried the planets around turned on eccentric centers (that is, that they did not share the same focus), which made their revolutions appear irregular to an observer on earth. As a device to transfer this conception to plane surfaces,

Ptolemy had devised the epicycle; a planet followed an orbit around an imaginary point, which point revolved in an orbit around the earth. Accumulating astronomical data made Ptolemy's device more and more necessary, for astronomers were attempting the impossible task of describing elliptical movement around the sun in terms of complex circular movements around the earth.

By the sixteenth century, accepted charts of the solar system included one hundred and forty epicycles, a complexity that raised serious doubts in the minds of some astronomers. Copernicus, a Polish astronomer-mathematician, saw the problem in its starkest terms. He came to believe that such complexity defied reason and that he must assume either that the observational work of his predecessors over several centuries was sloppy and inaccurate or that the theory was wrong. He chose the latter assumption and tried to fit the observations to a theory that the sun rather than the earth was the center, resolutely ignoring the problems this would create in physics and mechanics. The results were promising but inconclusive. Because Copernicus continued to assume that planetary orbits were circular, he could not achieve total harmony of data and theory, but he was able to cut the number of epicycles by about half. His conclusions were published in 1543, after his death, in a work titled, *The Revolutions of Heavenly Spheres,* and aroused violent controversy.

In the same year, 1543, another book challenged Aristotelian conceptions in the medical field. A young Italian, Vesalius, produced a book called *The Structure of the Human Body.* In this work the challenge lay not so much in any theory in the text but rather in the illustrations. For centuries the great medical authority had been Galen, a Greco-Roman doctor of the third century A.D., who had codified medical knowledge on an Aristotelian basis. However, Galenic medicine faced even more serious problems than Ptolemaic astronomy. Many early societies have strong taboos against desecration of the human body, and Greco-Roman society was no exception. Consequently, most of Galen's dissections seem to have been practiced upon apes and pigs, whose anatomy differs importantly from that of humanity. Moreover, Galen's treatises survived into the middle ages only in condensations, with many of his explanations drastically cut or abbreviated, and the Christian church of medieval Europe reaffirmed the traditional opposition to dissections, so his descriptions rarely were checked or criticized. In consequence, for centuries the teaching of basic anatomy was derived from animal analogies.

In the later middle ages, however, human dissection began to be practiced again, especially in Italy. It was mostly clandestine, depending upon grave robbers and sympathetic rulers who would give medical schools the bodies of condemned criminals, but it was sufficient to cause serious unease among anatomists who found results at variance with those described by Galen. Vesalius' book exemplifies the conflict well. His text is conservative, repeating a lot of Galenic error, but his illustrations showed what he actually saw, and new techniques of reproduction—engravings and woodcuts—quickly spread his sharply detailed illustrations throughout European medical circles, encouraging those who otherwise might have faulted their own methodology rather than Galen's theories.

Thus, in the mid-sixteenth century two important challenges were posed to traditional science. Yet this simple fact does not explain why these challenges launched a successful scientific revolution while other challenges had been discounted. The greater body of conflicting evidence that the new challengers could muster represents a difference of degree rather than of kind. And vague statements about a Renaissance spirit of inquiry are not satisfactory either, for the Renaissance was not an unmixed blessing to scientific investigation. The adulation of classical writers—very much a part of any definition of Renaissance spirit—tended to make challenges to Ptolemy and Galen and especially to Aristotle all the more scandalous. Recognition of the very real achievements of these men, especially Aristotle's logic and Ptolemy's geography, tended by analogy to lend authority to all of their theories, many of which simply were erroneous, such as Ptolemy's astronomy. In fact, the intellectual establishment offered enormous opposition to the new challenges. Classicists damned those who dared to criticize the ancient Greeks and Romans. Universities, which have a tendency to structure and formalize knowledge, opposed the radicals who would overturn traditional teaching. The church condemned the desecration of the human body and damned those who would assert that the divine drama of good and evil was played upon a stage that was but a speck of dirt spinning at dizzying speed through the universe.

Luther, who often is taken to represent the Renaissance spirit in religion, characterized Copernicus as a damned fool who would turn the universe upside down.

Nor can the traditionalists be faulted seriously for failing to adopt the new theories with enthusiasm. Copernicus could not offer an integrated and unified astronomy, only some simplification. Vesalius could not explain the mysteries of disease and death, only some structural errors of Galen. And to have accepted the theories of these men would have meant discarding all that was known of astronomy, physics, mechanics and medicine, to begin again fumbling into the vast unknown.

Nonetheless, the challenge was established successfully, and it did prove revolutionary. The printing press was one important factor, for it allowed dissemination of the new ideas not as ill-copied manuscripts with multiplying errors but as consistent treatises with careful illustrations. And the printing press was but one of several new tools, both physical and intellectual, that were developed about this time.

The ancient Greeks had not progressed beyond geometry, no mean achievement but only a first step in the development of mathematics, and they had instruments no more sophisticated than the astrolabe, a primitive device for measuring elevations above the horizon. The medieval period saw important additions to the mathematical tools known in Europe as well as some improvement in physical aids to research. From the Arab world had come arabic numerals (the advantage of which will be recognized readily by anyone who ever has tried to multiply or divide with Roman numerals) as well as the mathematics known as algebra. In addition, the Arab world had transmitted to Europe the Indian concept of zero, a concept terribly important to the continued development of mathematics. The most important new instrument to appear in medieval Europe was the compass, probably an import from China, and this was accompanied by a slow but steady increase in the availability of research data, such as compendia of astronomical observations. The early modern period saw both of these kinds of tools, intellectual and mechanical, proliferated further. By the end of the seventeenth century, mathematics had progressed to calculus, and laboratories and observatories were equipped with lens systems and all sorts of devices for measuring time, temperature and pressure.

Finally, the early modern period inaugurated a much fuller communication among experimenters. Sir Isaac Newton, originator of the hypothesis of universal gravitation, was to remark that he felt like a pygmy standing on the shoulders of giants, and although perhaps overmodest, the comment illustrates another important achievement. In Paris and London, in Naples and Salerno and as far away as Philadelphia and Warsaw, scientific investigators of the seventeenth and eighteenth centuries formed societies that began to publish papers and proceedings. No longer did the investigator work in a vacuum or from the basis of bits of other peoples' results that came to him by chance, but rather he could read of earlier experiments and could submit his own results for learned criticism.

In consequence of all these developments, the revolution launched by Copernicus and Vesalius progressed relatively rapidly despite opposition. There were those who tried to absorb the new theories into older ideas, such as the Danish astronomer Tycho Brahe (1546–1601), who postulated a universe in which the earth circled the sun while all of the other planets circled the earth. (Of greater long-range significance were the vastly improved astronomical instruments that he designed.) But there also were a few men who struck out boldly to substantiate the new ideas. In the late sixteenth and early seventeenth centuries, two men in particular contributed to the Copernican hypothesis, Galileo Galilei (1564–1642) and Johannes Kepler (1571–1630).

Galileo really was more important to mechanics than to astronomy, his experiments such as those with projectiles and with falling bodies providing some viable alternatives to Aristotelian notions. But probably he is most famous for his demonstrations with telescopes. It appears that he learned of experiments with lens systems that had been carried out in the Netherlands and that he undertook to duplicate them. In any case, he built telescopes, and with them he succeeded in giving visual refutation of the old astronomy. From observation of the phases of the inner planets, Venus and Mercury, he could show that they circled the sun, not the earth. With telescopic magnification he also could show that other planets, particularly Jupiter, had satellites, a serious blow to the defenders of Aristotelian astronomy. Over the course of a long life, he built hundreds of telescopes, progressing from early three-power models to something over thirty-power before his death. His dramatic descriptions of the universe revealed to him by his telescopes and his defense of the new astronomy attracted much attention and made him one of the foremost popularizers of the new astronomy.

Kepler, on the other hand, worked out the mathematics that established the sun-centered hypothesis beyond dispute. Discarding the Copernican theory of circular orbits, he tried and rejected other regular forms such as the oval, and he discovered ultimately that if orbits were assumed to be elliptical, the observational data could be fitted to the sun-centered theory without need for epicycles to explain discrepancies. A further problem remained in that planets moved at varying speeds along their elliptical orbits, and Kepler sought a regular and calculable basis for the variation. He found this basis in a relationship that linked the variations in a planet's speed with its distance from the sun. The results of these successes were Kepler's laws.

The latter seventeenth century saw continued scientific progress. Mathematics was advanced by the French philosopher René Descartes (1596–1650), who invented analytical geometry, a mathematical system that made it possible to express curves in algebraic equations and conversely to translate formulae back into curves on graphs, and by Blaise Pascal (1623–1662), whose work in combinations and permutations opened the whole field of number theory. A bit later, in independent but contemporary developments, the Englishman Sir Isaac Newton (1642–1727) and the German Baron Gottfried von Leibniz (1646–1716) invented calculus, a shorthand system of calculation and annotation to handle varying speeds and curves of movement.

In astronomy, these developments came to a sort of fruition in other works of Sir Isaac Newton, whose world view remained fundamental to science until whole new areas of consideration were opened up by Albert Einstein early in the twentieth century. That the sun-centered hypothesis was valid was obvious after Kepler, but Newton was intrigued to discover how it worked. The results of his investigations were the hypothesis of universal gravitation, which stated that all matter exercised an attractive force upon all other matter, and Newton's laws, which expressed the force of attraction between two bodies in terms of relationships between their masses and the square of the distance between their centers.

About the same time, the challenges posed by Vesalius were producing fruitful results. William Harvey (1578–1657), an English doctor who had studied in Italy, denied the old theory of two separate blood systems, venous and arterial, and propounded the circulation of the blood. He could advance his theory only inferentially, however, for he could not show the connection between the two systems; it remained for an Italian, Marcello Malpighi (1628–1694), using a microscope, to show the capillaries that passed the blood from the arteries to the veins for return to the heart.

By the early eighteenth century, Aristotelian science clearly was dying. Its greatest strength, overall unity, also was its greatest weakness. A challenge to part of it opened enormous problems, but if the challenge to part of it could be substantiated, then the whole structure had to be doubted. Vestiges of Aristotelianism lingered long. Aristotle's dictum that nature abhors a vacuum resulted in all sorts of imaginary substances filling outer space long after his crystalline spheres had been abandoned; Descartes spoke of celestial fluids, and as late as the early twentieth century many people found some sort of ether a notion more congenial than vacuum. Popular parlance still carries echoes of Aristotle in such phrases as "the sun is trying to shine." But by and large the scientific revolution was an established fact by the eighteenth century. Copernicus and Vesalius had posed challenges which men such as Galileo, Kepler and Newton, Harvey and Malpighi had substantiated. Not surprisingly, the new and radical scientific thought spilled over into other fields.

The late seventeenth century saw new speculation stimulated by patterns of stratification, such as those exhibited by the famous cliffs of Dover, by fossils unearthed in the Netherlands and by what appeared to be sharks' teeth found on mountain tops in Italy. These phenomena had disturbing implications; it appeared the earth was older than the Bible suggested and, moreover, that life forms had disappeared and new ones had appeared in ways not accounted for in Biblical accounts of Genesis and the Flood. Already in the eighteenth century, concepts of evolution were being suggested, though no one could advance any very persuasive arguments of how evolution might have worked until the mid-nineteenth century when Charles Darwin (1809–1882) published his *Origin of the Species* (1859), which suggested that natural selection by environment could transform species over the course of many generations. And the eighteenth century saw a variety of advances in a whole range of scientific studies: electricity (Galvani and Volta), chemistry (Lavoisier), botany (Buffon and Linnaeus), geology and paleontology (Hutton and Lamarck) and composition and behavior of gases (Boyle and Cavendish). Obviously a new and very productive approach to natural studies had evolved.

Inevitably there were those who tried to sum up and explain the new approach that had proved so fruitful, the discipline eventually called the scientific method. Most prominent among the explainers were the English Francis Bacon (1561–1626) and the French René Descartes. Neither described the whole of the scientific method, but each described a part of it in a way probably important to the continued progress of early modern science. Bacon stressed observation and careful recording of observed data, though it may be said in criticism that he seems to have assumed that explanations would pop into the head of the observer and that he probably was convinced that there existed a relatively limited set of general principles that would explain all scientific phenomena. Descartes, on the other hand, stressed the subdivision of problems into component parts that could be subjected to individual study and the casting of hypotheses susceptible to testing; he may be criticized for giving too little weight to careful and critical observation, for seeming to assume that once a part of the natural world had been studied, a great deal more could be explored by pure reason. Yet taken together, these two men caught the essence of the new science: an attempt at detachment from *a priori* assumptions, careful observation of quantitative data, construction of hypotheses to explain data, and exhaustive testing of the hypotheses to substantiate or refute them.

It is almost impossible to overestimate the impact of the new science, and especially of the scientific method, upon the mentality of early modern Europe's intellectual elite; for the new science destroyed age-old beliefs and set intellectuals to speculating in wholly new directions about the nature of the universe. In accord with Descartes's and Newton's basically mechanical conceptions, the European intellectual came to view his world—socially, politically, and physically—as a great machine in which understanding depended upon mathematics and quantitative data rather than upon theology and speculation. Descartes's method of analysis, blocking out separate problems within larger ones and using the solutions of these as building-blocks of a larger understanding, grew to be the dominant methodology of European thought. This geometric spirit, as it was called, was believed to hold the key to all fields of knowledge, and the French even coined a verb meaning "to Cartesianate" to express this mode of analysis that depended upon observation, experiment and reason. Explicit in this new intellectual methodology was the rejection of traditional authority unless that authority could bear the scrutiny of experimental analysis. In his *Discourse on Method,* Descartes specifically endorsed the value of skepticism, demanding that the researcher should doubt everything until he saw persuasive proof. Soon ethics, theology and politics also were adjusted to the new scientific and mechanical view of the world by Spinoza, Malebranche and Locke, and their followers were numerous. The eighteenth century English poet, Alexander Pope, summed up the universality of the impact of the new science in his couplet:

Nature and Nature's laws lay hid in night: God said,
Let Newton be! and all was light.

In a long perspective, the world view established by the scientific revolution, as distinct from the skepticism and the methodology that evolved from it, probably has been exaggerated in importance, for the twentieth century is overturning the conclusions of the seventeenth and eighteenth centuries with great rapidity, and acceptance for two or three hundred years is not nearly so good a record as Aristotle could claim. It is possible that relativity theory and investigations of sub-atomic structure, psychedelic drugs and genetic experiments with DNA and RNA, may leave Copernicus and Newton, Vesalius and Harvey, as antiquated as Aristotle and Ptolemy. But future investigators, however startling their discoveries, also should admit that they stand upon the shoulders of giants.

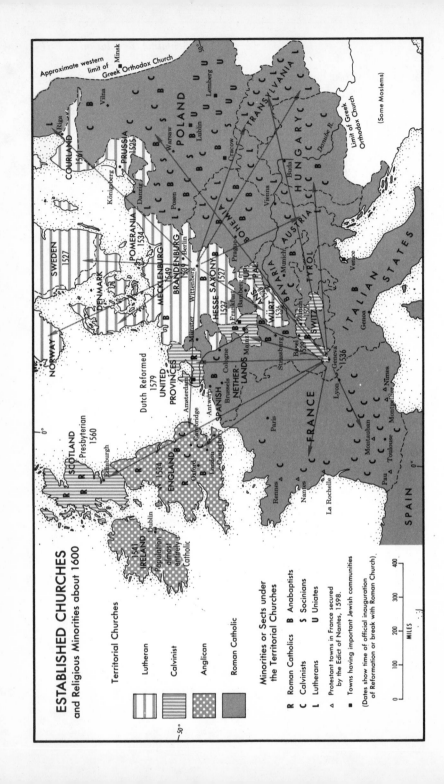

ESTABLISHED CHURCHES
and Religious Minorities about 1600

Territorial Churches

Lutheran

Calvinist

Anglican

Roman Catholic

Minorities or Sects under
the Territorial Churches

R Roman Catholics   B Anabaptists
C Calvinists   S Socinians
L Lutherans   U Uniates

△ Protestant towns in France secured
   by the Edict of Nantes, 1598.

■ Towns having important Jewish communities

(Dates show time of official inauguration
of Reformation or break with Roman Church).

0   100   200   300   400
         MILES

Approximate western
limit of Greek Orthodox Church

Limit of Greek
Orthodox Church

(Some Moslems)

Minsk
Vilna
Riga
COURLAND 1561
PRUSSIA 1525
Königsberg
Danzig
Warsaw
POLAND
Lublin
Lemberg
Posen
Cracow
TRANSYLVANIA
HUNGARY
Buda
Danube R.
Vienna
AUSTRIA
BOHEMIA
Prague
SWEDEN 1527
DENMARK
NORWAY
POMERANIA 1534
MECKLENBURG 1549
BRANDENBURG 1539
Berlin
Wittenberg
SAXONY 1527
HESSE 1527
Frankfurt
Bamberg
Munich
BAVARIA
TYROL
SWITZ.
Geneva 1536
PALAT.
WÜRT. 1534
Ulm
Augsburg
Münster
Cologne
Mainz
Strassburg
Basel 1529
UNITED PROVINCES
Dutch Reformed 1579
Amsterdam
Antwerp
Brussels
SPANISH NETHERLANDS
Utrecht 1576
ITALIAN STATES
Venice
Genoa
SCOTLAND Presbyterian 1560
Edinburgh
ENGLAND 1534
Cambridge
Oxford
London
Canterbury
IRELAND 1541
Dublin
Population almost
entirely Catholic
FRANCE
Paris
Rennes
Nantes
La Rochelle
Montauban
Toulouse
Pau
Montpellier
Nîmes
Lyon
SPAIN

THE HOUSE OF BOURBON

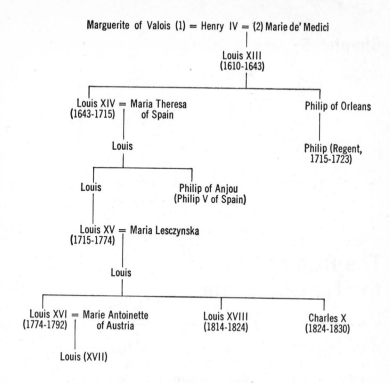

THE HOUSE OF ROMANOV

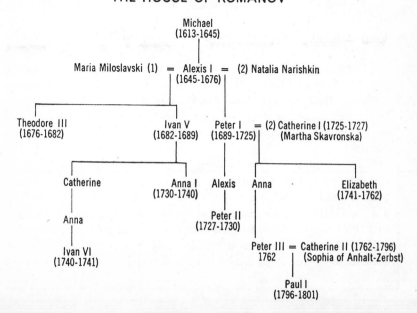

Chapter 5

The Rise of
the National State

When Philip II of Spain died in 1598, the Habsburg hegemony in Europe was far from ended. Despite the loss of the Great Armada and the rise of English naval strength, the reconsolidation of hostile royal authority in France and the *de facto* autonomy of Switzerland and the Dutch Netherlands, the two branches of the house of Habsburg still controlled vast territories. Spain remained the greatest military power in Europe, and though the Holy Roman Empire appeared still prostrate from the religious wars and the emperor weakened in relation to the princes, imperial claims to extensive authority throughout Germany never had been relinquished. Habsburg pretensions to universal monarchy still seemed a real threat, and England, France and the Netherlands were still very much on the defensive.

The beginning of the seventeenth century saw a few years of uneasy peace, but the situation remained far from stable. France was at peace officially after 1598, but King Henry IV continued to aid the Dutch in their war against Spain and to encourage the German Protestant princes in their political opposition to the emperor. In 1609 the Dutch signed a twelve years truce with Spain, but it seemed to be regarded by both sides as a pause to rearm and re-equip rather than as an opportunity to negotiate a peaceful settlement. Imperial claims in a succession dispute over Cleves-Jülich, a group of small territories on the lower Rhine, evoked the threat of French intervention in 1609. Revived religious quarrels in Germany led to the foundation of new armed alliances, the Protestant Union in 1608 and the Catholic League in 1609, and there were comparable difficulties in Bohemia. In 1606 the Austrians and the Ottoman Turks signed an inconclusive peace, but the Danube frontier remained insecure. The war between England and Spain was ended officially in 1604 by Queen Elizabeth's successor, James I, but beyond European waters, in the colonies and on the high seas, sporadic hostilities hardly were diminished. In sum, about 1610 none of Europe's major powers was at war officially, but old hostilities were still powerful forces, and many issues from colonial rivalries to religious clashes had the potential of precipitating great conflict.

The massive war that dominated the first half of the seventeenth century was triggered finally by religious incidents in Bohemia and by Habsburg reactions to them. This struggle usually is called the Thirty Years War (1618–1648) and often is designated the last of the religious wars, but neither of these appellations should be applied too rigorously. The Dutch long have talked of the Eighty Years War, considering the fighting in the early seventeenth century as part of their long effort to break Habsburg power, and a case can be made for considering the fighting of the whole period from the 1530s to the 1640s a second Hundred Years War, a struggle by non-Habsburg Europe to break the Habsburg encirclement. The designation "last of the religious wars" also must be considered carefully, for the implication that the war can be explained satisfactorily by religious motivation simply will not bear scrutiny. Religious factors were an important though not exclusive cause of the outbreak of the war, and they often complicated its course, but the conflict between Catholic France and the Catholic Habsburgs cannot be treated in terms of religious factors.

The Thirty Years War began with a Protestant revolt in Bohemia in the spring of 1618, over a combination of religious issues and a Habsburg succession question. Emperor Matthias (1612–1619), who also was king of Bohemia, was childless, and toward the end of his life he arranged to be succeeded by his cousin

Ferdinand of Styria. Ferdinand, however, was a strict Catholic and a leading exponent of the Counter-Reformation, so his accession was much feared in Bohemia, where Protestantism was well established, with roots going back to the fifteenth century Hussities. The Bohemian Protestants rose in revolt, and with help from German Protestants they drove Habsburg forces from Bohemia in 1619. At this juncture Emperor Matthias died.

The imperial electors awarded Ferdinand of Styria the crown of the Holy Roman Empire as Emperor Ferdinand II (1619-1637), which strengthened his position, but the Bohemian Protestants sought to prevent his accession to the Bohemian crown. Unfortunately the Bohemian estates once had elected Ferdinand successor to Matthias, but they reassembled, declared him deposed and offered the crown to Frederick Count Palatine; they hoped he could rally the Protestant forces of Europe to their defense, for he was one of the seven electors of the Holy Roman Empire, the leader of the Protestant Union and the son-in-law of King James I of England. Meanwhile, Emperor Ferdinand sought help from his Habsburg cousins in Spain and from Duke Maximilian of Bavaria, leader of the Catholic League.

The Protestant Union was divided internally by discord between Lutherans and Calvinists and by disagreement whether the Bohemian war was properly a religious or a political struggle, and in mid-1620 it abandoned Frederick. A few months later Bohemian forces were crushed by the army of the Catholic League at the Battle of White Mountain, and Frederick's Palatinate lands were invaded by troops from the Spanish Netherlands. By 1623 the Bohemian revolt was over, and Ferdinand's agents were eradicating Protestantism and political liberties.

The war that had begun in Bohemia spread quickly to Germany, however, largely as a result of Ferdinand's actions in the aftermath of the revolt. In addition to the repression in Bohemia, which frightened German Protestants by its display of the new emperor's fanaticism, Ferdinand also outlawed Count Frederick and other German princes who had supported the revolt and awarded part of Frederick's lands and his electoral vote to Maximilian of Bavaria. These actions raised a sort of constitutional issue, for traditionally, in the case of a prince, outlawry and confiscation could be decided only by the emperor and the other princes together, not by the emperor alone. Even those princes who had felt that

Ferdinand was justified in his policy in Bohemia had to fear the absolutist ambitions implicit in his unilateral action in Germany.

Christian IV, king of Denmark (1588–1648), was a prince of the Holy Roman Empire in his capacity as duke of Holstein. As a Lutheran he opposed the Counter-Reformation; as a German prince he opposed the emperor's political ambitions; as a dynast he aspired to secularized church lands as principalities for his sons. In 1625 he rallied some of the northern princes to oppose the emperor militarily, and in the summer of 1626 he marched south, opening what usually is called the Danish phase of the war. His campaign was supported by Bethlen Gabor, the Protestant prince of Transylvania (in Hungary) who attacked Austria from the east.

The emperor had new resources too, the army of Albrecht von Wallenstein. An adventurer who had made a fortune in land speculation in Bohemia during the repression, Wallenstein had offered to raise a force of twenty-five thousand men at his own expense if he might be allowed to command it. The emperor was delighted to accept the offer, for not only did it give him new resources in the spreading conflict but also a force which was not dependent upon the princes of the Catholic League, who were no more eager than Protestant princes to see a notable increase in the emperor's political strength. Wallenstein's army soon became infamous for living off the land, devastating any area it moved through like a swarm of locusts, but it was effective militarily. Part of this force turned back Bethlen Gabor, while the rest supported the armies of the Catholic League. Christian of Denmark was defeated at the Battle of Lütter am Barenberge in 1626.

Though Christian was forced to retreat, his army was still intact, and fighting continued for another two and a half years. Then Wallenstein thought he saw a new threat developing elsewhere and persuaded the emperor to make a moderate peace, the Treaty of Lübeck of 1629. By this treaty Christian got his lands back in return for a promise not to interfere further in German affairs; in addition, he abandoned his German allies, some of whom were outlawed and their lands given to Wallenstein.

The Treaty of Lübeck appeared to mark the collapse of opposition to the emperor's growing power. That Ferdinand II was determined to use this new power was made clear a few months before the treaty, when in March of 1629 he issued the Edict of Restitution. The Peace of Augsburg of 1555 had prohibited the confiscation of any more church lands, but this provision had proved unenforceable. During the succeeding three quarters of a century, Protestants had seized two archbishoprics, twelve bishoprics, and about one hundred and twenty monasteries. The Edict of Restitution proposed to restore all of these lands to the church and to break up all Protestant sects except Lutheranism, since only it had been given legal status with Catholicism by the Peace of Augsburg.

Concern over the emperor's growing power was not limited to German Protestants and princes, for a Germany firmly under the control of the Habsburgs also would have been a dangerous threat to France. During the 1620s the French crown was occupied with internal Protestant rebellions, but in 1629 the last of them was crushed, and the government at last could undertake a more aggressive foreign policy; having just concluded a costly civil war, it was not yet ready to send French armies across the Rhine, but French diplomacy and French gold were committed freely to persuade the king of Sweden, Gustavus Adolphus (1611–1632) to intervene in Germany. It was this threat which Wallenstein had seen when he advised the emperor to make a generous peace with Denmark.

Gustavus Adolphus was attracted by the role of Protestant champion, and he liked war and the command of armies; moreover, control of the German Baltic coast would have made the Baltic almost wholly a Swedish sea. He concluded a subsidy treaty with France, and in the summer of 1630 he landed an army in north Germany, beginning the Swedish phase of the war. The north German princes did not rally to Gustavus with enthusiasm, however, and a year was spent in negotiations to secure his base of operations and his supply line; but when his campaign began in the late summer of 1631, Gustavus Adolphus proved to be a military genius, and his army cut through Germany like a hot knife through butter. Wallenstein managed to cover the Danube Valley and protect Vienna, but for a year Gustavus Adolphus dominated the battlefields of the empire. Then at Lutzen, in November of 1632, the Swedish king was killed, and fighting was desultory for the next two years.

In 1634 the nature of the war changed again, when imperial forces with Spanish reinforcements won a great battle at Nördlingen which drove the Swedes and their Protestant German allies back almost to the Baltic. As in 1629, the emperor appeared again the military master of Germany, and in the spring of 1635 he consolidated his position by making peace with most of the German princes. The Peace of Prague granted amnesties and suspended most of the provisions of the Edict of Restitution. The emperor still refused to recognize Calvinism, but most of the German princes were satisfied.

As a result of the Peace of Prague, France increased her intervention, and the fighting continued, but this last phase of the war was fought by a new generation. Gustavus Adolphus had been killed in 1632 and Wallenstein in 1634. Emperor Ferdinand died in 1637, the French First Minister, Richelieu, in 1642 and the king of France, Louis XIII, in 1643. The new generation was less committed to the old issues of the early war years, and peace became possible at last.

The Peace of Westphalia of 1648 resolved a number of issues. The German princes gained effective independence from imperial control, and Calvinism was granted the same legal status as Lutheranism in the empire. The family of the Count Palatine got part of its lands back, and a new electoral vote was created for it (the eighth) so that Bavaria could retain the vote given to it in the 1620s. The independence of the Dutch and of the Swiss was recognized. Imperial hopes of Counter-Reformation and political consolidation were ruined, for the new Germany was a land of princely states and religious diversity. The peace also provided gains for the intervening foreign powers: Sweden obtained control of great stretches of Baltic coast and three commercially important river mouths as well as a financial indemnity, while France received the greater part of Alsace, which brought her frontiers to the Rhine. Perhaps the most significant aspect of the settlement was the division of the house of Habsburg. France refused to make peace with Spain, but the German Habsburgs settled nonetheless, abandoning their Spanish cousins to a solitary war with France that dragged on until 1659.

Within Habsburg Spain, the long years of war proved costly, and at the same time court favoritism and the crown's religious policy led to an enormous growth of noble estates and church foundations, largely tax-exempt, which reduced the government's resources. When Spain first joined the war in central Europe in the 1620s, she was still the greatest power in Europe, but about 1640 she began to experience serious problems. King Philip IV (1621–1665) had placed his government in the hands of the Count-Duke Olivarez, an able and loyal administrator who sought to increase royal power at home while maintaining Spain's hegemony abroad, but the program proved too ambitious. Olivarez' policy required heavy taxation at the same time that the crown was restricting the traditional privileges of local authorities, and revolts in Portugal and Catalonia resulted. With France supporting the rebels, the revolts became serious enough to cause Olivarez' dismissal and to win Portugal's independence, though Catalonia eventually accepted a compromise settlement. Moreover, these domestic disturbances were paralleled by reverses abroad: a French victory at Rocroy in May of 1643, a revolt in Naples in 1647, Spain's abandonment by the German Habsburgs in 1648. For another eleven years the war with France dragged on, but after another French victory in 1658, the Battle of the Dunes, Spain had to accept the costly Peace of the Pyrenees in 1659. She made important border concessions to France, both on the French frontier with the Spanish Netherlands and on the Pyrenees frontier, and she gave the king of Spain's eldest daughter as a bride to the young king of France, Louis XIV, which drew French interest more deeply into the troubled affairs of the Habsburg family. The Peace of Westphalia and the Peace of the Pyrenees marked the end of the Habsburg hegemony.

In France the war years, though costly, produced much more positive results. After the assassination of Henry IV in 1610 and the succession of his nine-year-old son, Louis XIII, the French crown was weakened at first by noble factions competing for favor, but in the mid-1620s, when the king put his confidence in the brilliant and dedicated Cardinal Richelieu, the French crown's policies of national consolidation and the overthrow of Habsburg domination were resumed. Richelieu often has been portrayed as unrestrainedly ambitious, threatening the authority of the king himself, and as a dictatorial tyrant seeking the destruction of the French nobility and the Huguenots, but such assertions are groundless. The king and his cardinal-minister worked in close harmony to promote the interests of the crown, and they sought not to destroy but to compel obedience. Richelieu, like Wallenstein or Olivarez, was a royal servant. All three appeared innovators to their contemporaries, and all three made many enemies, but Richelieu never lost the confidence of his royal master. That the work of national consolidation proved more effective and more enduring in France than in neighboring countries reflects the continuing importance of the person of the king in these nascent national states; without the intelligent and consistent support of royal authority, even able and dedicated ministers proved ineffective.

The increase of royal authority in France faced two major obstacles, the Protestants and the nobility. Despite Henry IV's Edict of Nantes of 1598, which had granted freedom of conscience and widespread toleration of Protestant public worship, extremist elements among the French Huguenots remained restive, still aspiring to destroy French Catholicism completely. These extremist elements involved the Protestants in several rebellions in the 1620s, but the key city of La Rochelle fell to the king's forces in 1628, and with it fell the political and military power of the Huguenots. Yet Louis XIII and Richelieu showed moderation in victory. The Protestants lost their private armies and their fortified towns, the special status that set them apart from other Frenchmen, but they kept their freedom of religion. The crown would allow diversity if coupled with obedience.

The same general policy governed Louis XIII's and Richelieu's treatment of the nobility. They had no desire to destroy it as a class; Richelieu himself was of the nobility, and the king depended upon noble families to supply personnel for his cavalry and the officer corps of his infantry. It was not the nobility but the endemic rebellions fomented by some noblemen that the king and his cardinal-minister attempted to control, and in this endeavor they were largely successful. The most dramatic incidents of their policy were the executions of the duke of Montmorency-Bouteville in 1630 and of the duke of Montmorency in 1632, two members of a family so great that it always had been considered beyond the reach of justice; the execution of the two dukes frightened the nobility into recognition of the fact that the king meant to be obeyed. Minor punishments for lesser offenders drove the lesson home; some were fined, some were imprisoned and others were compelled to destroy the fortifications of their chateaux at considerable expense. The nobility continued to be an important class, but it learned the meaning of obedience.

Both Richelieu and Louis XIII died in the midst of the Thirty Years War, and France again faced a long regency as Louis XIV (1643–1715) was only five years old. Direction of the regency government passed to the queen mother, Anne, and to her minister, Cardinal Mazarin, who brought the foreign wars to a successful conclusion but had to confront another internal upheaval before the accomplishments of the preceding reign were secure. This rebellion, known as the Fronde (1648–1652), was partly a protest against continuing the costly war against Spain after peace had been made with the Holy Roman Empire and partly an attempt to reverse the centralizing tendencies of the crown. The many disparate elements that participated in the revolt could never coordinate their efforts, however, and the government managed to defeat them completely. Subsequently, though there were occasional regional uprisings against royal officers or royal tax policy, there were no more rebellions aimed at forceful revision of the central government until the great French revolution of 1789.

When Cardinal Mazarin died in 1661, Louis XIV took personal control of his government. On the basis of earlier innovations by Richelieu, he created an extensive bureaucracy of officials called intendants to administer the provinces; with the advice of his finance minister, Colbert, he inaugurated tariff and subsidy policies designed to promote trade and encourage economic expansion; with the assistance of his war minister, Louvois, he raised the French army to a half million men, uniformed and better trained and equipped than any large army that Europe had seen since the Roman legions. Such consolidation did not proceed without setbacks, however: a new series of long and costly wars necessitated high taxation that negated some of the efforts at economic development; the construction of a new capital outside of Paris, at Versailles, largely isolated the king from the mainstream of French life and made the court a world in itself; and the revocation of the Edict of Nantes, in 1685, cost France tens of thousands of productive citizens, who fled abroad to escape religious persecution, and the sympathy of Protestant Europe. Nonetheless, by the end of the seventeenth century France was a national state, centralized and served by a fairly controllable modern army and an extensive bureaucracy.

In the aftermath of the Thirty Years War, the Dutch Netherlands also emerged as a powerful modern state. During the long war with Spain the Dutch fleets had expanded remarkably, and commerce ranging from the Baltic to Japan had brought fabulous wealth, so that though small in both population and area, the Netherlands was able to hire troops and play the role of a great power through the latter half of the seventeenth century. But the Dutch failed to solve political issues despite their commercial sophistication. Centralizing and aristocratic tendencies were represented by the house of Orange, which held the stadtholdership of the republic, a title that subsumed a number of military offices. The ambitions of the house of Orange were opposed by the seven provinces, which were fanatically jealous of states' rights; this opposition was expressed chiefly through the states-general, the republic's elected assembly, and through the office of the grand pensionary of Holland. Through the third quarter of the seventeenth century, the extreme youth of the heir of the house of Orange left power in the hands of the decentralizing party, and the able grand pensionary, John de Witt, piloted the Netherlands successfully through two trade wars with England. In the 1670s, however, war with France broke out, and in consequence of a French invasion, de Witt was murdered by a mob which called the now grown William III of Orange to power. The Netherlands then engaged in several wars with France, but their high cost and growing commercial competition from other states eroded the strong economic position that the Dutch had enjoyed in the middle of the century. An alliance with England appeared very advantageous to the Netherlands when William III secured the English crown in 1688, but as the Dutch economy weakened and the role of the central government remained unresolved, the republic became more and more a satellite of the English system. Nonetheless, by the end of the seventeenth century the Dutch Netherlands clearly was a modern national state if no longer a great power; the grim wars over more than a century had developed a sense of national consciousness in the populace, and despite political instability the republic had developed a modern fiscal administration and modern military and naval forces.

After some years of recuperation from the devastation of the Thirty Years War, signs of political revival began to appear in central and northern Europe in the late seventeenth century. With the Holy Roman Empire shattered, the government in Vienna focussed upon consolidation of the Habsburg family lands and achieved impressive results. Governmental reform in the late 1680s was effective, especially in financial administration. War with the Turks succeeded in freeing most of Hungary by the end of the century, and an extensive program of colonization began the revival of that country. In renewed wars with France, Austrian forces acquitted themselves well, and shortly after the turn of the century Austria replaced Spain as the controlling power in Italy and the southern Netherlands. While the multi-racial character of the population of the Habsburg lands impeded the sort of national consolidation that was developing elsewhere, the Vienna government did make some progress in developing the political and military apparatus of the modern state.

In north Germany, too, a modern state was beginning to appear on the foundation of the old Electorate of Brandenburg. In the middle of the seventeenth century, the electoral family of Hohenzollern held land all across north Germany from the Rhineland to Prussia, and in the chaos that followed the Thirty Years War, Frederick William the Great Elector (1640–1688) began hammering these scattered territories into some semblance of an effective power. He broke down local particularist privileges, established productive tax policies and rebuilt his army. He subsidized economic expansion, and when the Huguenots fled from France after 1685 he welcomed thousands of them to help repopulate his lands. His son Frederick (1688–1713), by using his armies wisely, obtained the emperor's consent to a royal crown in 1701, and proclaimed himself Frederick I, king in Prussia. As in the lands of the German Habsburgs, whether there was a national basis for the emerging new government remained uncertain, but it appeared to be developing rapidly the administrative and military components of a modern state.

Sweden also underwent an important transformation in the late seventeenth century. Domestic instability resulted from the abdication of Gustavus Adolphus' daughter Christina (1632–1654) and from the rivalry of aristocratic factions, while foreign policy was most notable for unsuccessful wars with Poland and Brandenburg. Toward the end of the seventeenth century, however, King Charles XI (1660–1697) succeeded in breaking the aristocracy's economic power by widespread confiscation of estates and its political power through limitation of the noble council's role. He established a strongly centralized royal government that was supported by highly developed popular national consciousness, and at his death in 1697, Sweden was a nascent modern national state. The royal victory was short-lived, however. Charles XII (1697–1718) had to fight to preserve Swedish control of the Baltic, but Sweden's resources were limited, and the series of wars he engaged in proved disastrous. Early in the eighteenth century Sweden's military power was broken, and an aristocratic resurgence undid the political achievements of Charles XI, so that Sweden declined to the level of a second rank power like the Dutch republic.

England experienced unique national development in the seventeenth century, moving from nascent absolutism through revolution and radical political experiment to restrained and responsible monarchy. When Elizabeth I died in 1603, she left a very delicate political balance to her Scottish cousin James I (1603–1625). The crown's frequent use of parliament had given that body the habit of regular assembly and a sense of institutional importance, especially in matters of money and religion. While it is certainly true that James I did not understand English political practice and that he lacked the Tudor's political skill, in all fairness it must be noted that England's peculiar interaction of king and parliament was without parallel anywhere and that the new king inherited difficult religious and financial problems from his predecessors. Further aggravating matters was the fact that James I, like most monarchs of his time, believed in the divine right of kings and sought to increase royal absolutism at the very time that the maturing parliament was seeking to increase the parliamentary role in government. Quarrels arose quickly, some over taxes and some over the demands of religious radicals called puritans, and these issues were aggravated by James's unpopular effort to achieve a Spanish alliance. In the early 1620s, tension reached a breaking point when parliament impeached some of the king's officers, criticized the proposed Spanish alliance and drafted the Great Protestation defending the parliament's right to debate any matter of government policy. In a rage, James destroyed the protestation and dismissed parliament.

Charles I (1625–1649) got on no better with parliament than had his father, and it presented him with the Petition of Right, a statement of parliamentary authority even more outspoken than the Great Protestation. Through the 1630s Charles attempted to govern without parliament, but severe religious troubles and shortage of money forced him to reconvene it in 1640, and the angry parliamentarians forced surrender after surrender upon him; he sacrificed counselors, agreed to summon parliament every three years, abolished unpopular courts and compromised on religious issues. Still the parliamentarians were not satisfied, and in 1641 when Charles refused further concessions, they raised troops and civil war broke out. After the war ended in victory for parliamentary forces in 1648, extremists wrested control from moderates, enacted radical religious reform and executed the king (January, 1649).

After the execution of Charles I, England attempted a Commonwealth (1649–1660), in theory a republic but in practice a military government run by Oliver Cromwell, a situation recognized in 1653 when Cromwell created a nominated parliament and adopted the title of Lord Protector. But despite almost dictatorial powers, even Cromwell had difficulties with parliamentary ambitions and continuing religious radicalism; when he died in 1658 English government was on no more stable basis than it had been in 1640, and a series of military *coups* led to the restoration of the Stuart monarchy in 1660.

The new king, Charles II (1660–1685), honestly sought compromise at first, but the old royal-parliamentary struggle soon flared again. The king tried financial expedients, including a subsidy treaty with Catholic France, to avoid dependence upon the parliament for money; he showed sympathy for Catholicism, and his brother and heir, James, joined that faith openly and married an Italian Catholic princess. These quarrels resulted in the emergence of two loose political factions, called Tories and Whigs; the former was strongly royalist and the latter generally parliamentarian, but both supported the English religious settlement. Hence, both groups were disturbed when Charles died and was succeeded by his Catholic brother. James II (1685–1688) was unpopular from the outset for his overt Catholicism, and when the queen bore him a son in 1688 it appeared that a Catholic royal line would be perpetuated. Consequently, the opposition invited William III of the Netherlands, who was married to James' daughter Mary (child of an earlier Protestant marriage) to save England from Catholic tyranny, and William accepted. Crossing to England with an army, he soon held the country, and James fled to France. Early in 1689 parliament declared James's flight to be an abdication and bestowed the crown jointly upon William and Mary. The Glorious Revolution had been accomplished quickly and with little bloodshed.

The settlement of the crown by parliament completed the emergence of England as a modern national state, for it established a stable centralized government composed of the king *and* parliament upon the basis of strong national consciousness. William and Mary agreed that laws and taxes needed the consent of parliament and that parliament should be convened frequently. Further, parliament excluded the Catholic Stuarts from the English throne and provided for a Protestant succession. The king retained extensive prerogatives, but parliament had achieved a secure place in the concept of crown government.

Hence, at the end of the seventeenth century Europe presented a political aspect very different from that of a century before. The Habsburg hegemony was broken; France and England were modern national states; the Dutch Republic and Sweden, though declining as great powers, seemed to be evolving in the same direction, and something comparable could be descried in Prussia and Austria. Not surprisingly, the emergence of a number of competing states changed the pattern of international affairs quite as much as those nations had changed internally.

Chapter 6

The Birth of
the Balance of Power

In the last quarter of the seventeenth century a new pattern of international relations began to emerge in Europe, stimulated chiefly by the ambitions of Louis XIV of France, for the collapse of the Holy Roman Empire and the decline of Spain had created a power vacuum which the French king sought to fill. Louis XIV's foreign policy is extremely complicated, for it was based upon both national and dynastic goals; but his ambitions, whatever their bases, threatened neighboring states. A changing pattern of coalitions developed to limit Louis XIV, and from the wars that resulted emerged the balance of power.

Louis XIV assumed personal control of his government at Mazarin's death in 1661, two years after the Peace of the Pyrenees. He was young, vigorous and eager to prove himself. Though his contemporaries sometimes thought him ill-educated because he was weak in the classics, Mazarin had trained him well for his responsibilities. That he would engage in war was almost certain; the tradition of the king as a military leader still was strong, and besides he had to provide honorable employment for his nobility. Within a few years France was involved in the first of the wars that were to dominate his reign.

Alleging rather obscure rights of inheritance called devolution, Louis tried to seize the Spanish Netherlands in his wife's name in 1667–1668, and Spain was too weakened to mount a very effective resistance. However, Europe had learned the effectiveness of cooperative resistance during the long struggle against the Habsburgs, and Louis soon found himself faced with a hostile coalition called the Triple Alliance: the Dutch, who feared to have France as a neighbor and commercial rival; the English, who feared the competition their trade might face if the port of Antwerp were in French hands; and the Swedes, whose commercial interests tied them to the Dutch and English. The French king was forced to content himself with a dozen fortified towns that strengthened France's northern borders.

Hardly was the War of Devolution ended when Louis XIV prepared an onslaught against the Dutch. He recognized them as the instigators of the alliance that had frustrated his first efforts and the chief opponents of French northern expansion; he resented their protection of French dissidents who published masses of hostile political tracts in the Netherlands; and he realized that Dutch commercial strength was one of the chief obstacles to French economic growth. By diplomacy and bribery he dismantled the Triple Alliance, concluding treaties with England in 1670 and Sweden in 1672, which drew them into co-operation with France. Then in the summer of 1672 he launched an army of 100,000 men against the Dutch while the English attacked them by sea. The Dutch war went well for France at first, and the southern Dutch provinces were overrun, but again Louis failed to achieve total success. The Dutch flooded their lands, stopping the progress of the French armies, and rallied around William III of Orange. Then France's allies abandoned her or were defeated. Again Louis XIV had to accept a negotiated peace. The Peace of Nimwegen of 1678 restored to the Dutch their conquered territories but allowed France some gains at the expense of Spain: border towns and the whole of the Franche-Comté.

In the 1660s and 1670s Louis XIV had aimed north and had met stiff opposition; about 1680 he began to aim eastward toward Germany. The Peace of Westphalia and subsequent treaties had given Alsace and other Rhineland positions to France, but the boundaries of these concessions were unclear. Louis established special courts, called chambers of reunion, to decide disputed cases and used his troops to enforce decisions. Naturally, French courts deciding

French claims on German lands tended to be prejudiced, and the result was a steady advance which the Germans called peaceful aggression. When the French seized Strasbourg in 1681, war seemed imminent, but the Empire was still weak, and negotiations resulted in a settlement in 1684. Louis kept most of what he had seized, and much of Germany was antagonized.

In the mid-1680s Louis XIV was at the height of his power. He had made significant territorial advances to the north and east, and he was respected and feared throughout Europe. But his neighbors were concerned to check his expansion, and the English and Dutch were fearful of the growth of French commercial power. Louis' policies were evoking general opposition such as had destroyed the Habsburgs. The hatred of Protestant Europe was increased further in 1685 when he revoked the Edict of Nantes; soon Protestant lands were flooded with Huguenot refugees who spread tales of the atrocities that had been committed in the king's name.

In 1686 the emperor, the kings of Spain and Sweden and some German princes concluded the League of Augsburg, aimed at containing Louis XIV. In 1687 the duke of Savoy joined. In 1688 William III of the Netherlands became king of England, and both the Dutch and the English joined the league, which then was called the Grand Alliance. Nine years of fighting resulted in a stalemate, however; Louis could not break the ring formed around him by his enemies, but neither could they crack his defenses and invade France. Peace was made finally at Ryswick in 1697, but it changed little except that France recognized William III as king of England, and the Dutch were permitted to garrison some towns in the Spanish Netherlands as a barrier against France.

The major powers agreed in 1697 to a settlement that settled almost nothing because of the growing crisis of the Spanish succession. The king of Spain was childless, and the Spanish branch of the house of Habsburg was about to die out. The French Bourbons and the Austrian Habsburgs had more or less equally good claims to the inheritance, though both faced legal complications. Because of the trade resources of Spain's colonies as well as possible effects upon the military situation in Europe, both the English and the Dutch felt their interests were involved and wished to prevent the union of Spain with either France or Austria. Thus, in the late 1690s all the powers sought to disengage so as to be free for whatever action their interests dictated when the king of Spain died.

The years immediately following the Peace of Ryswick saw a flurry of diplomatic activity in all the European courts, and the English and Dutch seem to have pursued the concept of a balance of power in which no one state could dominate Europe. Louis XIV understood this desire of the naval powers and was sympathetic to it; he was willing to forego the major inheritance, so long as it did not pass into Austrian hands, if that were the price of peace. For awhile it appeared that the issue might be settled peacefully, for though the Austrians were unwilling to accept a partial inheritance, they would have been helpless before a Franco-Anglo-Dutch agreement. Then a series of disasters befell the negotiators. In 1699 a Bavarian prince who had been chosen as a compromise candidate for the Spanish crown died, and hardly had new partition agreements been reached when the king of Spain died in 1700, leaving a will that prohibited partitions and left the entire inheritance to Louis XIV's grandson, Philip. When Louis XIV, as head of the Bourbon family, accepted the legacy, war with Austria was almost certain, but the English and Dutch were undecided at first. However, rapid French moves to exploit Philip's accession in Spain soon antagonized the naval powers, and in the autumn of 1701 the Grand Alliance was reestablished.

The War of the Spanish Succession was almost a replay of the War of the League of Augsburg except that Spain was allied with embattled France. Again France could not defeat her enemies and they could not invade France, though the brilliant English commander, Marlborough, won the Spanish Netherlands for the allies. Eventually the cost of the war forced the participants to the conference table, and the struggle ended in the Treaties of Utrecht in 1713 and Rastatt in 1714. The Spanish crown and its overseas colonies remained with the new Bourbon king, Philip V (1700–1746), but with the agreement that the Spanish and French crowns never would be joined. The Spanish Netherlands and most of Spain's possessions in Italy went to the Austrian Habsburgs. England made major gains: Newfoundland, Nova Scotia and the Hudsons Bay Territory from France and Gibraltar, Minorca and colonial trading privileges from Spain. The treaties also gave international recognition to the Protestant succession in England and to the royal crowns awarded to the duke of Savoy (Sicily, later exchanged with Spain for Sardinia) and the elector of Brandenburg (Prussia).

Most of all, the Treaties of Utrecht and Rastatt established the balance of power as the new pattern of European international relations. France remained the greatest power in Europe, but no longer could she threaten the security of the entire continent, for it had been proved that alliances could contain her. England had emerged as Europe's greatest naval power, but the Dutch, the French and the Spanish remained important in colonial affairs. Both Austria and Prussia had shown renewed vitality, and both had become significant politically and militarily. In the early eighteenth century western and central Europe counted England, France, Prussia and Austria as major powers with Spain and the Dutch Netherlands as secondary powers, but no one of them was strong enough to establish hegemony in Europe.

About the same time as the War of Spanish Succession, another struggle known as the Great Northern War was effecting equally significant changes in northern and eastern Europe. The basis of this war was the opposition of Russia, Saxony-Poland and Denmark to the Swedish hegemony in the Baltic area; the three powers allied in 1699 and attacked Sweden in 1700. However, the new Swedish king, Charles XII, proved to be a military genius, and he knocked Denmark out of the war, inflicted a humiliating defeat upon the Russians and then subjected the Poles and Saxons to a six-year struggle that ended in their defeat. But Peter the Great of Russia (1689–1725) was determined to continue the struggle until he held a secure harbor on the Baltic, giving access to the west, and during the half-dozen years that Charles was occupied in Poland the Russian armies were improved greatly. Thus, when Charles turned against Russia again, Peter was able to inflict a crushing defeat upon him in 1709, and the Swedish king had to flee southward into Turkey, where he spent several years in exile before returning to Sweden in 1714. Meanwhile, the Russians continued their conquests in the east, while in the west Denmark and Saxony-Poland revived and were joined by Hanover and Prussia. When Charles returned, he fought until his death in 1718, trying to restore the Swedish position, but without success. The war dragged on desultorily for a few more years until peace was made with the western allies in 1720 and with Russia in 1721. The Treaties of Stockholm and Nystadt dismembered the Swedish empire on the Baltic, giving Prussia and Hanover most of the north German lands formerly held by Sweden, while Russia secured most of the eastern Baltic coastal lands except Finland. Thereafter, Sweden was of secondary importance, while Russia became significant in Europe and a factor in the balance of power.

The first few decades of the eighteenth century were years of relative tranquillity, partly because the new balance of power brought international stability and partly because some of the major European powers were distracted by internal developments. In England, William and Mary died without children and were succeeded in 1702 by Mary's sister Anne (1702–1714). As Queen Anne also was without direct heirs, parliament passed a new Act of Settlement conferring the crown upon the related family of Hanover, excluding James Edward, the son of James II. Thus, when Queen Anne died, she was succeeded by the Hanoverian prince, George I (1714–1727), and England faced difficult adjustments. George I, who spoke little English and knew little of the laws and customs of England, was not a popular figure. Moreover, his succession caused a political reversal, for it was the Whigs who most strongly had favored transfer of the crown to him, while many of the Tories were Jacobites (from the Latin *Jacobus*, James) sympathetic to the claims of the Stuarts. Thus, in the new reign the Whigs formed the government instead of the Tories whom Queen Anne had favored. In addition, England was indebted heavily from the recent wars. Finally, the new government met serious crises at the very outset: in 1715 there was an armed rebellion in Scotland in support of the Stuarts, and in 1720 there was a financial crash and a scandal concerning illicit profiteering by members of the government. Out of this turmoil emerged a Whig government headed by Sir Robert Walpole, England's first real prime minister (who governed 1726–1742). Walpole concentrated upon pacification of the Tories and Jacobites, economic expansion, exploitation of colonial resources and retirement of war debts; the death of George I and the accession of George II (1727–1760) made little difference to these policies, so for many years foreign affairs held a subordinate place in English government.

At the same time France faced similar problems. Louis XIV died in 1715, at the age of seventy-seven, having outlived both his son and his grandson; he was succeeded by his five-year-old great-grandson, Louis XV (1715–1774), and France faced another long regency. Like England, the French government suffered financial strain from the wars, and a crash and scandal soon followed when a speculative financial scheme failed in 1720. As in England, the new government was insecure; young Louis XV's health was uncertain, and it was feared that if he should die Philip V of Spain might claim the French throne in defiance of the Peace of Utrecht and catapult Europe into another major war. Thus the regent, the duke of Orléans (governed 1715–1723), and after him Louis XV's first minister, Cardinal Fleury (governed 1726–1743), were inclined toward an unaggressive foreign policy and agreement with France's former enemies while encouraging economic development.

These programs of peace and economic growth also had their parallels in Prussia and Russia. In Prussia King Frederick William I (1713–1740) ran his state with what amounted to military discipline, rebuilt his treasury, and expanded his army to 83,000 men, an impressive force for a country with only two and a half million people. In Russia, Peter the Great launched a vast scheme of reforms that included breaking the power of the nobility in government and substituting a centralized and bureaucratized administration dependent upon the Czar, reduction of the independence of the Russian Church, and encouragement of commerce, manufacturing and education along western lines. Many of the Czar's reforms were superficial, and some proved impractical, but at his death in 1725 Russia had a modern army and navy, a revitalized economy, and a much stronger government than she had known previously. Peter's immediate successors were undistinguished rulers, but the effects of Peter's reforms and the influence of imported German advisors continued the modernization and strengthening of Russia as a great European power.

While the early eighteenth century was more tranquil than the seventeenth century, it was not unmarked by war. In 1717 and 1718 an attempt by Spain to seize Sardinia and Sicily resulted in joint military action by England, Holland, France and Austria to maintain the Treaties of Utrecht and Rastatt; but the affair was negotiated in 1720, and with a few territorial exchanges in Italy, peace was re-

stored. Another conflict arose in the mid-1730s, the War of the Polish
Succession, which set Austria and Russia against France, Spain and
Sardinia. The war began in a conflict between French and Austro-
Russian interests in Poland, but Russia quickly occupied Poland,
and most of the later fighting took place in Italy between French
and Austrian forces. Consequently, the treaty that ended the war not
only left Austro-Russian influence dominant in Poland but also confirmed the Austrians in much of north Italy while recognizing a
Spanish prince as king of the Two Sicilies (the island of Sicily and
southern Italy up to Naples). But these struggles of the early eighteenth century did not spread to engulf all Europe as had earlier
wars; the balance of power appeared to have established an equilib-
rium.

Toward the middle of the eighteenth century the issue of colonial supremacy emerged as one of the paramount questions in
Europe. The Peace of Utrecht had given the English important trading privileges in Spain's American colonies, of which the most profitable was the *Asiento,* a thirty-year contract for the supply of slaves.
In the late 1730s two factors made the situation explosive: as the
Asiento neared expiration, a growing rapprochement between
France and Spain seemed to threaten that France might replace England as a licensed supplier to the Spanish colonies, and the development of a more effective Spanish colonial coast guard threatened the
illicit but very profitable smuggling that the English had built up
around their legitimate trade. These threats evoked in England a
faction within the Whig party that clamored for war with Spain and
France, and in 1739 Walpole lost control of the situation. An English
captain named Jenkins was caught smuggling by the colonial coast
guard, and he and his crew were handled very roughly. At some
point in the fray the Spaniards cut off Jenkins' ear, and he brought
it back to England pickled. This atrocity story spread rapidly and
provided the war party the issue it needed to overcome Walpole's
objections. In 1739 parliament voted for war, and the ensuing struggle, which lasted until 1748, was known as the War of Jenkins' Ear.

About the same time, an equally serious issue was developing
in central Europe around the question of the Austrian succession.
Emperor Charles VI (1711–1740), who had no sons, hoped to see his

lands pass intact to his daughter, Maria Theresa (1740–1780). This arrangement was set forth in a document called the Pragmatic Sanction, and the emperor succeeded in obtaining endorsement of it from several European governments. Despite the Pragmatic Sanction, however, there were many diverse legal traditions in the Habsburg lands, and a female succession was likely to be disputed in at least some areas. In fact, no sooner was the emperor dead than the king of Prussia, Frederick II (1740–1786), claimed and occupied the rich province of Silesia, triggering the War of the Austrian Succession.

The two wars became linked when France, already engaged against England at sea, joined Prussia against Austria in 1741, and a year later England allied with Austria. In central Europe the war raged for eight years, interrupted by numerous truces and short-lived treaties, but by 1745 a pattern was clear: Prussia held Silesia and could not be pried out, but Austria was able to fend off her other enemies; this was the basis of the Treaty of Aix-la-Chapelle of 1748. The colonial war went badly for England except in North America, where colonial forces took the great French fortress of Louisbourg at the mouth of the St. Lawrence, and military reverses forced Walpole's retirement in 1742. Then in 1745 another great rebellion broke out in Scotland in favor of the Stuart pretender, Charles Edward, son of James Edward, and for nearly a year badly needed English forces were tied down. At the Peace of Aix-la-Chapelle England had to give up even her small gains in North America to get back the important town of Madras that France had taken from her in India, so the war had accomplished nothing. Probably the only power satisfied with the Peace of Aix-la-Chapelle was Prussia, which retained Silesia. Both Austria and England were humiliated while France remained eager to rebuild the colonial position she had enjoyed before the Peace of Utrecht. Consequently, the years immediately following 1748 were not so much a time of peace as a time of preparation for renewed war.

The chief area of colonial rivalry had shifted to North America, where vigorous French expansion threatened the future of the English colonies. Solidly established on the St. Lawrence and the lower Mississippi, the French were moving into the Ohio and upper Mississippi valleys, building forts and trading posts. The chief routes of communication in North America were the river valleys, and west of the Appalachian Mountains everything drained toward the Mississippi; hence, a French line following the St. Lawrence, the Ohio and the Mississippi threatened to limit the English colonies to the narrow coastal plain between the mountains and the Atlantic. Clashes were frequent, and in 1755 war broke out between the French and the English in North America, providing a catalyst to the plans of Maria Theresa's brilliant chancellor, Count Kaunitz.

Having concluded that Austria was not strong enough to defeat Prussia alone, Kaunitz had proposed an encircling alliance, and agreements had been reached with Czarina Elizabeth of Russia (1741–1762) and some of the German princes. However, Kaunitz also desired to reverse traditional patterns and bring France into the coalition against Prussia, and this proved more difficult. Kaunitz knew the French court, and he succeeded in building a pro-Austrian party that included the king's mistress, Madame de Pompadour, but the French government was hesitant. However, the undeclared Anglo-French war that had begun in North America brought Kaunitz' plans to fruition. Fearful of a French attack upon Hanover, King George II signed a neutrality treaty with Frederick II of Prussia in January of 1756, and this apparent abandonment by Prussia caused great indignation at Versailles; in May France signed the alliance Kaunitz had been seeking, and a month later fighting between France and England broke out in Europe. Frederick II followed these moves carefully, and in 1756 he seized the initiative with a late summer campaign that occupied Saxony and defeated an Austrian army. Thus, in the mid-1750s a diplomatic revolution had taken place, and in an effort to break the stalemate of the old balance of power the Seven Years War was begun with changed partners: France, Austria and Russia against England and Prussia.

On the continent Frederick II again won brilliant victories, but he also suffered defeats, and in the long run his resources could not match those of his enemies. When the new king of England, George III (1760–1820), decided to stop English subsidies in 1760, Frederick was in serious trouble, and only luck saved him from disaster. In January of 1762 Czarina Elizabeth died, and her successor, Peter III (January to July, 1762), was a great admirer of Frederick. Though he was deposed a few months later, Peter reigned long enough to pull Russia out of the war, and freed of the Russian threat, Frederick again defeated the Austrians in the summer of 1762. As negotiations between the English and the French made it likely that France, too, soon would quit the war, Austria was forced to accept failure. By the Treaty of Hubertusburg (1763) Prussia kept Silesia, an area that increased her size and population between a third and a half.

In the colonial war the English, under the brilliant political leadership of William Pitt, soon established their superiority. English command of the sea left French colonial forces isolated, and in both North America and India they were defeated; the Battle of Quebec delivered all of French Canada to the English, and the capture of Pondichéry destroyed the French position in India. By the Treaty of Paris of 1763, France ceded to England all of Canada, the eastern side of the Mississippi basin and positions in the West Indies and Africa. Spain ceded Florida to England, in return for which she received Louisiana from France and the restoration of the positions in Cuba that the English had conquered. Almost wiped out of North America and Africa, France was in little better condition in India; she was allowed to retain only two unfortified trading stations. England took the rest.

Despite the mid-eighteenth century wars, the balance of power had survived. Although England and Prussia emerged somewhat strengthened, Austria and France somewhat weakened and Russia somewhat more involved in European affairs, after 1763 there appeared no greater danger than there had been in 1713 of the domination of the entire continent by a single power. That the value of the balance of power was recognized by the European governments was demonstrated in eastern Europe early in the 1770s. The once great monarchy of Poland had been in a state of decline for a century, a pawn in the schemes of its neighbors; after the Seven Years War the dominant influences were Russia and Prussia, alleging protection of Greek Orthodox and Protestant minorities against the Catholic majority. A fanatically Catholic anti-Russian group, the Confederation of Bar, soon emerged and won French support, and civil war broke out. The Turks, with French encouragement, chose this moment to attack Russia, and there appeared a real danger that the Polish-Turkish question might embroil the great powers in a new general war; this danger increased when Russian victories over the Turks threatened Russian occupation of the lower Danube to the detriment of Austrian interests, and Austria seemed about to intervene. At this point Frederick the Great, fearful that a general conflict would destroy Prussia, proposed a compromise to preserve the peace and maintain the balance of power. Russia would abandon her Turkish conquests and be compensated with Polish lands, gains not objectionable to Austria; to compensate for the increased Russian strength and westward advance, Austria and Prussia also would take slices of Poland. Thus, a sacrifice to the balance of power, Poland lost about a third of her territory and half her inhabitants. This unhappy solution to eastern European rivalries set a precedent; in 1792 Poland was partitioned a second time, and in a third partition in 1795 she disappeared altogether.

The late 1770s and early 1780s witnessed a sort of epilogue to the eighteenth century colonial struggles, the American War of Independence. Questions of political authority and powers of taxation that long had been irritants in Britain's relations with her North American colonies became serious issues after 1763. The territories that Britain had won in the Seven Years War had lengthened enormously the colonial frontiers that had to be defended against Indian attacks and the shipping lanes that had to be protected. Not unreasonably, the British government expected the colonies to bear some of the costs. The colonists, while happy to be relieved of the French menace, had economic problems of their own, for some of which they blamed crown policy, and they had seen enough blundering of the colonial administration that they were unwilling to accept further taxes without some voice in their expenditure. Ever more violent colonial protests and British attempts at compulsion grew into open fighting in 1775, which led a year later to a declaration of independence by the colonies. Almost immediately France took an interest in the affair.

France's position was delicate. Her resources strained by the costly mid-century wars, she could not afford to plunge recklessly into a new struggle with England. On the other hand, a colonial rebellion that might humiliate the British, weaken their Atlantic position and transfer important colonial trade to France could not fail to interest the government of Louis XVI (1774–1792). The French crown chose to remain neutral officially while giving the colonies large amounts of covert aid. A dummy company was set up, which sold arms to the rebels (the weapons actually financed by the French treasury), while the French government waited to see what the colonists could do against the British. It was not a long wait.

The British plan for 1777 called for dividing the colonies; General Burgoyne was to move down the Hudson Valley from Canada while Lord Howe was to ascend the valley from New York, a campaign that would have isolated New England. But inexplicably Howe turned aside for an attack upon Philadelphia and the Delaware Valley instead. Meanwhile, the colonial General Gates used his Indian allies to annihilate Burgoyne's scouts, and Burgoyne's army, alone and blinded, was left stumbling in near wilderness; after two engagements Burgoyne surrendered at Saratoga in October of 1777. That winter the colonies signed the Articles of Confederation creating the United States of America, and in February of 1778 France signed treaties of alliance and commerce with the new government. Of course this meant war between France and England, and the following year Spain joined in on the basis of a French promise to help retake Gibraltar and Florida.

Aside from such famous volunteers as Lafayette and de Kalb, Franco-Spanish overt assistance to the colonialists was chiefly in the form of naval support until Rochambeau arrived with six thousand French troops in 1780, but even the naval support was very significant. It helped assure the safe arrival of essential supplies, and it played a crucial role in the last campaign of the war. British strategy was founded upon command of the coasts, her fleets embarking and disembarking troops where they wished while colonial forces had to march great distances overland. After the disaster at Saratoga, the British attempted to overpower the southern states; Clinton took Charleston in 1780, and in 1781 Cornwallis fortified himself in Yorktown while awaiting support from the British fleet, preparing to hold off the forces of Washington, Lafayette and Rochambeau, which were concentrating around him. The arrival of Admiral de Grasse with a French fleet upset the British plans, for de Grasse blocked the seaward approaches to Yorktown, and Cornwallis was bottled up so that the British fleet could neither reinforce his army nor evacuate it. In October of 1781 Cornwallis surrendered with seven thousand men, and in the Treaty of Paris of 1783 Britain recognized the independence of the United States.

It is surprising how little immediate effect the success of the American War of Independence had upon the balance of power. The stability that had developed in Europe in the eighteenth century had spread around the shores of the Atlantic and was not upset by an armed conflict and a political readjustment. Trade with England, interrupted by the war, soon picked up again, and French hopes for a revival of French influence on the Atlantic came to nothing. The new nation, beset with economic and political problems in the aftermath of independence, exerted no great force on the international scene. Calm returned and the eighteenth century balance of power appeared secure for another decade until it was swept away by the new forces unleashed in the French revolution.

Chapter 7

Man, God, and Reason

During the eighteenth century, Europe experienced an intellectual revolution, the twin bases of which were skepticism toward accepted beliefs and a mechanical interpretation of both natural and human phenomena. Drawing heavily upon the discoveries and speculations of their immediate predecessors, eighteenth century intellectuals undertook to reexamine critically the very foundations of European society. Newton's description of a mechanistic universe was a major influence in this revolution, as was Descartes' skepticism, the doubting attitude which he advocated as essential to scientific inquiry; but in addition to the scientific revolution, eighteenth century Europe also had to assimilate the impact of foreign cultures and the discrediting of many of its beliefs concerning its own history.

Europeans traveled widely in the seventeenth century, often writing accounts of their travels which posed disturbing contradictions to Europe's ethnocentric confidence and sense of superiority, and after 1700 these were supplemented by fictitious voyages in which imaginary peoples and societies further challenged western values. Europeans tended to become self-critical, and eighteenth century literature became studded with idealized types, of which the simplest was the noble savage, derived from the American Indian; the idealizations exemplified the virtues of simplicity, honesty and loyalty which European writers found lacking in their own culture, and it was a short step from such idealized accounts of real people and societies to the invention of peoples and societies whose governments and morals made the Christian monarchies of Europe appear barbarous.

Religion also was challenged by the impact of foreign cultures and by European speculation stimulated by that impact. In the seventeenth century most Europeans were convinced, on the basis of Biblical chronology, that the world had been created about 4000 B.C., and it came as a shock to find that the Egyptians, the Babylonians and the Chinese traced their history back beyond that date; despite the tendency to discount the reliability of such "heathen" traditions, by 1700 confidence in Biblical chronology had weakened greatly. Moreover, study of Egyptian records revealed the striking similarity of Egyptian and Hebrew beliefs and raised the disturbing possibility that the Jewish prophets had derived many of their ideas from Egypt rather than from direct divine inspiration. Since early modern Christians of all varieties tended to take their Bible literally, the implications of derivative prophecy were distressing, and such problems were compounded by studies of fossils which made it clear that early life-forms had disappeared and new ones had appeared during the earth's history, neither phenomenon accounted for in the Bible.

Scholars as well as travelers and scientists contributed to the growing skepticism concerning the historical accuracy of Scripture. In the last years of the seventeenth century, Pierre Bayle's *Historical and Critical Dictionary* demonstrated the implausibility of some Biblical tales, ridiculed the moral examples in others and generally treated religious doctrine as ludicrous superstition. At the same time, Catholic scholars were preparing massive editions of the lives of the saints, trying to sift truth from myth and to establish the authenticity of texts; inevitably, the textual criticism of documents that they developed, summed up in Jean Mabilon's *De Re Diplomatica* (1681), soon were applied to Scripture itself. By 1679 Richard Simon, a Catholic priest and Biblical scholar, published *A Critical History of the Old Testament,* and this was followed in the 1680s and 1690s by his *Critical History of the Text of the New Testament* and comparable works on other versions of and commentaries upon the New Testament. With the best of intentions, a desire to establish a reliable text, he proved transpositions, interpolations and omissions, and skeptics used his work to deny the value of the Bible as revealed truth.

Under the impact of such challenges, large numbers of the European intelligentsia lost their belief in the traditional doctrines of Christianity, and many who tried to defend the old faith, such as John Locke in England and Malebranche and Fénélon in France, did so on the basis of the reasonableness of God as the architect of the Newtonian world-machine rather than on the basis of dogmatic theology; even Christianity's supporters were finding it difficult to accept their faith's revelation and miracles as more than superstitions or symbolic tales for the instruction of the ignorant and were trying to justify themselves on rational and secular grounds. This intellectual revolution had enormous implications, for rationalism and secularism left no possibility of justifying governments on religious grounds, and such attitudes set the intellectuals ever farther apart from the great mass of the population, which was reacting to the formality and coldness of the state churches with popular pietistic and revivalist movements.

Another basis for novel opinions developed out of seventeenth century England, where tumultuous political development inspired new reflections upon society and politics. In 1651 Thomas Hobbes' *Leviathan* sketched a purely secular and naturalistic basis for ethics and politics, proposing the theory that in a state of nature anarchy would prevail and life would be "nasty, brutish and short." Hobbes suggested that government was originated by men seeking security of life and property. Hobbes' idea that government was initiated by men through a social contract rather than instituted by God was not as shocking as his conclusions that the state must have complete domination over churches and, with few exceptions, over all aspects of the subjects' lives if the society were not to revert to the anarchy of the state of nature. Obviously Hobbes' thought was conditioned by the political troubles of England in his day, but it remains notable for its purely secular postulates, and his conceptions of the state of nature and the social contract were very influential.

Secular and rational approaches to man and society were continued by John Locke, who was convinced that all understanding derives of experience. Rejecting theories of innate ideas, he asserted that a child was born with its mind blank and that experience wrote upon it, a conception that demanded new analyses of man as a social and moral animal. In considering politics Locke also posited the idea of a state of nature, but because of his concept of human psychology it was a different condition than that suggested by Hobbes. Locke felt that even in the state of nature man was bound by natural law interpreted by reason and experience and that men always established general principles for the safeguard of life and property, conventions that created society; this idea introduced an intermediate step in the agreement between subject and monarch, and repudiation of the monarch did not dissolve the social contract but only left society to make new arrangements for its governance. Because Locke's *Two Treatises on Government* appeared in 1690, because it was an easy step to interpret parliament as the voice of society and because he lauded William III, the author has been accused of acting as apologist for the Glorious Revolution, but his political ideas seem to have been worked out well before that event and to have proceeded from his basic philosophy.

Locke was read widely in the eighteenth century, and translations made both his *Two Treatises on Government* and his *Essay Concerning Human Understanding* accessible to continental readers; he became for psychology and philosophy what Newton was to physical science, a guide to fruitful areas of investigation and the architect of new conceptions. Though always moderate himself, he provided potent intellectual weapons to those who mounted an ever more aggressive attack upon tradition, and those who sought only security and stability were drawn into this attack. Locke's summation of the bases of social order as security of life, liberty and property is a fair outline of what many articulate men were concerned to protect in the early eighteenth century, and threats seemed to come less from a few intellectual innovators than from old institutions. For two centuries, sectarian quarrels and dynastic struggles had kept Europe immersed in civil conflict and international war; if life, liberty and property were to be protected by reasonable laws, it appeared that the claims of the theologians and the ambitions of dynastic monarchs would have to be restrained.

The leadership of England in the development of secular, rational and humane thought was founded on Newton and Locke, and it was reinforced by writers on both sides of the channel during the second quarter of the eighteenth century, but by the middle of the century intellectual supremacy had passed to France. The early writers of the French Enlightenment acknowledged their debt to the English, as in Voltaire's *Elements of the Philosophy of Newton*, but Paris quickly became the center of the new philosophy. The scope of the Enlightenment and the range of individual variation from one writer to another make generalizations difficult, but some common positions can be sketched briefly. At the foundation of most Enlightenment thought was a mechanistic view of a world governed by natural law that was discoverable by reason. Such an assumption implied that not only natural science but all aspects of life were integrated in a vast mechanical scheme such as Newton's laws of gravitation. Skepticism toward traditional beliefs and authorities was reinforced by the rapid advances in natural studies produced by the scientific method and by contemplation of exciting new possibilities in human and social studies; by comparison with the natural sciences, the social sciences were still primitive, but they had become empirical and inductive, and they had developed methods that could be used to judge traditional institutions and authorities by new standards.

Most writers of the Enlightenment shared the expectation that great discoveries would continue to be made, that reason would uncover further natural laws and that much that remained mysterious would become explicable. In this context, mysteries were but natural phenomena as yet unexplained, and miracles were fanciful explanations of natural phenomena, not only inaccurate but also an offense to human intelligence. The confidence in right reason and experience as tools leading ultimately to complete understanding was almost limitless. Few figures of the Enlightenment asserted atheism, however, for they still required a creator for their world-machine, an architect or engineer whose designs were the foundation of natural law, but their rejection of the miraculous generally meant a denial of concepts of an afterlife of salvation or damnation. Life no longer was a mere preparation, the world a vale of tears; life was reality, the world the place where fulfilment or frustration had to be found, and it began to be perceived that happiness in itself might be a valid goal in life.

Reluctant to affirm a thoroughgoing atheism, most eighteenth century intellectuals adopted a religious creed called deism, characterized as natural religion. Deists accepted a God, usually impersonal, who had fabricated the universe, and they accepted a set of morals that God had engraved on the hearts of all men. To some extent deism was a reaction against the arid arguments of Christian theologians and the horrors of persecution and religious wars that had resulted from Christian dissension; to some extent it was the outgrowth of the impact of foreign cultures which showed common religious tenets in many faiths and of the new science which stressed the orderliness of the physical universe and the unity of mankind. God was assumed to be rational, not capricious, so the deists had no patience with miracles, which would require the suspension of natural law, or with metaphysical revelation, which claimed knowledge of God other than through understanding His natural laws. Comparative religious studies convinced the deists that their tenets were the core of all the world's religions and that the varieties of religious belief were but superstitious error derived from false claims of particular revelation.

It was not angry Christian theologians but the Scotch skeptic, David Hume, who challenged these opinions most effectively; his *Natural History of Religion,* published in the late 1750s, attacked the fundamental assumption of the advocates of natural religion by denying that men allowed themselves to be guided by reason or that there was any universality of human motivation. Hume contended that reason was not and could not be a guide to principles but only a tool for devising the means of gratifying irrational impulses and desires which varied among individuals and societies; thus he negated, to his own satisfaction at least, the whole concept of rational natural religion and, incidentally, challenged the very basis of Enlightenment rationalism and its derivative structure of universal morality and self-evident truths.

Another common element of Enlightenment thought was optimism. This attitude was encouraged by the great scientific progress that had resulted from the new methodology, but its roots ran much deeper. On the one hand, the great German scientist, Leibnitz, was convinced of the existence of a beneficent deity, and his endorsement of optimism had some influence through his popularizer, Christian Wolff. But in a broader sense, the general optimism of eighteenth century intellectuals derived from their convictions about the nature of the universe. They believed firmly that all phenomena were explicable through natural law, and they were convinced that in reason they had found the key to understanding natural law; hence, they fully anticipated that further application of reason would make both the physical and social world more explicable and more predictable and that men would be able to plan their lives and their societies to avoid catastrophes. Some of the more superficial aspects of this optimism, especially the idea of a beneficent deity, were satirized brilliantly by Voltaire in his *Candide,* but general confidence in human progress continued to be characteristic of most eighteenth century intellectuals.

It was in specific applications to man and society that Enlightenment thought had its most far-reaching effects, in such concepts as the theory of natural rights. Grounded originally in principles of natural law, as time passed the theory of natural rights was justified more and more on the basis of empiricism, on the conviction that history showed that security of life, liberty and property was essential to the stability of society and the development of the potential of humanity. Fused with the older theories of the state of nature and the social contract, the doctrine of natural rights provided a standard against which to measure the performance of governments. To the extent that a government contributed to the greater security of life, liberty and property, it was fulfilling its function; when corruption of its purposes, as through subservience to dynastic ambition, for instance, weakened the security in which these basic rights were held, to that extent it failed to fulfill its purpose. Implicit, of course, was a notion of the right of revolution.

An important corollary of these ideas was the conception of society based on individuals who were born free and equal, in contrast to older notions of society based upon family units enmeshed in a web of divinely ordained social inequality and obligations to church and king. By born free and equal, the eighteenth century writers understood free to mean the individual's right to choose his own goals and equal to mean that all started life with minds the blank slate on which experience wrote; they quite accepted that qualitative differences of experience would produce human inequality, and they were not disturbed much by that so long as inequality was not institutionalized in law. Perhaps the best summation of the socio-political thought of the Enlightenment, natural rights and social contract with vague deistic overtones, is provided by the American Declaration of Independence of 1776:

> We hold these truths to be self-evident, that all men are created equal, that they are endowed by their Creator with certain unalienable Rights, that among these are Life, Liberty and the pursuit of Happiness.—That to secure these rights, Governments are instituted among Men, deriving their just powers from the consent of the governed,—That whenever any Form of Government becomes destructive of these ends, it is the Right of the People to alter or abolish it. . . .

The substitution of "pursuit of happiness" for Locke's "property" usually is attributed to the existence among the Americans of radical elements who were seeking to weaken property rights and would not agree to any endorsement of them in the declaration, but the idea that the "pursuit of happiness" was a natural right certainly was deep-rooted in Enlightenment philosophy and existed independent of the political maneuvers surrounding the framing of the Declaration of Independence.

Perhaps the most effective demonstration of the scope and variety of Enlightenment thought is provided by a brief survey of some of its leading advocates. In France, one of the earliest of these was Baron Montesquieu. As a young man, Montesquieu embarked upon the judicial career traditional in his family, but he soon turned to writing, and in 1721 he published his *Persian Letters;* the literary device of letters purporting to be written by two refined Persians traveling in Europe provided an opportunity for amusing but merciless satire of church, state and society in France, and the book became very popular. It was the first of the devastatingly witty works of social satire that were to typify the eighteenth century French rationalist critics who called themselves *philosophes.* In the 1730s he published some reflections upon Roman history, and then in 1748 appeared his greatest work, *The Spirit of the Laws;* a comparison of various constitutional patterns, this work demonstrated the sociological and anthropological relativism that was to transform the study of history and social science in the eighteenth century. The concepts of the separation of powers and checks and balances that Montesquieu presented in his idealized analysis of English practices proved very influential upon later writers of constitutions.

Of the same generation as Montesquieu was Voltaire, a notary's son who produced his first successful play in his mid-20s. A penchant for writing political satires resulted in occasional arrests and frequent exile from Paris; three years spent in England during his early 30s had a strong influence upon him, for he came to admire England's toleration of free thought and general absence of censorship. This influence showed itself in 1733, when he published his *Philosophical Letters on the English* and behind the pretense of comments on English society attacked the church and government of France. Official reaction to the *Philosophical Letters* was violent; the work was seized and burned, and the author escaped arrest only by another flight out of the country.

The continued development of Voltaire's critical spirit was marked in the late 1730s by the appearance of the *Elements of the Philosophy of Newton* and a *Treatise on Metaphysics,* which endorsed the value of experience and reason and renewed the attack upon religion. In 1751 he had to leave Paris again, and after sojourning for two years with Frederick the Great of Prussia, he settled near Geneva in a house that was in France but very near the Swiss border, in case escape should prove necessary. There he spent the last quarter century of his life, entertaining friends and writing voluminously, except for a final visit to Paris, where he died in 1778 at the age of eighty-four. During these last years he produced masses of letters, essays and lampoons attacking the establishment in church and state with bitter sarcasm, denouncing oppression and ridiculing the extremes of other rationalists. Some of the best of these efforts were his many contributions to the *Great Encyclopedia,* which involved him with the next generation of Enlightenment writers, who dominated the third quarter of the eighteenth century, and especially with the encyclopedia's general editor, Diderot.

Denis Diderot, a craftsman's son, first appeared on the literary scene in the mid-1740s with a translation of Shaftesbury's *Inquiry Concerning Virtue and Merit;* this was followed by his own *Philosophical Thoughts, The Promenade of a Sceptic* and a *Letter on the Blind,* the latter an assertion of man's total dependence upon his senses. The vigor of his skeptical criticism cost him three months in prison, but after his release he undertook a massive and even more daring work, the *Great Encyclopedia.* A Parisian publisher, André-François LeBreton, had conceived the idea of publishing a translation of the popular Chambers' *Cyclopedia,* but the project quickly grew into an original multivolume collection surveying the whole range of human knowledge, and as Diderot had some reputation as a translator and author, he was drawn into the venture, first as a staff writer and then as general editor. The series eventually comprised seventeen volumes of text and eleven volumes of illustrations, and most of France's great eighteenth century writers contributed to it. This encyclopedia reflected the unorthodox views of the *philosophes,* and it soon became a center of controversy; there were two attempts at governmental suppression in the 1750s, and in the 1760s Diderot discovered that the worried publisher, LeBreton, was censoring some of his more extreme articles. Nonetheless, the *Great Encyclopedia* emerged as a statement of faith of eighteenth century rationalism; more than a compendium of information, it was an arsenal of weapons and ammunition for the critics of eighteenth century society. Its explanations of science, its easy assumption of universally valid, simple mechanical laws of nature and its brilliant list of contributors offered reason, optimism and confidence to critics of the world as it was, and it became an enormous success. Published by subscription in advance, the work was issued first in fifteen hundred, then two thousand and finally four thousand copies, and hardly was it completed in 1772 than reissues and pirated editions began to appear; despite the protests of the establishment, the publisher and his associates made something in the range of four million dollars profit from the venture, for the spirit and the content of the *Great Encyclopedia* had caught the cosmopolitan and iconoclastic temper of the eighteenth century literate public.

One of the most direct influences of the Enlightenment was its impact upon progressive rulers who admired the *philosophes.* Few exponents of the Enlightenment had enough confidence in the common man to advocate a democratic society; most, like Voltaire, were supporters of enlightened despotism and aspired only to persuade the governing powers of Europe that rational law guaranteeing "natural rights" was the best basis of the state. They found some audience among Europe's crowned heads, and though enlightened despotism generally remained more theory than practice, it deserves notice. Most notable among governing powers who endorsed the idea were the sovereigns of Prussia, Russia and Austria, though there were others.

Frederick the Great of Prussia (1740–1788) was a cultured man as well as an able administrator and a distinguished soldier. Despite the mid-eighteenth century wars, he was the most effective of the enlightened despots, rationalizing and codifying Prussian law, adopting policies designed to improve the economic condition of his subjects and reforming the judicial system in an effort to assure equal justice; his attitude toward government was summed up best in his famous comment, "I am the first servant of the state." Catherine the Great of Russia (1762–1796) is more difficult to evaluate. She endorsed the *philosophes,* admired Voltaire greatly and entertained Diderot; but as she depended upon the conservative Russian nobility both for the maintenance of her domestic authority and for the support of her aggressive foreign policy, her avowed intention of governmental reform, such as codification of Russian law, produced no results. The most dramatic attempt to establish enlightened despotism was that of the Emperor Joseph II (1780–1790). When the death of his mother, Maria Theresa, delivered power into his hands, he plunged into rapid and radical legislative experimentation aimed at breaking the power of the church and the nobility and destroying provincial privileges. Joseph II achieved impressive results on paper, but in practice he aroused a storm of opposition that blocked the effective implementation of his intentions, and his brother and successor, Leopold II (1790–1792), had to revoke most of the radical decrees in order to undertake more moderate and more practical reforms. Probably even Louis XVI of France (1774–1792) thought of himself as an enlightened despot, at least in the early part of his reign, when he encouraged his minister Turgot to undertake reforms in justice, taxation and economic regulation; and other governments in Portugal, Italy and the German states were influenced by the principles of enlightened despotism.

Despite the Enlightenment, however, there were many people who supported different values and denied that the *philosophes* had discovered great new truths. Often their feelings were expressed through an emotional religious revival. In the late seventeenth century, France had the earliest experience of this movement, with a group called Quietists, whose faith was so mystical as to be dangerously close to a rejection of clerical authority, and another called Jansenists, who sought to introduce into Catholicism a puritanical and predestinarian doctrine reminiscent of Calvinism; the Quietists were suppressed quickly, and early in the eighteenth century the Jansenists were condemned, but the currents of emotional commitment to a more personal Christianity that they stirred flowed strongly among the common people in France while the intellectuals were debating reason and natural religion. The religious revival in Germany occurred in the middle of the eighteenth century, led by the Moravian Brethren who sought to find personal religious experience and preached a religion of the heart; genuinely tolerant on an individual basis, they condemned both rationalist deism and the dogmatic theology of the established Christian churches. The movement had a strong influence through many German states, encouraging the abandonment of an artificial French culture, and contributed importantly to the richness of the German language and the emotional sensitivity that marked Germany's late eighteenth century literary blossoming with Herder and Goethe.

Probably the most influential of the eighteenth century pietistic movements was English Methodism, organized by the devout and energetic John Wesley and inspired by the emotional evangelism of George Whitefield. Throughout England the Methodists preached and published the love of God, the assurance of salvation and the horror of sin; unfortunately, in their reaction against the cold rationalism of the elite they also were rather anti-intellectual, condemning science and critical study of Scripture as paths to atheism. Their meetings often aroused emotional hysteria repugnant to the fastidious upper classes, but whatever their shortcomings, the emotional preaching and the simple fundamentalism of the Methodists communicated to the horribly depressed masses of the eighteenth century and began their integration into modern English society.

Eventually distrust of the doctrine that reason and the senses were man's only reliable faculties penetrated even the intellectual elite. Dissenting voices were a minor counterpoint in the thundering acclamation of rational empiricism, but some of them spoke too forcefully to be ignored. As noted already, Hume, though no antirationalist, had challenged the psychological assumptions of his contemporaries in the 1750s, and another dissident of formidable reputation appeared in the person of Jean-Jacques Rousseau. A member for awhile of the Paris circle of *philosophes* and a contributor to the *Great Encyclopedia,* he broke with his associates in the mid-1750s over differences of principle, for the *philosophes* were reformers and Rousseau was a true radical who sought the overthrow and replacement of contemporary society. In his search for the nature of man, upon which a moral regeneration might be based, Rousseau reached conclusions radically different from those of Locke. He asserted that natural man was neither corrupted by original sin nor simply blank but filled with good impulses which society negated. Alienated from the world and the people he would have liked to have claimed as friends, Rousseau found himself committing actions he disapproved, and he concluded that he had been corrupted and degraded by society. With lashing invective, he damned the social order and pleaded for a return to nature, which he sought within himself; sweeping aside all of the sociological and anthropological inquiry of his contemporaries, he asserted the sole validity of his own experience and intuition. Proceeding from such tenuous foundations and susceptible to his own changing perceptions, Rousseau's philosophy often is contradictory, for at times he endorses unrestrained individualism, and at other times he projects a stringent collectivism. The unifying rationale is his passion for simple, unspoiled humanity at the same time exercising freedom and associating harmoniously, and these general ideas are more important than his specific theories. His love of nature and the beauty he discovered in it found a wide audience; his passion and his sensitivity offered a valuable counterpoise to the chill rationality of the *philosophes;* and his endorsement of human values provided a glow of warmth in the impersonal mechanistic universe of the Enlightenment.

The negation of the Enlightenment was a strong current by the late eighteenth century, revealed by English poets such as Gray and by a growing enthusiasm for things medieval, such as a revival of gothic styles and a fondness for old castles and abbeys in contrast to the classical enthusiasm of the mainstream of eighteenth century culture. A cult of sentimentality was growing that found the sterile intellectualism of the Enlightenment as much a prison for humanity as the metaphysical otherworldliness of the medieval churchmen.

Chapter 8

A Harvest of Violence

All over Europe the eighteenth century ended in a cataclysm of social upheaval and political innovation that began in France in the late 1780s. The French revolution developed from many factors: arbitrary government which, though not tyrannical, was unresponsive to important interests in the kingdom; the unpopularity of the royal family, which weakened traditional loyalty to the crown; the discredit of the government in consequence of military failures and its inability to relieve economic distress; and political awareness intensified by the critical literature of the Enlightenment. All of these problems were aggravated by inequitable taxation, which generated particular grievances as focal points for discontent and left the government tottering on the verge of bankruptcy in a prosperous nation. By the 1780s some sort of far-reaching reform probably was unavoidable, but there was nothing inevitable about the revolution that grew out of efforts at reform.

In the late eighteenth century France had a population of about twenty-six million and a complex social structure. At the top of the society stood the church and the aristocracy, both groups closely linked to the monarchy and both enjoying privileged positions with regard to taxation. The church depended heavily upon the king, for most of its high offices were filled by royal nomination, and it was exempt from direct royal taxes paid by commoners, for each year it

made a free gift to the government. While this sum was less proportionately than that paid by the peasantry, it should be remembered
that the church supported at its own expense most of the educational, charitable and hospital services of the society as well as
its religious obligations. The princes of the church, archbishops,
bishops and abbots, often were wealthy, powerful and urbane members of aristocratic families, active in politics, while parish priests
and simple monks were commoners, usually impoverished and often
ill-educated. Though all were considered together as the first
estate—the church—the social and economic gulf between the worldly
bishop at the king's court and the simple priest in a country parish
was enormous.

The aristocracy held a position comparable to that of the
church, both in its dependence upon the king and in its privileged
exemption from most direct taxation. Honorific and remunerative
positions at the court, commissions in the army, and offices in the
administration and the church depended upon the king's will, and
royal pensions formed an important part of aristocratic income. The
aristocracy was variegated, its common feudal and military character long lost. The distinction between nobility of the robe, with
titles earned in the royal administration, and nobility of the sword,
with older feudal origins, that had divided the aristocracy in the
seventeenth century had been blurred through marriage by the late
eighteenth century, but another equally divisive distinction had
grown up with the development of the court: the courtier nobility
that lived near the king and the country nobility that lived on its estates. Generally the courtiers depended heavily upon the king; they
drew rents from their lands as absentee landlords, but their chief income derived from royal appointments and royal pensions. They
lived in some luxury, and vast sums of money passed through their
hands to meet the high expenses of court life, but most were deeply
in debt and would have been ruined financially as well as socially by
loss of the king's favor. By contrast country noblemen lived upon
their estates and generally depended upon them for their income,
but even the country nobility was not homogeneous. Some were
modestly prosperous and lived as comfortable country gentlemen,
renting out their lands on relatively short-term leases that allowed
them to raise rents from time to time to keep pace with inflationary

costs. Most of these country gentlemen were important figures in the life of their districts, experimenting with new crops and livestock, adjudicating disputes among peasants, and articulating local grievances or needs to the government; generally they were regarded with respect and often with affection. By contrast, there was another class of country noblemen that was impoverished, frequently because family lands had been divided too often or because the lands were rented on perpetual or near-perpetual leases, leaving the owners defenseless against inflation. Often these impoverished noblemen, called *hobereaux*, were distinguishable from the peasantry only by their right to wear a sword and by the traditional dues they could collect from their tenants.

By the late eighteenth century the urban middle classes formed an important group in French society. At the top of the urban social structure was the *grande bourgeoisie*, wealthy bankers and large-scale merchants. Beneath them was the *petite bourgeoisie*—shopkeepers, artisans and small tradesmen, a class which had grown large with the urban and commercial development of the eighteenth century. And beneath these classes was the urban working force, not a vast modern proletariat, but a considerable group, nonetheless. These groups did not enjoy the general tax privileges of the clergy and the aristocracy, but many of them were privileged. Wealthy bourgeois often achieved exemption on a personal basis by buying royal offices which carried such privilege. Whole towns often enjoyed partial privilege, having negotiated special tax rates with the crown in return for extraordinary contributions or some other service. Thus, in the upper levels of the third estate the incidence of taxation was quite uneven.

At the base of the society were about twenty million peasant farmers, most of them free of any vestiges of personal servitude and many of them small landowners. The peasants paid rents, dues and tithes to landlords and to the church and heavy taxes to the government, but probably they were freer and economically better off than anywhere else in Europe; their participation in the revolution certainly was not a blind rebellion motivated by hopeless conditions. But upon the peasantry fell the major burden of taxation, and even at this level there were great differences in the burdens imposed. About two-thirds of the French provinces, the older ones, were called *pays d'élection;* there the crown's authority was great, and the *taille,* the major direct tax, depended largely upon the assessments of the tax collector. By contrast, the newer provinces, called *pays d'états,* had maintained local assemblies, and the *taille* was negotiated between royal and local officials.

Given this vast web of privilege—by class, by region and by person—it should not be surprising that the government faced bankruptcy in a prosperous country; the wealthy usually escaped taxation, and the government was left in the awkward position of taxing primarily the poor. Moreover, the mechanism of collection was costly and inefficient; the *taille* was collected by government personnel, but indirect taxes, such as the hated *gabelle* on salt, were contracted to private collectors called tax-farmers, and their charges often were exorbitant. Generally rising costs and the military expenses of the eighteenth century wars had forced the government to borrow heavily, and by the 1780s about fifty per cent of the crown's expenditure went to interest charges on the debt; another twenty-five per cent went to military expenditures, leaving only twenty-five per cent for all the costs of administration, public services and the court. Thus, the expenses of the court, while undeniably extravagant, were less significant than angry critics believed. The root of the fiscal difficulties was privilege, which protected France's wealth from governmental exactions; for political reasons it was not possible to reduce governmental expenditures significantly, and because of traditional privileges it was not possible to increase income to meet expenses without the consent of the groups that would have to pay. In the 1780s a number of finance ministers attempted various expedients to relieve the fiscal crisis, but the best of them always came to the same conclusion: those who were privileged would have to be persuaded to accept taxation. The question was how.

Early in 1787 the crown convened an assembly of notables, a hand-picked group of prominent people, and submitted new tax proposals to it, but this group refused to accept the responsibility and was dismissed without results. Then new tax edicts were submitted to the parlement of Paris, the high court that registered royal laws and provided the judicial machinery for their enforcement, but the parlement refused to accept them. Though a nonelective and nonrepresentative body, the parlement had become spokesman of the opposition to royal absolutism, and when the crown tried to put pressure upon the court, the parlementarians became public heroes for their resistance. They claimed that neither they nor the assembly of notables had the authority to approve what the crown asked and insisted that for such momentous decisions the estates general had to be revived.

France's privileged classes did not refuse adamantly to consider assuming some of the national burden, but they aspired to political power as the price of their support. The French admired England greatly, and though English government often was ill-understood, the French privileged classes understood clearly enough that in England royal power had been limited through parliamentary control of governmental finance; what they sought in the 1780s was to force the crown's officers to negotiate with a large and representative body dominated by the aristocracy and to concede some measure of political authority to that body in return for new taxes. They scored a victory when the crown agreed that an estates general should be convened in the spring of 1789, the first such assembly since 1614.

Unfortunately for the intentions of the aristocrats, they did not constitute the only politically ambitious group in France. The large middle class—prosperous, vocal and influenced by the *philosophes*—also desired a political voice as the price of their taxes, and their influence persuaded the government to authorize for the estates general as many representatives for the third estate as for the first two estates combined. The aristocracy quickly countered this maneuver by having the king declare that the estates would vote separately upon all resolutions. This was a desperately important issue, for if votes were taken by head the commoners could expect that with double representation and a little support from sympathetic lower clergy and country noblemen they could dominate the assembly; but if the estates voted separately, it could be anticipated that the two upper estates would stand together to evoke concessions from the crown in their own interest while blocking the ambitions of the third estate. Thus, when the estates general assembled in May of 1789 the commoners already were restless and angry, and there was an atmosphere of tension.

The royal financial position was worse than ever, and bad harvests had caused widespread economic distress. In the countryside there was violence, and rumors spread that the food shortages were the result of an aristocratic conspiracy to starve the commons into submission. The third estate was in an ugly mood. In June of 1789, in defiance of the king's order, it assumed the title of the National Assembly and invited the representatives of the other two estates to join it, and several of the clergy and some nobles did. Uncertain what to do, the king suspended the assembly and closed its meeting hall, but the delegates gathered in a nearby indoor tennis court and took an oath not to disband until they had given France a constitution; the king capitulated, ordering the remaining members of the upper estates to join the National Assembly, and the reform movement launched by the aristocracy had slipped from its control.

Despite this victory, the third estate remained distrustful of the vacillating king, for royal troops were concentrating around Versailles and Paris, and there were rumors that the government would break up the assembly; these rumors acquired more force early in July when the king dismissed the popular minister, Necker, who had convened the estates general, and violence erupted in Paris. On July 14, 1789 a crowd stormed the Bastille, a royal fortress, massacred the garrison and seized the arms stored there, ready to fight if the king should try to use troops to suppress the National Assembly and its Parisian support. About the same time, peasant uprisings broke out all over France against the exactions of aristocratic landlords. In this revolutionary atmosphere a number of great nobles began to leave France, rioting spread, and popular militias and provisional governments were formed.

In August the pace of change accelerated. Liberal aristocrats began a voluntary surrender of feudal rights, and the National Assembly abolished titles and adopted a Declaration of the Rights of Man. Hunger and fear of repression caused more popular demonstrations in Paris, and a mob marched to Versailles and forced the royal family and the National Assembly to transfer to the city. A liberal monarchical constitution was adopted under which legislative power resided in a unicameral assembly, and the king's power was limited to a suspensory veto which could delay legislation for two terms of the assembly. Declarations of war and foreign treaties also required the consent of the assembly. In the summer of 1790 regional privileges were destroyed as the old provinces were abolished and France was redivided into eighty-three departments. The assembly then moved to the establishment of a new currency, a national reorganization of the clergy and the establishment of new political mechanisms (which included financial qualifications for voting). The revolution appeared to have been accomplished with the victory falling not to the aristocrats who had begun it but to the middle class.

There were groups that wanted the revolution to continue, however, most notably the radical political clubs of which the Jacobins, under the leadership of Robespierre, was most prominent. These groups tended to be republican and to favor abolition of the monarchy. Shortly before the elections that were to establish a legislative assembly under the new constitution, an attempted flight by the king and his family strengthened these radical groups by demonstrating the king's implicit hostility to the new limited monarchy, and the Legislative Assembly of 1791–1792, though still primarily representative of the bourgeoisie, had a republican majority. War with Austria and Prussia, which broke out in the spring of 1792, further stimulated republican and national extremism, and new elections in the fall of 1792 produced an assembly, called the National Convention, that was composed entirely of republicans elected by universal manhood suffrage. The new assembly was more radical than either of its predecessors; one of its first acts was to abolish the monarchy under mob pressure, and in July of 1793 Louis XVI was executed.

In the midst of foreign war, political activity in the capital became more and more radical, and by mid-summer of 1793 Robespierre and the Jacobins dominated the government through its Committee of Public Safety, backed by the revolutionary Commune of Paris. Alleging the dangers of counterrevolutionary activity, Robespierre inaugurated a reign of terror, with mass arrests, trials by revolutionary tribunals and summary executions, which lasted until his enemies overthrew and killed him in the summer of 1794.

The overthrow of the Jacobins and French victories in the foreign war brought more moderate policies, and in the summer of 1795 a new constitution provided for a two-house legislature with executive authority vested in a committee of five called the Directory. Radical Paris objected to the new arrangements, but in October a young Corsican general, Napoleon Bonaparte, protected the government by firing artillery into a mob, and the projected elections took place.

The foreign powers reacted with indifference to the first stages of the French Revolution, for they were distracted by other problems. Britain had just gone through a governmental crisis concerning her interests in India, she faced rising unrest in Ireland, and in 1788 King George suffered the first of his fits of insanity. English opinion generally was hostile to the rising tide of violence in France and shocked by the execution of Louis XVI, but the British held aloof until the French Republic declared war on them in 1793. Similarly the interests of the eastern monarchies (Austria, Prussia and Russia) were committed elsewhere, to traditional involvements in Poland and to new rivalries consequent upon the decline of the Turks. After 1789, however, refugee aristocrats from France began to pour into foreign capitals, particularly Vienna and Berlin, where they begged foreign intervention to restore their positions and the authority of Louis XVI. In August of 1791 the Austrian emperor and the king of Prussia met at Pillnitz to discuss various issues, and with reference to the French situation they announced that they would intervene only with the unanimous consent of all the great powers. Since such agreement was quite unlikely, the declaration of Pillnitz was not a very dangerous statement, but in France it appeared a serious threat, particularly as it came only two months after Louis XVI's attempted flight abroad.

Developments early in 1792 made war almost certain. In Austria the new Emperor Francis II (1792–1835) was sympathetic to the war party, and an Austro-Prussian alliance against France was signed in February. In France the republicans wanted a war which they anticipated would intensify national and revolutionary sentiment. Both sides were eager for the conflict when the French Republic began it in April of 1792.

At first the war went badly for the French, but about the same time that the Convention proclaimed the republic, they managed to stabilize the military situation by winning an artillery duel at Valmy, and then one French army swept the Prussians back over the Rhine while another conquered the Austrian Netherlands. These victories were followed by a French offer of assistance to any people that wished to overthrow its government, by the reopening of the Scheldt to commerce and by the execution of Louis XVI. This series of events brought Britain, Holland, Spain and the Holy Roman Empire into alliance against France, and in the summer of 1793 the republic was in real danger, for the allies overran the southern Netherlands (which France had annexed) and invaded northern France, while internally a number of revolts threatened political chaos. However, the war had the political effects that the republicans had sought. They were able to intensify the terror against their political enemies and to institute radical measures of price controls and rationing, and in August of 1793 they called to military service all males capable of bearing arms, putting fourteen armies into the field. In the autumn the French began achieving military success, and in 1794 and 1795 they were victorious everywhere. Both the Austrian and Dutch Netherlands were conquered and turned into a Batavian republic under French influence; Prussia and the lesser north German states were forced out of the war, and France annexed the left bank of the Rhine. In the summer of 1795 British troops and emigrant French royalists attempted a landing in Brittany, but they were defeated quickly. Thus, when the Directory took office the situation appeared quite favorable.

The successes of the rapidly levied and ill-trained French armies astonished their enemies. Part of the credit belongs to the splendid artillery and sound officer training of the eighteenth century royal army and part to Carnot, the brilliant member of the Committee of Public Safety who undertook the organization and logistical support of the armies of the republic, but the greatest credit belongs to the revolution itself. The abolition of privilege and the political reorganization of the country enabled the republic to mobilize the vast resources that had been beyond the reach of the royal government. Popular participation in political processes, the terror and a campaign of hatred against royalists and foreigners who

would undo the revolution all contributed to a wave of unprece-
dented national and patriotic sentiment.

The crucial factor in the new armies was morale, which enabled
them to survive reverses and withstand casualty rates that destroyed
the professional forces of the eighteenth century, but though morale
was crucial, it should not be overlooked that France rapidly developed new methods and tactics adapted to the large but raw armies
she was putting into the field. The exodus of masses of aristocrats
deprived the French army of many of its senior officers, some of
them competent professionals but many of them titled bunglers who
held their rank through favor; thus rapid promotion was open to
talented junior officers, such as Bonaparte, and the battlefield
quickly sorted the talented from the merely competent. New junior
officers were chosen from among sergeants with experience in
the old royal forces, and new recruits were organized around cadres
of old professionals. The most startling innovation, however, was in
tactics. The French lacked the time to train masses of new recruits in the complex drill of rapid fire musketry and swift field
maneuver that was the basis of eighteenth century tactics, so they
relied upon the bayonet charge after artillery bombardment had
softened enemy ranks. In early encounters, casualties were very
high, but in the new French forces casualties were replaced more
easily than in the professional armies of Austria or Prussia, and as
the new French armies acquired experience, their casualties de-
creased while their victories increased. Though a few precedents
might be found in the Dutch forces that fought Spain in the sixteenth century, in Cromwell's army in the seventeenth century, or
in the American colonial forces in the eighteenth century, Europe
had never seen anything like the new French armies of the republic
for sheer size and dedication. The revolution had mobilized both the
economic and human resources of the wealthiest and most populous
nation in Europe, and it soon reestablished French military domination of the continent.

The Directory, which lasted from 1795 to 1799, faced acute
financial crises, and accusations of corruption swirled around its
members, but it provided an effective war government. In 1795 the
only great powers still in the field against France were Austria and
Britain, with the support of the south German states. After some ini-

tial successes, two French armies invading Germany were checked by the Austrians in 1796, but a third army under Bonaparte swept the Austrians from north Italy and established two republics there under French domination; in 1797 Austria accepted a peace that recognized the new Italian states and ceded the Austrian Netherlands to France. The next year the French invaded both the Papal States and Switzerland, setting up two more republics. Thus, already by 1798 the French had altered the political organization of Europe greatly, and of all the great powers only Britain remained in the war.

Desirous of forcing Britain to terms and convinced that an invasion of England was not feasible, Bonaparte proposed the seizure of Egypt, from which position the French could threaten the British empire in India. Early in the summer of 1798, Egypt was occupied easily, but in August the British destroyed the French Mediterranean fleet, which negated the strategic value of the success. French forces remained in Egypt until 1801, but Bonaparte returned to France in the summer of 1799. The Directory never had won popular support, while military success had made a hero of Bonaparte, and in November of 1799 the general overthrew the constitution and seized control of the government. A consulate of three men was established (1799–1804) which was dominated by Napoleon Bonaparte as First Consul.

During the course of the fruitless Egyptian campaign, a second European coalition had been formed against France, this time including Russia. Early campaigns of Russian and Austrian forces drove the French out of south Germany, Switzerland and north Italy, but a British invasion of the Netherlands failed, co-operation among the allies broke down, and the Russians quit the war. The French then inflicted crushing defeats upon the Austrians in 1800, both in Germany and Italy, and in 1801 Austria had to sign the Treaty of Lunéville, which conceded to France everything west of the Rhine and recognized the client princes and the satellite republics that France had established. In the same year, long negotiations with the pope produced a concordat by which part of the Papal States was restored in return for papal acceptance of the situation of the church in France: high clergy appointed by the government, all clergy paid by the government, confiscated church lands in

France not to be restored and all education to be controlled by the state. Finally, in March of 1802, England also made peace with France by the Treaty of Amiens.

In 1804 Bonaparte abolished the Consulate, proclaimed the French empire with himself as Emperor Napoleon I and established a brilliant court with an aristocracy based on talent and service. The Corsican general had succeeded in establishing the absolute monarchy that the Bourbon kings had sought, and he appeared secure. War with England had broken out again in 1803, but the rest of Europe was at peace, and France was the strongest nation on the continent. The situation remained basically unstable, however, for the English felt that their security was threatened by French control of the southern Netherlands, and Austria was humiliated and determined upon vengeance.

In 1805 a third anti-French coalition was formed, including England, Austria, Russia and Sweden, and Europe plunged into war again. At sea the English victory at Trafalgar in October of 1805 broke French naval power definitively, but on land a series of French successes, culminating in the victory over the Austrians and Russians at Austerlitz in December, quickly knocked Austria out of the war again. In the aftermath, the greater part of west Germany was organized into a Confederation of the Rhine under French "protection," the Holy Roman Empire was dissolved, Austria confirmed earlier territorial concessions, and Napoleon made one of his brothers king of Naples while establishing another as king of Holland (the former Batavian republic). The war was far from over, however, for Russia was still in the field, and Napoleon's new arrangements in Germany brought Prussia into the war against him. In 1806 he broke the Prussians completely at Jena and Auerstädt, and in 1807 he defeated the Russians at the Battle of Friedland, which left the French in control of all of Europe to the Nieman River. By the Treaties of Tilsit, signed in July of 1807, Prussia was reduced to half of her former size, and Russia accepted the French reorganization of Europe. A few months later Russia joined France in the war against England.

Napoleon's policy at this time was dominated by the war with England and by new provisions for his family. In 1806 he had proclaimed the Continental Blockade, banning English goods from all the ports of Europe to break the economy of the nation of shopkeepers, and the desire to make the blockade effective led him to occupy Portugal and Spain, areas that he was never to succeed in pacifying. At the same time, he created a new kingdom of Westphalia in northwest Germany for another of his brothers and moved his elder brother from Naples to Spain, giving Naples to a brother-in-law. In 1809 Austria once again tried to raise Germany against Napoleon, but again she suffered defeat, at Wagram, and had to accept another humiliating peace that cost her much territory and three and a half million subjects.

About 1810 Napoleon was at the height of his power, but there were many signs of discontent. An English expeditionary force in Portugal received strong local support, and the French were unable to complete their conquest of that country; though the French occupied Spain, guerilla resistance never ceased, and large French forces were tied down; in Germany there were a number of uprisings against French domination; and in new quarrels with the pope, French armies reoccupied the Papal States in 1809, whereupon the pope excommunicated Napoleon and the pope himself was taken as a prisoner to France. All over Europe Napoleon's creation and dissolution of new states were resented, and all governments were strained by the large levies of men and money that Napoleon constantly demanded of them. But the greatest danger was the growing tension with Russia. Personal rivalry between Napoleon and Czar Alexander I (1801–1825) was reinforced by a conflict over a number of issues, such as the Continental Blockade, the future of Polish lands and Russian ambitions for expansion in the Balkans. As Franco-Russian relations deteriorated, Napoleon assembled the Grand Army, a multinational force of about six hundred thousand men, and in June of 1812 if advanced into Russia. The Russians fell back, forcing Napoleon to depend upon very long supply lines; then at Borodino they stood and fought a bloody engagement with heavy losses on both sides. After Borodino the Russians had to fall back again, and the road to Moscow was open, but the French could claim no great victory; the Russian army was still intact and dangerous. When Napoleon's army occupied Moscow, the Russians burned the city, leaving the French with neither shelter nor provisions, and Napoleon had no choice but to withdraw. He was caught by the Russian winter, while cold and hungry men and horses were harassed by Cossacks and armed peasants and sometimes had to fight the pursuing Russian army; only about one hundred thousand men of the Grand Army lived to recross the Niemen. Napoleon hurried back to Paris.

The disaster in Russia encouraged France's other enemies. In 1813 the Prussians allied with the Russians; England was already in the war, of course, with forces in Portugal and Spain. As Russian and Prussian forces gathered, Napoleon raised another army and prepared to defend his control of Germany, winning the first encounters in May of 1813. Then in August Austria once more declared war against France, and the ensuing conflict became a German war of liberation with strong Russian support. In October of 1813 the Battle of Leipzig, called the Battle of the Nations, was fought, and Napoleon was defeated decisively by the combined allied forces. The war in Germany had forced the recall of French troops from Spain, and the English army under Wellington soon crossed the Pyrenees and besieged Bayonne. The allies made steady progress in Germany, and in December of 1813 they crossed the Rhine into France; despite some brilliant defensive actions against superior numbers, Napoleon could not halt the allies, and on March 31, 1814 they entered Paris. The imperial senate declared that Napoleon had forfeited the throne, and on April 11 he abdicated, being granted by the allies the island of Elba and a pension. The victorious powers then settled to the task of shaping the peace, a major problem because the Europe of the 1790s had disappeared during two decades of the revolutionary and Napoleonic wars.

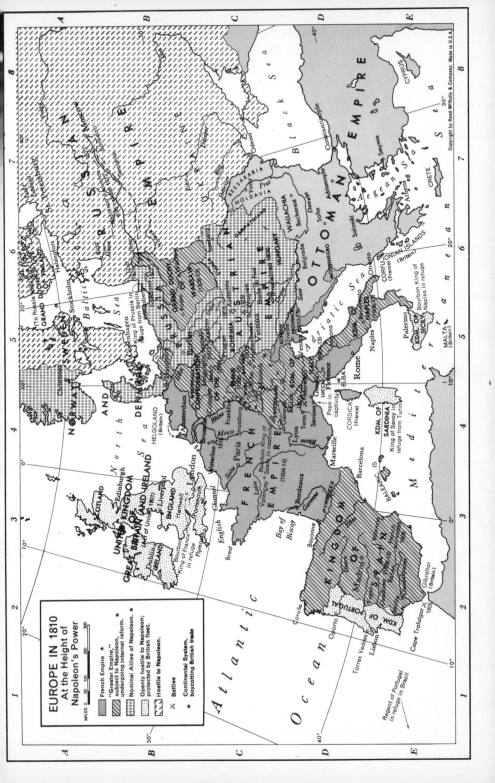

EUROPE IN 1810
At the Height of Napoleon's Power

MILES 0 50 100 200 300

French Empire ★

"Greater Empire," subject to Napoleon. ★

Nominal Allies of Napoleon, undergoing internal reform. ★

Openly hostile to Napoleon; protected by British fleet. ★

Hostile to Napoleon.

✕ Battles

★ Continental System, boycotting British trade.

Copyright by Rand McNally & Company, Made in U.S.A.

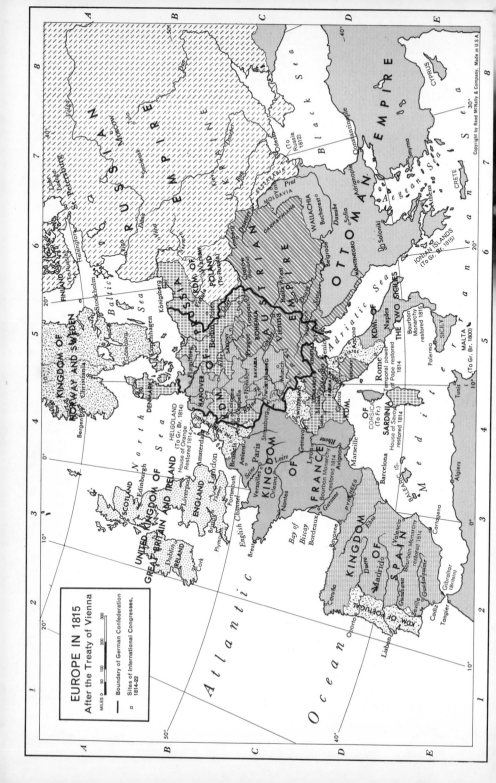

EUROPE IN 1815
After the Treaty of Vienna

— Boundary of German Confederation

▫ Sites of International Congresses, 1814–22

MILES 0 50 100 200 300

Chapter 9

Restoration and Reaction

Peace and stability were the dominant themes of the settlements made by the victorious powers in 1814 and 1815, and the first Treaty of Paris, signed in May of 1814, dealt fairly generously with their former enemy. France was restored to the rule of the Bourbon monarchy, and she had to recognize the independence of the European states that Napoleon had subjected and promise to abolish the French slave trade, but her frontiers were returned to those of 1792, allowing retention of the early revolutionary conquests, and England returned most of the French colonies she had captured.

In September of 1814 the Congress of Vienna assembled to expand this rudimentary treaty into a general European settlement. Strictly speaking, it was not a congress at all, for there were no plenary sessions, and representatives of Russia, Britain, Prussia and Austria made all the major decisions. Before negotiations had proceeded very far, however, the four great powers divided over an explosive issue, the future of Poland and Saxony. The Russian czar, Alexander I (1801–1825), wanted to reestablish Poland as a Russian dependency, while the Prussians wanted to annex Saxony. Austria and Britain opposed these ambitions, fearful that Prussian aggrandizement would threaten Austria's domination of Germany and that Russian expansion westward would upset the new balance of power that they hoped to create in Europe. This division among the former allies was exploited by the astute French diplomat, Talleyrand, to gain admission to the inner councils at Vienna, and in January of 1815 Britain, Austria and France signed a secret treaty committing them to fight if Russia and Prussia would not abandon at least part of their demands. At this point the whole effort to make a general settlement might have collapsed but for a new crisis that reunited the former allies.

The discord at Vienna was paralleled by the failure of France to rally to the restored Bourbon government, and Napoleon, well aware of both of these situations, determined to make an attempt to recover his throne. On March 1, 1815, he crossed from Elba to the south of France and began to march north; in the middle of the month the king fled abroad, and on March 20 Napoleon entered Paris. Since the allies refused even to negotiate with him, he realized that he would have to fight again, and he hastily gathered an army to oppose the English, who were first in the field. On June 18, however, he was defeated overwhelmingly at Waterloo and was exiled to the barren island of St. Helena in the south Atlantic.

While Napoleon was attempting to reestablish himself, the diplomats at Vienna continued their work, and early in June of 1815 the Act of the Congress of Vienna was signed, creating a new political framework for Europe. Czar Alexander's ambition was satisfied partially by the establishment of a kingdom of Poland (smaller than he had hoped) with himself as king, and Prussia got two fifths of Saxony as well as some other small territories, while Austria was compensated for the increased strength of Russia and Prussia by being given large parts of north Italy. No effort was made to reconstitute the eighteenth century maze of petty German states; instead, German lands were divided anew, in accordance with the wishes of Austria and Prussia. Thirty-nine states emerged, former petty princelings being compensated with titles and pensions, and a German confederation was created to replace the old Holy Roman Empire. The Dutch Netherlands, the former Austrian Netherlands (Belgium) and Luxemburg were combined into a kingdom of the Netherlands under Dutch rule, and a whole series of articles provided for the retention by England of some colonial conquests, the restoration of former dynasties in Spain and Sardinia and the reestablishment of an independent Switzerland.

After Napoleon's return from Elba, usually called the Hundred Days, a second Treaty of Paris was signed in November of 1815; this treaty reduced France to her boundaries of 1790, forced her to return the art treasures that Napoleon had stolen, and imposed an indemnity and an army of occupation. The regions that France lost through the adjustment of the frontiers were given to the Netherlands, Prussia and Sardinia in an effort to strengthen further the obstacles to any renewed French expansionism, and at the same time the major powers made arrangements for continuing enforcement of the settlements. In September they signed an idealistic document called the Holy Alliance, a mutual agreement to be guided by Christian principles, and concurrent with the second Treaty of Paris, they established a firmer basis for continuing cooperation; through the Quadruple Alliance they bound themselves to maintain the territorial arrangements and the exclusion of the Bonapartes for twenty years, and they agreed to hold further meetings to oversee the implementation of the treaties.

Meanwhile, with the Napoleonic adventure finally ended, the reconstituted European states groped for internal settlements that might produce stability and order, but the task was not easy, for during two decades of revolutionary warfare, legal and political changes had been inaugurated all over Europe. The lands of nobles and of churches had been confiscated, divided and sold; laws had been promulgated upon a basis of legal equality; and men had grown accustomed to the idea that in Napoleon's service advancement was open as far as their talents and energies could carry them. The violence and anarchy produced by the French revolution in large measure had discredited the idealistic liberalism of the Enlightenment, but with more cautious goals and more sharply defined principles, of which the most prominent was a doctrine of governmental noninterference, liberalism survived as a political creed with wide support.

The economic theorist Adam Smith had asserted in the 1770s in his *Wealth of Nations* that economic expansion would proceed most rapidly if governments would refrain from extensive regulation and would permit almost unrestricted private capitalism, and this opinion was endorsed on a broader basis in the late eighteenth and early nineteenth centuries. Liberals such as Jeremy Bentham maintained that government was a necessary evil, and that it ought to be restrained from interference with political and economic liberty so as to assure "the greatest good of the greatest number." Only a few radicals supported broadly democratic reform at the beginning of the nineteenth century, but many liberals desired constitutions which would set limits upon the scope of governmental activity, some form of representative political institutions and public education free of ecclesiastical control.

The other political conception that took root solidly in Europe during the Napoleonic era was nationalism. First stimulated in France by popular involvement in political and military affairs during the revolution, nationalism grew in other parts of Europe as both positive and negative responses to the French imperium. On the one hand the concept was transmitted positively by law codes and administrative and military structures based on French models and by geographical rearrangements such as Napoleon's creation of a kingdom of Italy; on the other, it developed spontaneously as a reaction against exploitative French domination, as exemplified by the stubborn resistance of the Spanish and by the national rising of the Germans.

The fortunes of war could transfer political power back to kings and aristocrats, but it could not undo the transformation of social and political consciousness that had taken place. Restoration could not mean the reestablishment of eighteenth century Europe, but most of the governing powers of the European states in the years just after 1815 were singularly incapable of comprehending this. Years of exile had put them out of touch with their own countries and had taught them nothing except to hate revolution and to be violently suspicious of all innovation.

The intellectual and cultural expression that characterized these dominant classes of early nineteenth century society is called Romanticism, a matrix of thought and attitudes composed of piety, emotional sensitivity, respect for authority and reverence for the past. To some extent Romanticism developed as a reaction against the rationalism, empiricism and anticlericalism of the Enlightenment, which were blamed for the chaos and bloodshed of the revolutionary and Napoleonic years, and to some extent it grew out of the dissenting subculture of the eighteenth century, the religious revival exemplified by pietists and Methodists and the admiration of nature and of simplicity voiced by Rousseau in France and by Robert Burns in Scotland. As well as affecting the arts, Romanticism also influenced political thought, its reverence for piety, tradition and authority encouraging conservatism. On the basis of ancient lineage, returning exiles were given responsibilities in the restoration governments for which they had no preparation at all; the anticlericalism of the revolutionary years was matched by the exaggerated piety of postrevolutionary governments, and the restorations were proclaimed as a victory of religion over atheism, most governments regarding organized religion as one of their most important defenders. In governmental circles, piety and caution replaced wit and boldness as the ideals of the courtier, and tradition replaced experiment as the foundation of policy. Most of the new rulers committed themselves mildly to reestablishing the aristocracy and the church, to trying to make history run backwards.

The only notable exception to the general incomprehension and inability of the restored monarchs was Louis XVIII of France (1814–1824). He showed clearly that he understood the need for a new fusion when he remarked that the problem was to nationalize the monarchy and to royalize the nation, but he found no support at all for this program, and his reign is one of the tragedies of the early nineteenth century. Shortly after returning to France he issued a declaration promising that he would grant a constitution, would honor the public debt and would uphold property rights and freedom of the press and of religion; it was obvious that he considered many of the revolutionary changes in France permanent and that he intended to rest his government upon the new society and not upon some idealized version of the old. However, the king's brother, the count of Artois, organized a reactionary party of ultra-royalists who hoped to restore the nobility and the church to their full prerevolutionary position; the extremism of these ultras, and the postwar reduction of the army, which scattered unemployed and dissatisfied officers all over the country, quickly eroded the king's position, and the necessity of flight during the Hundred Days diminished his prestige yet further. When he came back to Paris after Waterloo, it was said that he "returned in the baggage of the allies," but courageously he tried again to bridge the gulfs that separated Frenchmen from Frenchmen.

Despite Louis XVIII's desire that the past be forgotten, a White

Terror was launched by extremists who were, in an old French phrase, "more royalist than the king." All over France, men who had been active in the revolutionary or Napoleonic regimes were assaulted and sometimes killed by inflamed royalists, and in the midst of this hysteria, elections were held for the assembly created by the constitutional charter that the king had granted. A majority of those elected proved to be ultras, and the extremist measures that they enacted worsened the situation in a country already suffering the economic dislocation normal in the aftermath of great wars, but nonetheless this was an important experiment in representative government. Slowly the antagonists were learning the techniques of effective debate and party organization, while newspapers were stimulating a considerable public interest in the legislative quarrels. The king's moderation was winning respect, new elections produced a majority of moderate royalists and prosperity was returning. The prospect justified cautious optimism, but then disaster struck.

In 1820 the duke of Berri, Louis XVIII's nephew, was assassinated by a fanatic, and this event so inflamed the political situation that it ruined the king's hopes for a compromise policy that would merge liberalism and monarchy. The moderate center waned, and even the king himself no longer could resist the pressure of the ultras. A new ministry and new electoral laws marked the beginning of a more reactionary policy, intensified when Louis XVIII died in 1824 and was succeeded by his brother who reigned as Charles X (1824–1830). During the late 1820s the situation continued to deteriorate, for the liberals won a majority in the chamber, the business classes were antagonized by indemnification of the nobility at their expense and moderate royalists were driven into the opposition by reactionary legislation. In August of 1829 the king precipitated a crisis by appointing as head of a new ministry Prince Polignac, a dedicated ultra. Unable to obtain support in the chamber, in July of 1830 Charles X and Polignac issued five ordinances by royal prerogative, an action popularly interpreted as the beginning of government by decree. The Parisians revolted, throwing up barricades and rioting in the streets, and within a few days Charles X fled to England, leaving France committed to further political experiment.

In radical Paris there was a rather strong movement which sought to abolish the monarchy, proposing to create another republic with Lafayette as president. To many Frenchmen, however, republicanism recalled the Jacobins and the Terror, and liberal deputies in the chamber preferred constitutional monarchy under the duke of Orléans, the reputedly liberal head of the younger branch of the Bourbon family. To avoid a serious breach between the two groups, Lafayette accepted the duke of Orléans, and he was proclaimed Louis Philippe, king of the French (1830–1848). Revision of the charter of 1814 outlined a constitutional monarchy, and French liberalism appeared to have achieved an easy victory.

Disillusionment came quickly, however, when Louis Philippe proved to be no revolutionary king, refusing to aid the revolutions in Italy and Poland or to make concessions to the workers of Paris. Instead, he appointed cautious governments, and radical agitation continued, erupting into revolutionary violence in both Paris and Lyons. These insurrections were suppressed savagely, and in 1835 repressive laws were enacted censoring the press and providing for more severe treatment of insurgents, after which successive governments followed ever more conservative policies. Radical liberal and republican movements continued, however, and conditions consequent upon rapid industrial development soon added a socialist movement to the growing opposition. In 1846 and 1847 an economic depression worsened an already tense situation, and the opposition organized a series of protest meetings disguised as banquets. When the government tried to prohibit one of these banquets, in February of 1848, a street demonstration turned to rioting, and revolution was let loose again.

Nowhere else on the European continent in the years following 1815 were the good will and clear understanding of Louis XVIII found. The restored Bourbon king of Spain, Ferdinand VII (1814–1833), was greeted with wild enthusiasm upon his return, for he had become the symbol of national resistance to Napoleon, but this popularity waned quickly. The nation was impoverished from its long struggle against the French, but the king's sole interest was the restoration of ecclesiastical and aristocratic property and the reestablishment of the nobility's seigneurial rights. In 1820 dissatisfaction led to a mutiny of some of the army, and it required foreign help to suppress it, after which Ferdinand inaugurated a program of repression that lasted for the remainder of his reign; this policy failed to reestablish order, as also did his successors' programs of limited, controlled reform, and for the next fifty years Spain continued to be torn by revolutionary violence.

Elsewhere, comparable situations were developing. In the kingdom of Naples, reactionary policy evoked revolutionary ferment which broke into open violence in 1820, and the next year saw a rising in Piedmont-Sardinia. Again foreign intervention crushed the revolutions, but throughout the 1820s all of Italy remained restive, and the overthrow of Charles X in France in 1830 stimulated a new wave of revolutionary agitation. Secret societies espousing liberalism and nationalism recruited widely, and throughout the 1830s and 1840s only the strong Austrian presence in Italy maintained the reactionary governments that dominated the peninsula.

After the defeat of Napoleon German political development pivoted upon Austria's chancellor, Prince Clement von Metternich, one of the architects of the Vienna peace settlement and a firm conservative. Inevitably Metternich was concerned to repress any expression of the revolutionary movement, for Austria's subjects comprised half the races and religions of Europe, and national and liberal ideas threatened the very foundations of the Austrian empire. German resistance to Napoleon had been motivated largely by rising national feeling, and initially the Vienna settlement was not unsatisfactory to this still nascent sentiment; the more important units of German political life were reestablished, and the confederation appeared to provide loose unification. Liberals and nationalists were disturbed by the lack of constitutional guarantees, and they were distressed to see a conservative internationalist such as Metternich in control of Germany's political development; then their hopes for effective national and liberal leadership from Prussia, Austria's traditional rival, were disappointed when the king of Prussia proved unwilling to challenge Austrian predominance.

Finding no governmental support, liberal and national feeling was expressed through popular movements with no very clear goals. Almost immediately after Napoleon's defeat, German students began organizing nationalist societies, a movement highlighted in 1817 by a mass rally at Wartburg castle, Luther's famous sanctuary, and in 1819 by an assassination and another attempted one in the name of the liberal and nationalist cause. The chief result of this agitation, however, was a meeting of representatives of the foremost German states at Carlsbad in 1819 and the issuance by them of the Carlsbad Decrees, repressive measures aimed against student organizations and against the press. Despite some sporadic outbursts of revolutionary violence, Metternich and his sympathizers retained control until the late 1840s.

Although liberalism made no progress in Germany during the first half of the nineteenth century, one development was encouraging to nationalists. The existence of thirty-nine states, each with tariff barriers, was an obvious obstacle to the development of German economic life; in 1819 Prussia took the lead in the establishment of a customs union called the *Zollverein,* and it grew steadily. By the late 1820s Prussia had established a large free trade area in north Germany, which was copied by some of the south German states, and in the mid-1840s the organizations were fused to create an economic unit comprising most of non-Austrian Germany. At the same time, steady administrative reform was establishing for Prussia a reputation for honest and efficient government. These developments prepared Germany for unity under Prussian leadership, excluding Austria, but the achievement of this political unification still lay many years in the future.

In Britain, the end of the war brought unexpected difficulties as governmental purchase of war supplies ceased, continental markets failed to open up rapidly, about 400,000 demobilized men were dumped into the job market and poor harvests drove food prices up. This situation was made worse by high tariffs enacted to protect the grain interests of large landowners and to compensate for the cancellation of a ten per cent wartime income tax. High prices and widespread unemployment caused serious popular unrest, but the conservative Tories governing Britain believed that victory over the French had demonstrated beyond challenge the merit of the existing social and political structure, and they were unwilling to change anything. The Whig opposition was moribund, and there appeared to be no parliamentary alternative to a government which, in the midst of widespread economic hardship, thought only of protecting vested interests and of begging the country to appreciate the blessings of peace and order. Consequently, the discontent tended to focus in private liberal clubs outside of parliament, and they organized mass rallies and open-air protest meetings. The government failed to distinguish between acts of violence and these controlled demonstrations demanding reform, and in 1817 it began a program of repression.

The repressive measures and the demonstrations disturbed the consciences of some members of the governing classes, and parliamentary elections returned more Whigs and some young Tories who were at odds with their own party on the issue of repression versus reform. Then in 1819 another economic slump sharpened the political crisis, and two issues rallied support through a broad political spectrum, parliamentary reform and repeal of the 1815 grain tariffs called the Corn Laws. Workers and factory owners alike were concerned with these matters; the unreformed parliament allowed no representation to the new industrial areas, and the grain tariffs appeared to the working man to keep his food costs high while to the employer they appeared to inflate his wage bills by forcing him to base wages upon an artificially maintained high cost of living. Thousands turned out for mass protest meetings in the north and in the midlands, and the government panicked.

In the summer of 1819 troops were sent to an open-air meeting at St. Peter's fields in Manchester with orders to disperse the crowd and to arrest the speaker. In the confrontation that ensued some people were killed and many were injured, and the affair became a national scandal. Satirists called it the battle of Peterloo, and many members of the establishment protested vehemently, but the government pressed on doggedly with a program of further repression. At the end of 1819 it passed the Six Acts, which facilitated the prosecution of agitators, restricted public meetings and limited the operations of radical journalists. England appeared to be drifting towards a serious confrontation between a reactionary government and a populace stirred to revolutionary agitation, but before any more serious crisis developed, economic revival and new men in the cabinet eased the tension and made possible evolutionary rather than revolutionary solutions.

In 1822 Castlereagh, the dominant figure of the old Tory

cabinet, committed suicide, and a reshuffle of the cabinet brought some young liberal Tories into it. These men were limited by what they could persuade their own party to accept, but through the 1820s they managed an important revision of the criminal code, abolishing the death penalty for many offenses; a revision of tariffs, lowering duties on many imports (but not on grain); and an easing of the laws concerning combinations and conspiracies which, in effect, made unions legal while forbidding strikes. A reaction on the part of the right wing of the Tory party forced the Tory liberals to resign, and from 1828 to 1830 the government was entrusted to the conservative duke of Wellington, Napoleon's conqueror. Reform had won such strong support, however, that even he was forced to amend the Corn Laws in an unsuccessful endeavor to bring about lower prices without abolishing protectionism entirely and to carry an emancipation bill allowing Catholics to sit in parliament. These partial measures further stimulated reformist sentiment without satisfying it, and in new elections in 1830 the Whigs, who had committed themselves to reform, won a majority.

The momentum of the legislation of the 1820s, the Whigs' electoral commitment and the stimulus of the 1830 revolution in France combined to press the English government into a decade and a half of far-reaching reforms. Despite the opposition of Tory peers in the House of Lords, in 1832 a bill was passed which redistributed many seats in the Commons and lowered the requirements for voting; this bill gave representation to new centers of population and increased the electorate by half. In 1833 one bill eliminated slavery in Britain's colonies and another began effective regulation of abuses of the industrial working force; 1834 brought a new poor law and 1835 an act reorganizing and democratizing local government. Minor reforms continued for another decade under both Whig and liberal Tory governments, and in 1846, under the pressure of famine in Ireland, Sir Robert Peel enacted the long-demanded repeal of the Corn Laws. Thus, by the late 1840s when continental Europe again was swept by revolution, England had moved far in the direction of the consolidation and democratization of a national society.

Concerned to preserve Europe's security, the members of the Quadruple Alliance had agreed to continue meeting from time to time after the war. The first of their conferences, at Aix-la-Chapelle in 1818, appeared innocuous; they rearranged some details of the peace with France and admitted France to their alliance. Later meetings dealt with much more sensitive issues, however, and the Quadruple Alliance and Holy Alliance soon became symbols of reaction and repression to liberals and nationalists.

When revolt broke out in Naples, Metternich felt that Austria's Italian interests were endangered, and he called a meeting at Troppau in 1820 to seek support from his allies. Although Britain and France refused to agree, the three eastern powers issued a statement announcing their intention to intervene wherever necessary to crush revolutions before they could spread, and after further consultation with his eastern allies at Laibach in 1821, Metternich sent Austrian troops to Naples. In 1822 a crucial meeting was held at Verona to consider a Greek revolt against the Turks and the revolutions raging in Spain and its colonies. Because of conflicting interests, the allies agreed to ignore the Greek revolt, but Spain became an issue on which congress diplomacy foundered. Castlereagh had died shortly before the conference, and his successor in office, Canning, had less commitment to the alliance and even greater determination to avoid the involvement of Britain in another country's internal affairs. Ultimately, to avoid the use of Russian troops in western Europe, it was agreed that France should send aid to Ferdinand VII of Spain, but western suspicion of Russia and England's intransigent refusal to be a party to the project marked the breakdown of the alliance. Equally as serious was Canning's determination that the repression should not extend to Spain's American colonies, where English trade was developing rapidly, and his discussions with the government of the United States were directly responsible for the proclamation of the Monroe Doctrine in 1823.

Despite the breakdown of congress diplomacy as a mechanism of the Quadruple Alliance, however, international cooperation continued to function, as in the Belgian revolution of 1830. The overthrow of Charles X in France stimulated the Belgians, who were dissatisfied with Dutch rule, to rise against the king of Holland. International reactions were uncertain at first, with Britain and France favorable to the revolution and the eastern powers opposed, but diplomacy avoided overt intervention and the possible clash of great power interests, so the independence of Belgium was achieved without escalation into a major international conflict. In retrospect, it may be said that the reactionary purposes that the eastern powers attempted to develop in the postwar alliance had little effect beyond a few specific interventions in Italy and Spain, but the principle of international cooperation in peacetime and the more sophisticated diplomatic mechanisms developed in the aftermath of the Vienna peace enjoyed moderate success and contributed importantly to the international stability of the nineteenth century.

Chapter 10

Industrialization
and Its Consequences

The nineteenth century witnessed an economic transformation as fraught with consequences for European development as the political and social innovations of the revolutionary and Napoleonic experience. Beginning in Britain in the eighteenth century and spreading to the continent in the nineteenth century, heavy industrialization of manufacturing processes changed both the techniques and the capacities of European production and brought in its wake a whole series of new problems: urbanization, modern industrial labor forces, mass political movements united by economic interests, and reinvigorated international competition for markets and raw materials.

The beginnings of heavy industrialization in eighteenth century Britain turned on two major technological developments, a revolution in metallurgy and the successful application of steam power to manufacturing. The metallurgical improvement of such vast consequences was the discovery of the technique of smelting iron with coal purified by coking. By the eighteenth century, Britain, and indeed most of western Europe south of the Baltic, were experiencing severe shortages of the hardwoods traditionally made into charcoal for the smelting of iron. Early attempts to substitute coal, which

Britain had in quantity, were unsuccessful, as the impurities in the coal produced gases which caused bubbles in the iron, making it brittle and unreliable. It is uncertain exactly when the coking process to remove impurities was developed, but it was being used in the north of England in the early eighteenth century and had become rather widely known by the middle of the century. In the days of charcoal smelting, blast furnaces had to be small enough to be transported from one fuel source to another, whereas the utilization of coke allowed enormous facilities to be built over England's extensive coal fields; thus, in addition to solving a critical fuel problem, the use of coke increased productive efficiency and made much greater quantities of iron available at substantially reduced prices.

Besides its uses in construction, relatively cheap iron encouraged one of the most revolutionary developments of human inventiveness, the steam engine. Men long had dreamed of harnessing the power of steam, but only in the early years of the eighteenth century did such dreams become reality, when Thomas Newcomen built the first economically feasible steam engine. Its efficiency was so low that it was used only to pump water from coal mines, where cheap fuel was abundant, but it proved that steam could be put to work; James Watt began experimenting with improvements in the 1760s, found a partner to finance him, and by the 1780s was producing successful steam engines for general industrial use. It would be difficult to overestimate the significance of this invention, for until the eighteenth century, despite the development of some very sophisticated machinery, men depended for power upon wind, water and muscle; the steam engine was the first source of power that was independent of the vagaries of the elements and the fatigue of muscles, and despite the limited efficiency of the early engines, they represented an enormous technological advance.

Steam power first was applied widely in the production of cotton textiles, and study of this industry has prompted many historians to speak of an industrial revolution. It should be recognized, however, that cotton manufacture in many ways was an atypical industry, and one cannot generalize from it safely. The production of cotton cloth was a new industry in eighteenth century Europe, which previously had depended upon domestic wool and linen, so the industry was more susceptible to innovation than most, and it became centralized into factories or mills dependent upon steam power long before other industries were affected significantly. Moreover, traditional textile production was one of Europe's most decentralized industries, so the contrast was the more startling.

At the end of the middle ages and during the early modern period, the voyages of discovery had opened enormous new opportunities for trade, but the guild organizations that dominated Europe's manufacturing processes were oriented to ideas of stable markets and the security of the craft rather than to speculative production for expanding markets. Consequently, a number of entrepreneurs developed new sources of production outside the guild-dominated towns, particularly in textiles which were important trade goods. They instituted production through specialization of labor in villages; thus, their agents would deliver wool in one village for spinning into yarn, transport it to another village for weaving, to another for dyeing, and so on. Because this production was carried on in the workers' homes, it often was called the domestic system, and it was the most decentralized manufacturing to be found. By contrast, the new cotton industry soon came to depend upon cumbersome and costly machinery that necessitated centralized production. Even before the significant application of steam power, the development in the 1760s of the "water frame," a water-driven machine that spun yarn in quantity, established this pattern, and when it was converted to steam in the 1780s the process was accelerated by the cost of the new installations. The consequent availability of practically limitless supplies of yarn stimulated the invention of an economically feasible steam loom just after 1800, completing the centralization of cotton textiles into large factories and providing Britain the export product she needed for expanding nineteenth century markets.

The rapid development of some aspects of Britain's manufacturing industries was enormously costly, for construction of large blast furnaces and factories with steam engines required heavy investment. Moreover, the growth of large factories required a labor force, and this in turn depended upon a rather high degree of mobility of men able and willing to accept employment in the new enterprises. In both of these matters, eighteenth century England was singularly well equipped to take the lead in European industrialization. On the one hand, highly successful colonial expansion had built some great commercial fortunes in England; on the other, an accelerating transformation of English agriculture was producing both capital growth and a mobile work force.

At the end of the seventeenth century there began in England what sometimes is called an agricultural revolution. The foundation of this agrarian transformation was a process called enclosure, which created large consolidated farms from the common fields which had been characteristic of manorial practice. Enclosure negated the rights that many small farmers held under the common law, so it required an act of parliament, but as the large landowners dominated parliament, hundreds of enclosure acts were passed during the eighteenth century. On the resulting large farms production increased markedly through careful crop management and selective stock breeding, which often made the landowners wealthy, but traditionally small farmers had depended heavily upon their rights of usage of common lands, and when this usage was denied them many had to sell out. In addition, enclosure displaced cottagers, impoverished individuals with no actual ownership who built hovels on common land and eked out a meager existence. Small farmers and cottagers uprooted by enclosure often drifted toward the cities, where they formed a labor pool for the new factories.

The combination of export markets, risk capital, technological development and mobile labor catapulted Britain into the forefront of European manufacturing in the eighteenth century, and after the fall of Napoleon the new techniques and new patterns of industrial organization spread slowly to the continent. There, however, they were changed significantly. Mercantilist practices of the continental states in the eighteenth century had tended to make long-distance trade a government enterprise through colonial companies, so there were fewer private commercial fortunes. Moreover, continental Europe had not undergone an agricultural revolution; rather, the revolutionary and Napoleonic years had tended to confirm the organization of arable land into small peasant farms, so great agrarian fortunes were rare, too. Finally, heavy taxation to pay for two decades of massive war had diminished both capital and its owners' willingness to risk it. Inevitably, governments were much more involved in underwriting industrialization on the con-

tinent than was the case in England, for often it was only governments that had the necessary resources to take the risks involved
and to await long-term return on heavy investment, whether direct—
as when the Prussian government built railway lines, or indirect—
as when Napoleon III's government provided subsidies and guaranteed loans to private developers.

The second stage of the economic transformation of Europe
was the revolution in transportation that occurred because of steam
power. As early as the eighteenth century horse-drawn railways
were being used to move heavy loads such as coal, and the substitution of engines for horses was a natural step. During the 1820s and
1830s reasonably reliable locomotives were developed, and the
next few decades saw a great era of railway construction, not only
in Europe but also in its colonial dominions and in North America.
About the same time, steam power and iron construction were being
applied to problems of ocean transport. Ships were using a combination of steam and sails before 1820, and in 1826 a Dutch ship crossed
the Atlantic wholly under steam power; in the 1830s the screw
propeller replaced the paddlewheel, while the use of iron allowed
construction of vessels large enough to utilize the power of steam
efficiently. By 1840 regular steamship service had been established
between England and Egypt and on a transatlantic route. The
development of railways and steam-powered iron ships had enormous impact upon commerce, especially after the opening of the
Suez Canal in 1869. Relatively cheap long-distance transport made
it possible to gather raw materials from anywhere and to reexport
finished goods to anywhere, and western Europe quickly became
the industrial center of the world.

The most immediate social consequence of industrialization
was rapid urbanization, as thousands of people poured into the
burgeoning industrial cities seeking unskilled employment in the
factories. Since labor was plentiful and unorganized, wages tended
to be very low and hours very long. Moreover, many manufacturers
hired women and children, who could be had more cheaply than
adult males, and some factories were death traps with unshielded
machinery and massive fire hazards. The inhumanity of early in-

dustrial society, discovered by governmental investigating committees and popularized in the novels of Dickens and Zola, defies belief. Since antiquated legislation encouraged orphanages to apprentice their charges in useful employment, children as young as six worked fourteen hours daily, and foremen beat them regularly to keep them awake at their work. Wages were far too low to allow an unskilled laborer to support a family, and factory owners assumed no responsibility for workers who fell ill or were injured in industrial accidents, so, typically, among industrial families husband, wife and children worked.

Industrial workers were housed in vast rapidly built slums where whole families lived in one room, and usually these slums lacked sanitary facilities, safe water supplies or any of the other amenities needed to protect life in crowded conditions. In these sprawling districts there were, of course, no schools, no nurseries and no medical services, so people of all ages who fell ill generally lay untended until they either died or recovered, while wasting diseases such as tuberculosis simply were accepted as normal to life. Compounding these horrors were the activities of unscrupulous and vicious individuals, typified in some of Dickens' novels: men who sired numerous children so as to live by the pittances they could earn in the mills and foster parents who collected unprotected children whom they destined to factories and mines or apprenticed to crime. The industrial slums became teeming jungles where humanity was reduced to the level of predatory animals.

The horrendous conditions that accompanied industrialization have tempted some historians to draw sharp contrasts between factory labor and earlier guild, domestic and agricultural employment, but the differences easily can be exaggerated. Producers under the guild and domestic systems worked equally long hours and were equally susceptible to unemployment due to market fluctuations, while agricultural labor always had been back-breaking drudgery. Industrialization even represented some improvement, for under the older form of production the workman usually had to buy or rent his tools, which left him to bear the cost of idle capital equipment during periods of unemployment. It is undeniable that early industrial conditions were frightful, but this does not mean that the previous condition of unskilled labor was much better. Rather, growing population meant that there were many more people experiencing this miserable existence, and urbanization meant that they were gathered together where their plight was more obvious to the rest of society. Certainly the health hazards and the degradation of life in the industrial slums represented a deterioration of the condition of the poor, but the long, grueling hours of underpaid work and the callous unconcern of the upper classes did not originate with industrialization.

The concentration of masses of the laboring poor in the new industrial cities made it impossible for the rest of society to ignore their plight. Many people called for government regulation, and this group included some industrialists who disapproved in principle of the practices to which they were forced in order to meet competition; they saw in regulation a device that would force the added cost of more humanitarian practices equally upon all producers, and it was a cotton magnate who pressed the first English factory legislation through parliament.

Economic regulation met serious resistance, however, not only in defense of profit but also on the basis of a relatively new economic doctrine called *laissez-faire*, a justification of unrestricted private enterprise that grew out of Adam Smith's *Wealth of Nations*. Generally the *laissez-faire* economists held that economics should be regulated only by natural laws, such as supply and demand, and that productivity and consequent national wealth would increase most rapidly in an environment of free trade and unrestricted competition. This school of thought also formulated the iron law of wages which held that the working force always must live at a level of bare subsistence because any increase in real wages only would encourage the poor to breed more children, who would eat up the increment.

As the nineteenth century developed, the massive contrast between the wealthy few and the numerous poor encouraged ever more fanciful rationalizations. Observing the immorality and lawlessness spawned by the industrial slums, the upper classes theorized that to allow leisure time to working people would be to encourage social instability and violence, and they concluded, therefore, that long hours of work were a good thing. In 1850 Herbert Spencer's *Social Statics* expounded the view that the lower classes were basically inferior, that the reason there *were* lower classes was because they were lazy and/or incapable of betterment, and this theory was reinforced in succeeding decades by pseudo-scientific analogies. In 1859 Charles Darwin's *Origin of Species* suggested that the explanation of evolution lay in the fact that the fittest examples of a species lived to breed and pass on their characteristics. This line of reasoning, and particularly the catch phrases "natural selection" and "survival of the fittest," soon were applied to social analysis, producing theories loosely termed "social Darwinism." According to this school of thought, not only were reformist movements doomed because the poor generally were incapable of betterment, but such reform would endanger the human race by encouraging the survival and procreation of the unfit. Both the classical liberals, as *laissez-faire* economists were called, and the later social Darwinists advocated the unhampered operation of private capitalism, holding that general welfare was achieved best through the unrestrained pursuit of self-interest.

These theories did not go unchallenged. In England those who wanted to use the power of government to pursue greater social justice, like their *laissez-faire* opponents, were inspired generally by Jeremy Bentham's "greatest good of the greatest number," while on the continent such aspirations usually derived of the French Revolution. On both sides of the channel, however, a number of men came to support a doctrine called radicalism. Though they often differed among themselves, most radicals sought extensive democratic reform, such as universal manhood suffrage; most tended to be republicans, at least until Queen Victoria made the monarchy popular in England, and most were anti-clerical. Under the impact of industrialism, some of the radicals extended their political thought to economics, developing doctrines called socialism.

Until the late 1840s socialism was rather amorphous, but all socialists agreed that the socioeconomic system as it existed was grossly unfair, for industrialization was making a few manufacturers unbelievably wealthy while workers continued to live in poverty. The socialists rejected the whole concept of private ownership and control of capital assets in favor of communal possession, with profits to be shared through the entire society, and they rejected the value of competition in favor of economic and social coordination through governmental planning. Early socialists tended to be utopian dreamers such as the English factory owner Robert Owen and the French theorists, the Count de Saint-Simon and Charles Fourier. More practical was Louis Blanc, who proposed the establishment of governmentally financed factories where workers might have the benefit of industrial employment without private owners taking all the profit; this idea was supported enthusiastically by Parisian workers whose disenfranchisement and isolation under the restored monarchy rekindled revolutionary ferment and hostility to the bourgeoisie, and despite England's industrial preeminence, it was in Paris that socialism found the strongest support during the 1830s and 1840s.

Industrialization and the problems it brought in its wake soon began to influence the political development of Europe. In Britain, working class unrest provoked the Peterloo massacre in 1819, but in the 1830s political and legal reforms and the beginning of protective legislation resolved some problems and seemed to promise early resolution of others, so the British labor movement did not develop a very deep radical and socialist commitment. By and large, such tendencies were subsumed in the chartist movement in the 1840s, and when this movement died, the aspirations of British labor began to reorient toward unionism.

The chartists derived their name from a People's Charter which was drafted in 1838 to draw together all those desirous of continuing reform; it incorporated six points, of which universal suffrage was the most important, and it rallied widespread working class support. In 1839 the charter was presented to parliament as a petition signed by one and a quarter million people, but parliament rejected it; it was presented again in 1842 with more than three and a quarter million signatures, and again it was rejected. These rejections sparked widespread rioting but when the immediate reaction had worn itself out, chartism went into a decline. Inspired by revolutions on the continent, there was a brief revival in 1848, and yet another petition was presented without effect; then chartism withered away, undermined by its failure to achieve results and by an improvement in the standard of living after repeal of the Corn Laws in 1846 lowered food prices.

On the continent industrialization had not yet progressed far enough nor socialist doctrine evolved sufficiently for the industrial labor force to have much effect upon the revolutions of 1830. In Paris workers formed a significant part of the republican movement, but they were unable to prevent Lafayette and the bourgeois leaders from accepting the Orléanist monarchy; in Belgium and in Piedmont-Sardinia the revolutions served national and liberal aims; and in the rest of Europe they were crushed. However, in the 1840s socialism became stronger and more self-conscious, and it formed an important element in the violence of 1848.

The political eruptions that shook Europe at the end of the 1840s varied widely both in causes and results from one area to another. In eastern and central Europe, where national feeling had not yet achieved institutional expression and where the liberal constitutionalism attained in the west had not yet developed, nationalism and liberalism were major forces, as they had been in the western upheavals of 1830–32. By contrast, in England, France and Belgium, where the bourgeoisie had achieved political power in the 1830s and industrialization had advanced markedly, the chartist movement and the revolutions of 1848 reflected a conflict of interest between the dominant bourgeoisie and the new industrial labor force. England escaped serious violence largely because socially conscious Tory landowners provided some counterbalance to bourgeois government and secured the passage of legislation that ameliorated laboring conditions somewhat, but in western continental Europe the more or less unrestrained domination of the capitalist classes led to a new confrontation. Since the upheavals that took place all over Europe in 1848 were sparked by a new outbreak of revolutionary violence in Paris, in which the working class played an important role, industrialization must be considered an important causative element even though only a small part of the continent was as yet industrialized.

The protests against Louis Philippe's government in France were organized by an opposition that was basically bourgeois-liberal and probably could have been contained within the constitutional monarchy by a few concessions, but when the king's minister, Guizot, proved intransigent and tried to repress even the protest banquets, the opposition broadened. The working class announced its adherence to the cause of change by raising barricades in the streets of Paris and rioting in front of Guizot's house, and it sought more than minor electoral reform. When Louis Philippe abdicated and fled abroad in February of 1848, radicals, including socialists, invaded the Chamber of Deputies and forced the proclamation of another republic; three of the ten members of the provisional government then formed, most notably Louis Blanc, favored socialism. Between February and April of 1848 they were able to obtain some concessions to their desire for broad economic and social reform, especially the creation of national workshops; these were public works projects rather than the collectivist factories that Blanc long had advocated, but at least they provided some relief from the high unemployment that had resulted from depressed economic conditions during 1847 and 1848. Socialist strength was limited to the Paris area, however, the rest of France being dominated by bourgeois and peasant conservatism, and the constituent assembly elected on a nationwide basis in May created a five-man executive that was intensely hostile to Blanc and his followers. A struggle soon developed between the Paris socialists and this cautious constituent government.

In May the Paris radicals revolted again, and the Constituent Assembly used troops to suppress them, but Paris continued to seethe with unrest, and when the government tried to abolish the national workshops in June, believing correctly that they were the centers of much of the sedition, it sparked an insurrection of the working classes. The government's solution was to entrust something near to dictatorial power to General Cavaignac, and toward the end of the month there occurred the Bloody June Days when class warfare raged through the streets of Paris. Cavaignac succeeded in restoring order, but thousands were killed, and in the aftermath thousands more were deported to the colonies. The events of June 1848 terrorized France, especially French property owners, and prepared the way for a revival of Bonapartism.

In December of 1848 elections were held for a president of the republic, based upon universal manhood suffrage, and the victor was not one of those who had been active in the revolutions of February and June but Louis Napoleon Bonaparte, nephew of Napoleon I. Louis Napoleon was not well known in France; he had written two books that indicated a strong sense of nationalism and a responsible concern for social welfare, but his chief strength in the election was the popularity of the Napoleonic legend. After three decades of monarchical experiment, bourgeois domination and lack of national purpose, the Napoleonic years were remembered not for their cost in blood and taxes but for the glory, the excitement and the temporary French hegemony that they had achieved. The general populace hoped the new Napoleon could restore some of these attributes to France; moderate republicans hoped he could control radicals; and conservatives, frightened of socialism and anticlericalism and divided between Bourbonists and Orléanists, hoped he could maintain order and protect the church. Thus, by early 1850 the radical revolution had evolved into a very conservative republic relying upon disparate groups held together only by nationalism and their desire for stability.

Once again revolution in Paris inspired uprisings in other European capitals. In March of 1848 an insurrection broke out in Vienna, whence rioting spread rapidly through Germany and Italy. Metternich resigned and fled; the king of Prussia was forced to promise the issuance of a constitution; and lesser governments collapsed one after another. In Hungary the diet adopted a constitution establishing autonomy within the empire; in Venice and Tuscany republics were proclaimed. The king of Piedmont-Sardinia issued a constitution before his government was overtaken by revolution and then tried to turn popular agitation in Italy to advantage by declaring war upon Austria, in which he was joined by volunteers from all over the peninsula. In March of 1848 the carefully balanced systems that Metternich had created collapsed, both within the Habsburg empire and beyond it in Italy and Germany, and everywhere governments yielded to nationalist and liberal demands for constitutions and political and legal reforms. Probably the most ambitious efforts of the nationalists were the convocation of an all-German assembly at Frankfort and a Pan-Slav Congress in Prague.

As in France, however, the force of revolution could not be sustained, and in the summer of 1848 conservatives in central Europe began to reassert themselves. In June Habsburg military forces succeeded in reoccupying Prague and broke up the Pan-Slav Congress; then in July they defeated the Sardinians in north Italy and reestablished Habsburg authority in Lombardy and the Venetia. In the autumn the non-Magyar population of Hungary rallied to the Habsburgs for protection against the excesses of Hungarian nationalism and by October the Hungarian insurrection was broken; at the same time, a last resort to violence in Vienna failed when Habsburg forces from Bohemia compelled the city to surrender. Conservatives were encouraged and forced the abdication of Emperor Ferdinand, who had made frightened promises of reform in March, and began to rebuild the Habsburg government around Emperor Francis Joseph, so 1848 ended with the Austrian empire shaken but intact.

In 1849 another wave of revolutionary violence swept central Europe, marked by widespread rioting in Germany, the proclamation of a republic in Rome and renewed Magyar insurrection in Hungary, but again the movement waned after initial successes, and by late summer traditional governments were in control again. At the same time, the all-German assembly at Frankfort, having failed to persuade the king of Prussia to lead a nationalist movement, began to disintegrate and a stubborn remnant finally was broken up by Prussian troops. In central Europe as in France, by 1850 the revolutions had run their course and had achieved little or nothing that the revolutionaries sought. Nationalism still lacked institutional expression in Germany and Italy, and in the few states where the constitutions extorted by the revolutions were maintained, they tended more to obstruct than to advance the cause of liberalism.

Chapter 11

The Nation Deified

Just as the cataclysm of the revolutionary and Napoleonic wars had discredited the Enlightenment's optimism and faith in reason, so the general failure of the revolutions of 1848 tended to discredit the Romantic's faith in popular nationalism and mass agitation. The new generation of nationalists was composed of hardheaded pragmatists who planned to further their ambitions through the manipulation of political machinery and the use of military force. In central Europe the major goal remained national unifications, while in Britain, France and Russia, where unified states already existed, nationalism tended to express itself in pressure for social consolidation and an aggressive international role.

In Britain the 1850s and 1860s were marked by increasing stability of government, a realignment of the party structure and a much more assertive foreign policy. During the quarter century following the Vienna peace, the prestige of the monarchy had eroded badly: George III (1760–1820) had suffered fits of insanity; George IV (1820–1830) had scandalized the nation by the debauchery of his private life and by inaugurating divorce proceedings against his wife; and William IV's reign (1830–1837) was too short and too much dominated by the great reform ministries to have much effect in reestablishing public respect for the crown. By contrast, Queen

Victoria (1837–1901) enjoyed a long reign and she showed dignity and strength of character that impressed her subjects very favorably; without attempting to intrude upon the rights of parliament she asserted herself forcefully to maintain her household's independence from politial questions, insisted on being consulted concerning foreign affairs and occasionally rebuked her ministers sufficiently to remind them that they were ministers of the crown and not republican officials. Queen Victoria refused to allow the crown to become either a political pawn or a meaningless anachronism, and the monarchy came to be a symbol of national unity.

The middle years of the nineteenth century also witnessed a transformation of the British party structure. Repeal of the Corn Laws in 1846 split the Tory party beyond repair, for Peel's conversion to free trade threatened the economic security of Tory landowners, while rifts appeared between the old Whig aristocrats and younger Whigs influenced by the sociopolitical theories of Bentham and his successors. Among the Tories, Benjamin Disraeli led a revolt against Peel, claiming he had betrayed the party and adopted the Whigs' principles, and traditionalist Whigs gravitated toward this conservative group, while the "Peelite" Tories and progressive Whigs began to cooperate with each other. By the end of the 1850s the Liberal and Conservative parties had evolved, but no great gulf separated them; both were committed fully to the constitutional monarchy and to further amelioration of the living conditions of the lower classes, and they differed chiefly on how these ends best might be served. Generally the Conservatives favored Tory democracy, with monarchy, aristocracy and church leading the nation and showing responsible concern for the physical improvement of living conditions, while Liberals were oriented more to the burgeoning industrial middle class and to continuing political reform, but in the 1850s and 1860s the new alignment was still a bit amorphous.

By 1840 Britain's increasingly nationalist foreign policy had been illustrated by the Opium War with China, when bombardments by British gunboats were used to settle a quarrel with the Chinese government, and this aggressiveness was shown again in 1850 against the Greeks. Don Pacifico was a Moorish Jew resident in Athens who held British citizenship; when the Greek government refused to settle claims he had against it and an anti-Semitic mob burned his house, a British naval squadron blockaded Athens and forced the Greeks to make restitution. While defending his action before the Commons, Foreign Secretary Palmerston compared British citizenship to classical Roman citizenship, and his bold appeal to nationalism won him an ovation. In the 1860s this aggressiveness was reaffirmed during the American civil war by Britain's friendly attitude toward the southern states, with whom she had important commerce in cotton, despite the risk of war with the United States.

These years of political growth and economic expansion in Britain were capped by another reform bill in 1867, more radical than its predecessor in 1832. Essentially a Liberal measure forced upon a Conservative government by popular pressure, it provided a redistribution of seats in the commons, and it reduced voting qualifications drastically, doubling the electorate and admitting most urban workers to the franchise. This extensive reform consolidated the nation thoroughly and prepared the way for the great imperial expansion of the late nineteenth century.

In France, the 1850s and 1860s were dominated by the efforts of Louis Napoleon to balance the contending factions of the French political scene. He attempted to rally various sorts of conservatives to his government, and since all that united these disparate groups was Catholicism and fear of radicalism, his early policy favored the church and repressed anticlericals and radical extremists. In the spring of 1849 French troops intervened in Rome to crush a revolutionary republic and restore the pope, and early in 1850 new laws extended considerably the role of the clergy in French education, limited the suffrage indirectly by establishing long residency requirements and prohibited political organizations and public meetings. But Louis Napoleon was no reactionary, and he had no intention of becoming a tool of conservative interests. He tried to inhibit the reestablishment of an absolutist papal government in Rome, and he agreed only with reluctance to extensive Catholic educational influence in France. His goal was the reestablishment of a popularly supported imperial government, and he wanted to encourage nationalism and economic growth and to practice moderate policies that would unite Frenchmen rather than divide them.

Unfortunately for Louis Napoleon, the issues of French politics were serious and the divisions bitter. Proclerical and anticlerical groups hated one another; property owners detested socialists, while socialists damned factory owners as exploiters; and monarchists despised the republic while republicans hated the monarchy. Moreover, these issues tended to align the nation in two great blocs; monarchists usually were proclerical property owners, while republicans usually were anticlerical and sympathetic to more moderate forms of socialism, so any policy threatened to evoke a massive political confrontation.

Louis Napoleon honestly believed strong leadership was needed in the maelstrom of French politics, but the constitution limited him to one four-year term, so at the end of 1851 he overthrew the constitution by a *coup d'état,* restored universal manhood suffrage, and went to the voters with a plebiscite asking for extraordinary powers to draft a new constitution. When the plebiscite was overwhelmingly successful, he proclaimed a constitution that put free and unfettered authority in the hands of the president and made him emperor in everything but title. Then, at the end of 1852 another plebiscite approved the reestablishment of the empire, and the president assumed the title of Napoleon III (out of respect for Napoleon I's son who had died without reigning).

In many ways Napoleon III's career exemplifies the first practice of modern popular dictatorship. He based his government upon nationalism and prosperity, using the plebiscite to affirm his personal popularity and offering a few material benefits to everyone: insurance and employment on public projects for workers, government contracts and subsidies for buisness interests. At the same time he employed all the awesome power of the modern state to repress opposition; newspapers were controlled rigidly, and thousands of political opponents were deported to Algeria (which France had conquered toward the end of Charles X's reign). The material success of Napoleon III's policies was impressive: during the 1850s railway trackage increased almost fivefold; Paris was rebuilt, and from a cluttered, jumbled town it became a beautiful modern capital of broad avenues and beautiful perspectives; and business and industry expanded rapidly.

Napoleon III pursued an aggressive foreign policy that he hoped would submerge domestic quarrels and promote nationalism as a unifying force, but in this he was singularly unsuccessful. When he intervened in Rome in 1849, his honest desire for a reformed papal government brought charges of interference with the church from

French Catholics, while the repression of the Roman Republic antagonized French liberals. The emperor enjoyed his only real success in foreign affairs in the mid-1850s, when a Russo-Turkish war broke out and he was able to persuade Britain to join him in intervention since both France and Britain were opposed to Russian expansion to the Mediterranean. The Crimean War succeeded in limiting Russian expansion, and it aroused considerable enthusiasm in the west, partly because war correspondents using the telegraph were able for the first time to provide fresh, vivid accounts to newspapers, but it did not heal the rifts in French domestic politics.

Napoleon III had particular sympathy for Italian national aspirations, for his family had an Italianate background and during his years in exile he had lived in Italy and had associated with Italian nationalists. He hoped to do something for the Italians, and his intentions were reinforced early in 1858 when an Italian terrorist, who thought his cause abandoned, threw a bomb at him. Napoleon III agreed to provide French help to the liberal monarchical government of Piedmont-Sardinia to expel the Austrians from Italy in return for the province of Savoy and the port of Nice, and in 1859 French and Italian forces quickly overran Lombardy. The Austrians withdrew to prepared positions in the Venetia, however, and it became evident that there could be no quick end to the war, while popular risings in Tuscany, Parma, Modena and the Papal States indicated that the unification movement was spreading farther than intended. French Catholics, fearful for the safety of the pope, became angry, and to avoid disaster Napoleon III quit the war, which led both the Italians and the French liberals to damn him.

In 1860 Napoleon III was criticized seriously both for the Italian fiasco and for an unpopular free trade policy, and in an effort to retrieve his position, he decided to liberalize the empire. Far from responding with gratitude, however, the emperor's enemies used the new freedoms to denounce him bitterly, and a strong opposition developed rapidly, so he determined to intervene in a Mexican revolution in hope that another foreign adventure might calm domestic disputes. The Mexican revolutionaries were violently anticlerical, so intervention that protected the church might mollify French Catholics; the French business community was antagonized by the emperor's free trade policy, but it might be appeased by investment opportunities in Mexico; relations with Austria, embittered by the French role in Italian unification, might be reestablished on a cordial basis by offering a Mexican throne to the Austrian emperor's brother, Maximillian; and the military glory of a successful campaign might revive flagging nationalist enthusiasm for the French emperor. Unfortunately, the adventure ended in another fiasco, for the French found themselves in a guerilla war that could not be won, the government of the United States demanded a French withdrawal, and because of growing political problems in Europe Napoleon III needed to recall his troops. In the aftermath of a Mexican total victory in 1867, Maximillian was shot, the church was expropriated and French investments were confiscated.

Another disaster further weakened the French emperor in 1866 when war between Prussia and Austria ended with a startlingly rapid Prussian victory. France received no compensations for the potential threat to her security, and as a result, Napoleon III's prestige suffered badly, while at the same time internal opposition to him was growing stronger and his health was failing. He liberalized the government further in an attempt at appeasement, but elections in 1869 showed a dangerous increase in monarchical and republican strength, while in a deteriorating international situation the French government was isolated. In 1870 the emperor staked everything on a final gamble and precipitated war with Prussia, but the French armies were defeated everywhere, and Napoleon III himself had to surrender at Sedan. Two days later, in Paris, the assembly proclaimed the dissolution of the empire and the establishment of yet another republic.

Though ultimately Napoleon III's government collapsed, his efforts cannot be judged futile. The French economy underwent tremendous expansion, his capital was rebuilt and became the most beautiful city in Europe, and even his foreign policy was not without important results, though it failed to preserve his government; the Crimean War undoubtedly kept the Russians off the Mediterranean, and French intervention launched the successful struggle for the unification of Italy. Napoleon III played a major role not only in the development of France but in the shaping of nineteenth century Europe.

Italian nationalism was the major issue of southern Europe in the middle of the nineteenth century, and when the failure of the widespread risings of 1848 discredited both republican nationalist groups and their terrorist tactics, the focus of the unification movement shifted to Piedmont-Sardinia, the only state in Italy that had maintained the constitution granted in 1848. This reorientation was encouraged both by King Victor Emmanuel II (1849–1878) and by his prime minister, Count Camillo di Cavour, the latter a moderate constitutional monarchist deeply influenced by English political practices and deeply committed to economic and particularly industrial expansion.

The first stages of the wars of unification already have been considered. By the spring of 1860, Austria was confined to the Venetia, and Piedmont-Sardinia had annexed Parma, Modena, Tuscany and some of the northern papal territories. At this point, the colorful adventurer, Garibaldi, secretly encouraged by Cavour, sailed from Genoa with a band of a thousand volunteers known as the Red Shirts to aid revolutionary ferment in Sicily; this band, supported by local uprisings, soon captured the whole of the Bourbon kingdom of Naples. Cavour then sent Piedmontese troops to the support of a revolution in the remaining papal states and secured central Italy while avoiding Rome, which was garrisoned by French troops. Plebiscites in Sicily and southern and central Italy produced overwhelming majorities for union with Piedmont-Sardinia, and in March of 1861, the kingdom of Italy was proclaimed. The new kingdom soon made an alliance with Prussia which proved advantageous in 1866, when one of the consequences of Austria's defeat by Prussia was that she was forced to cede the Venetia to Italy. Then, in 1870, when French troops had to be called home for the Franco-Prussian War, Italian forces crushed the papal garrison in Rome, and it became the Italian capital.

Even in conservative eastern Europe currents of nationalism ran strongly. A Polish national revolt in 1863–64 was repressed and cost Poland her autonomous administration as direct Russian control was reestablished; in 1867 Hungary succeeded in evoking massive concessions to nationalism, and the Austrian Empire was reformed as a dual monarchy with an autonomous government for Hungary; and in the Balkans there were many insurrections against Turkish rule all through the mid-nineteenth century. In Russia, Czar Nicholas I (1825–1855) suppressed any opposition movements successfully, while limited reforms and the national stimulus of foreign wars tended to reinforce his authority, and Czar Alexander II (1855–1881) freed Russia's serfs and made reforms of local government and the judiciary, which relieved some of Russia's most pressing problems and rallied considerable national support for expansion into central Asia and for development of the far eastern provinces.

Beyond a doubt, however, the most influential national movement in Europe was the unification of Germany. The failure in 1848–1850 of both a liberal parliamentary union and an appeal to Prussia left German nationalists stalemated for a decade, but the successes of the Italian nationalists in the early 1860s stimulated a new wave of German agitation, and about the same time Prussia became more sympathetic to German nationalism. In the face of Napoleon III's aggressive foreign policy, the Prussian king, William I (1861–1888), wanted to reform and modernize the Prussian army, but the Prussian parliament demanded further liberalization of the constitution as the price of voting the necessary funds, and the king was unwilling to make such extensive concessions. The resulting deadlock became serious, and in 1862 the king entrusted the government to his former ambassador to St. Petersburg and Paris, Otto von Bismarck, a man reputed for his boldness, his loyalty and his steady conservatism. Bismarck took up the struggle with the Prussian liberals, and for four years he governed extralegally, but meanwhile he so advanced the cause of German unity that nationalists rallied to him even if somewhat distrustfully.

In the 1860s there were two schools of thought concerning the form a unification movement should take. Austria and the governments of the smaller southern states tended to favor a big Germany to be established through closer integration of the German Confederation; this solution would have included the German parts of the

Austrian domains and would have offered some greater security for the independent traditions and Catholic religion of the south, which tended to orient toward Vienna. Bismarck, for nationalist reasons, and German liberals, because of distrust of Austria's extremely conservative and internationalist policies, tended to favor a little Germany solution, which would exclude Austria and create a unified state with a strong central government dominated by Prussia. Bismarck recognized that to achieve his aims it would be necessary to assert Prussian leadership in Germany aggressively and that it probably would be necessary to employ military action to force Austria to accept exclusion from a future union, and he adopted a policy of flexible opportunism, waiting to seize any occasion to strengthen Prussia's position.

The first opportunity that presented itself occurred in 1863 when the king of Denmark attempted to incorporate the duchy of Schleswig into his monarchy. This action inflamed German nationalism, for while Schleswig long had been an autonomous possession of the Danish kings, there also were strong traditions supporting its close association with the duchy of Holstein, which was a member of the German Confederation, and the inseparability of Schleswig-Holstein had been confirmed by recent international agreements. In the name of the German Confederation, Prussia protested strongly and provoked a war with Denmark, though she had to act in concert with Austria, for the Prussian government dared not commit its forces to the north while leaving Austria free to act in the south. Nonetheless, the Danish war affirmed Prussia's parity with Austria in national leadership, and its aftermath provided extended opportunities to further Prussian ambition. Austrian and Prussian troops quickly overran the disputed duchies, and arrangements for a joint occupation brought the two German powers into a close association in which friction was a distinct possibility.

Convinced that Austria would not accept exclusion from Germany willingly, Bismarck began to prepare for an Austro-Prussian war. Discussions with Napoleon III, which appear to have included hints of compensations for France, had assured French neutrality in the approaching conflict, and negotiations with Italy won its support in return for a promise that Austria would be forced to cede Venetia to the new Italian kingdom. Then, in the spring and summer of 1866, the Prussian government deliberately escalated disputes with Austria over both the reform of the German Confederation and the administration of Schleswig-Holstein, and in June war was declared. Contrary to the expectations of everyone, and especially of Napoleon III, who had anticipated a long war exhausting both belligerents, the Austrians were crushed in seven weeks, and Prussia was free to make peace on her own terms.

During the short war most of the smaller states had opposed Prussia, and after the defeat both they and Austria were totally vulnerable, but with a thought for future cooperation Bismarck imposed moderate terms. Austria was forced to accept exclusion from any German union, and she had to cede Venetia to Italy, but she suffered no other penalties; Prussia annexed some north German territory and forced the remaining northern states into a new North German Confederation under Prussian domination. The southern states, which remained quite fearful of Prussia, were allowed to maintain their independence, but playing upon their fears of French ambitions and the evidence of Prussian moderation, Bismarck managed to draw them into close military alliances.

The successful war with Austria also had important internal consequences for the Prussian government. Although they still found Bismarck's conservative policies distasteful, many liberals rallied to him because he was furthering their hopes for unification, and in September of 1866 the Prussian legislature passed an indemnity bill which approved retroactively the government's extra-legal action during the four year constitutional quarrel. Thus, by 1867, Prussia had returned to constitutional government, had asserted her leadership of Germany successfully, had excluded Austria from the national movement, and through annexations and a Prussian-dominated northern confederation had achieved the unification of the area north of the Main River. But there were serious obstacles to completing the unification and Prussification of Germany since both Catholicism and the traditional southern orientation toward Vienna separated the south from the Prussian north; the fear of France was the most potent force pushing the southern states into a Prussian orbit, and Bismarck played upon it cleverly.

The swift Prussian victory in the war with Austria and the subsequent consolidation of northern Germany discredited the already much-criticized foreign policy of Napoleon III, and the evolution of strong new political units on France's frontiers, the kingdom of Italy and the North German Confederation, caused many Frenchmen serious and justified concern for France's security. In a desperate attempt to redeem himself in the opinion of his subjects, the French emperor rather clumsily sought Bismarck's support for French aggrandizement at the expense of the Netherlands or the south German states, and Bismarck allowed these suggestions to leak to both foreign governments and the German public. The twin results were an intensification of French diplomatic isolation and a wave of nationalist concern and agitation in southern Germany. Circumstances favored Bismarck's ambitions when a Spanish revolution in 1868 expelled Queen Isabella II and the revolutionaries offered the crown of Spain to a relative of the king of Prussia.

The possibility of being caught between two Hohenzollern monarchies upset the French, and the Paris government tried to exert pressure upon the king of Prussia to reject the offer. Bismarck was able to represent the French efforts as an intrusion upon Prussian sovereignty and an affront to German national pride, and he escalated the issue into a major confrontation. In the summer of 1870, Napoleon III, who already was in political difficulty over a number of issues, declared war on Prussia, and both the collapse of the French empire and the fulfillment of German nationalist ambitions followed rapidly. The military alliances that Prussia had concluded with the south German states quickly made the conflict an all-German war against France, and the combination of united effort and decisive German victories stimulated unionist sentiment. One by one the southern states agreed to unification within the Prussian scheme, and in January of 1871 a federated German Empire was proclaimed with the king of Prussia taking the title of German Emperor. This union solved the German problem, one of the most disruptive issues of nineteenth century Europe, but it also upset the European balance of power and created new issues that were to plague European development for three-quarters of a century.

The failures of the revolutions of 1848 affected socialists as profoundly as nationalists in the sense of discrediting idealism in favor of pragmatism and persuasion in favor of force. That the conflict of interest between the impoverished working classes and the prosperous owning classes was potentially violent was illustrated indisputably by the Bloody June Days in Paris, and the hostility of established governments toward even moderate socialist measures seemed to suggest that socialist goals could be achieved only through violence. The most influential of the tougher socialist doctrines were those of Karl Marx and Friedrich Engels, but in 1848 they were only two members of a minor radical socialist group that was little more than a secret society of German emigrants in London, and at that time they were unknown beyond their own narrow circle. Early in 1848 they had published some of their ideas in a tract entitled *The Communist Manifesto,* however, and these ideas had a wider appeal after the events of 1848 and 1849.

At the root of Marxian socialism was a deep pessimism concerning the possibility of improving working class conditions within society as it existed. Marx and Engels accepted the iron law of wages with its implicit inevitability of bare subsistence pay for workers; they observed that political power was confined to the prosperous owning classes; and they concluded that improvement by evolutionary progress through existing political institutions was impossible. They were persuaded that the working man was exploited by his employers, who expropriated to themselves the fruits of his labor, used the power of the state to repress his protests and used the promises of religion to persuade him to passive acceptance of his condition. The situation might have appeared hopeless but for the example of the great French revolution of 1789 by which society had been forced to massive civil and legal changes. Marx and Engels believed that what the bourgeoisie had done, the working classes could do, that the proper application of violence could remold society.

To these concepts based upon industrialization and revolution, Marx added a philosophical element, dialectical materialism. Derived of the German philosopher Hegel, the dialectic was an explanation of change in terms of syntheses produced by conflicts; since a synthesis itself could evoke an opposition, a new conflict then would arise, producing a new synthesis, and so on. Marx applied this philosophical concept to an interpretation of history based upon the idea of classes, explaining social evolution in terms of class conflict, and this pseudo-scientific theory suggested that industrial society confronted the last stage of social evolution, bourgeois-working class conflict, and that revolution was inevitable. To socialists these theories were reassuring, for they confidently announced ultimate victory, and they were inspiring, for they gave direction to socialist efforts—encouragement of working class solidarity and education of workers to recognize how they were being exploited. Through most of the west, however, trade unionism and extension of voting rights provided an alternative to revolution in the struggle for emancipation of the working classes, and though Marxism retained an important influence in socialist thought, especially its concepts of solidarity and activism, its revolutionary character diminished greatly and might have disappeared altogether but for its revival by Lenin and its institutional establishment in Russia in 1917.

UNIFICATION OF ITALY

MILES 0   50   100   150

TUSCANY	Independent states in 1815
- - - - - - -	Northern boundary of Kingdom of Italy, 1866-1919
1859	Joined by plebiscite with Sardinia
1860	Joined by revolution and plebiscite with Sardinia, to form Kingdom of Italy, proclaimed 1861
1866, 1870	Joined with Kingdom of Italy

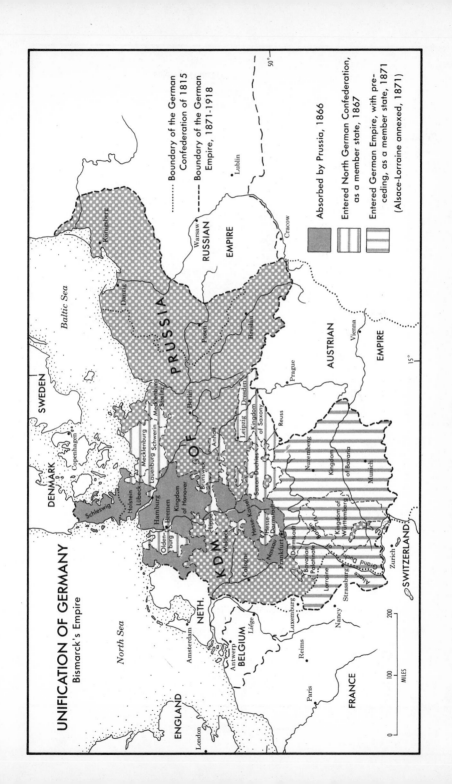

UNIFICATION OF GERMANY
Bismarck's Empire

Boundary of the German Confederation of 1815

Boundary of the German Empire, 1871–1918

Absorbed by Prussia, 1866

Entered North German Confederation, as a member state, 1867

Entered German Empire, with pre-ceding, as a member state, 1871 (Alsace-Lorraine annexed, 1871)

ENGLAND

London

North Sea

NETH.

BELGIUM

Amsterdam

Antwerp

Liège

FRANCE

Paris

Reims

Nancy

Luxemburg

SWEDEN

DENMARK

Copenhagen

Baltic Sea

Schleswig

Holstein

Lübeck

Hamburg

Bremen

Mecklenburg Schwerin

Mecklenburg Strelitz

Lauenburg

Königsberg

Danzig

PRUSSIA

Posen

Breslau

RUSSIAN EMPIRE

Warsaw

Lublin

Cracow

Olden-burg

Kingdom of Hanover

Waldeck

Lippe

Brunswick

Anhalt

Berlin

Leipzig

Dresden

Kingdom of Saxony

Reuss

Prague

AUSTRIAN EMPIRE

Vienna

K D M

O F

Cologne

Hesse Kassel

Saxon Duchies

Hesse-Darmstadt

Nassau

Frankfurt

Nuremberg

Kingdom of Bavaria

Munich

Bavarian Palatinate

Kingdom of Württemberg

Baden

Grand Duchy

Strassburg

Alsace

Lorraine

Zurich

SWITZERLAND

50°

15°

MILES

0   100   200

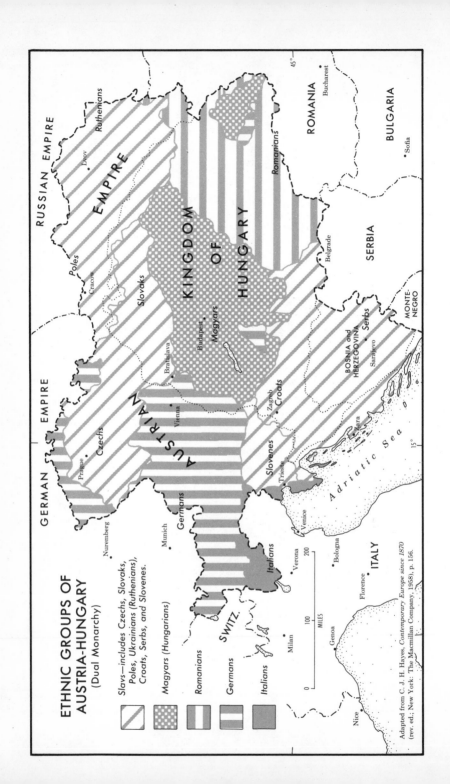

ETHNIC GROUPS OF AUSTRIA-HUNGARY
(Dual Monarchy)

Slavs—includes Czechs, Slovaks,
Poles, Ukrainians (Ruthenians),
Croats, Serbs, and Slovenes.

Magyars (Hungarians)

Romanians

Germans

Italians

MILES
0   100   200

Adapted from C. J. H. Hayes, *Contemporary Europe since 1870*
(rev. ed.; New York: The Macmillan Company, 1958), p. 156.

RUSSIAN EMPIRE

GERMAN EMPIRE

AUSTRIAN EMPIRE

KINGDOM OF HUNGARY

ROMANIA

BULGARIA

SERBIA

MONTE-NEGRO

BOSNIA and
HERZEGOVINA

ITALY

SWITZ.

Adriatic Sea

Ruthenians

Poles

Czechs

Slovaks

Magyars

Romanians

Serbs

Croats

Slovenes

Germans

Italians

Lvov

Cracow

Prague

Nuremberg

Munich

Vienna

Bratislava

Budapest

Belgrade

Zagreb

Trieste

Venice

Verona

Bologna

Florence

Genoa

Milan

Nice

Sarajevo

Zara

Bucharest

Sofia

45°

15°

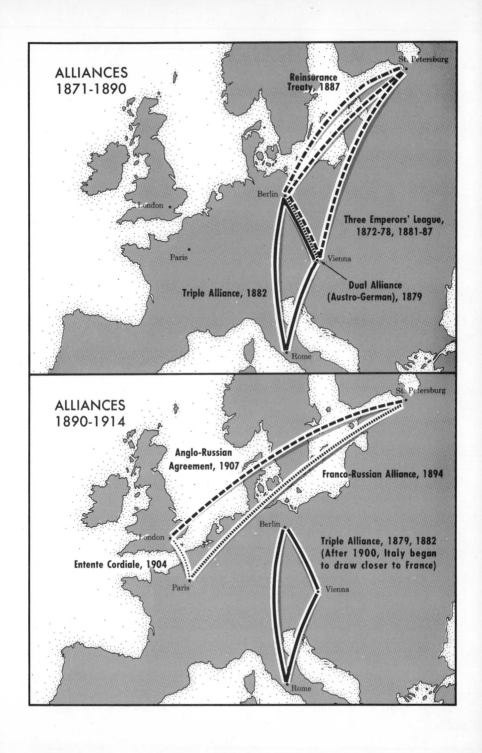

ALLIANCES
1871-1890

Reinsurance
Treaty, 1887

St. Petersburg

London

Berlin

Paris

Vienna

Three Emperors' League,
1872-78, 1881-87

Triple Alliance, 1882

Dual Alliance
(Austro-German), 1879

Rome

ALLIANCES
1890-1914

St. Petersburg

Anglo-Russian
Agreement, 1907

Franco-Russian Alliance, 1894

London

Berlin

Triple Alliance, 1879, 1882
(After 1900, Italy began
to draw closer to France)

Entente Cordiale, 1904

Paris

Vienna

Rome

Chapter 12

The New Europe

Ever since the fall of the Roman Empire, the monarchy in France generally was the strongest power in Europe; sometimes it was weakened by internal divisions, as during the Hundred Years War, or overshadowed by external combinations, such as the great alliances that checked Louis XIV and defeated Napoleon; but it had human and natural resources that exceeded those of any other power, and those resources were organized by one of the most highly developed governments in Europe. During the nineteenth century this situation changed completely, for industrialization doubled and redoubled Britain's strength, and the unification of Germany created a state that was both larger and more populous than France. Thus, in the last quarter of the nineteenth century, in addition to confronting social problems consequent upon industrialization and political problems resulting from self-conscious and enfranchised working classes, the European states had to confront one another in an ill-defined international scene in which precedents had little value and the strength of allies and opponents only could be guessed.

Britain's major concerns, thanks to the stability of a highly consolidated national society, were to find raw materials and markets to serve her industrial economy. France was committed to another republican experiment while still experiencing the turbulence of rapid industrial development, and she had to grapple with the results of defeat in the Franco-Prussian War and the threat to her security implicit in the existence of a unified Germany. The new central European states, Italy and Germany, had to seek means of national development; and Austria had to struggle to maintain the stability of a multinational empire in an age of virulent nationalism while flanked by a reorganized Germany from which she was excluded and a hostile Italy whose government had further designs upon Habsburg lands. Finally, Russia, humiliated and isolated after the Crimean War, had to redefine her international position, settle and develop her territories in central and eastern Asia and build the industrial basis for a modern economy. Considerations of the late nineteenth century often are overshadowed by European imperial expansion, but this also was a period of internal European development that was fraught with consequences for the twentieth century.

During the 1870s and 1880s Britain's government was dominated by the towering personalities of William Gladstone and Benjamin Disraeli. During Gladstone's first ministry (1868–1874), liberal reform was continued, and many of the vestiges of an older and more authoritarian society were abolished. In an attempt to pacify Ireland, where violence was endemic, Gladstone ended the requirement that the Irish support an Anglican church to which few of them belonged and revised the legal structure of Irish land tenure to provide the Irish peasantry some protection against English absentee landlords. Within England, where there were educational facilities for only about half the children of school age, he established a system of public schools with government support and removed religious qualifications from access to higher education. In an attempt to open government service more broadly, he provided for competitive examinations in the civil service and ended purchase of military commissions. Finally, he provided for the use of the secret ballot in elections and reformed English courts to provide more rapid and more equitable judgments. In the spirit of Tory democracy, a Disraeli government (1874–1880) carried bills establishing minimal standards for public health and for workers' housing and providing safety regulations for merchant shipping. The second Gladstone ministry (1880–1885) returned to liberalization, further developing legislative protection of the Irish peasantry, extending voting rights in England again, enacting another parliamentary redistribution and attempting to limit corrupt practices in elections. During the last decade and a half of the nineteenth century Britain witnessed a notable expansion of trade unionism, culminating with the foundation in 1893 of the Independent Labour Party with an evolutionary socialist platform, but chiefly British politics after about 1885 were dominated by a fast-changing international situation.

Queen Victoria's death and the accession of Edward VII (1901–1910) brought no dramatic changes. Continuing prosperity maintained stability, and the government pursued a moderate program aimed at the gradual improvement of social conditions. A new Education Act in 1902 extended public education to secondary levels; a Trade Disputes Bill and a Workman's Compensation Act in 1906 improved the position of unions and provided further protection to laborers; an Old Age Pension Law in 1909 made provision for minimal support of every aged British subject; and a National Insurance Act in 1911 introduced both health and unemployment insurance. Britain experienced some political agitation—labor unrest over rising prices, conflict over the perennial question of home rule for Ireland and a movement to disestablish the Anglican church in Wales—but questions of foreign policy remained predominant, and most domestic quarrels were smothered by the outbreak of war in 1914.

In France, Napoleon III's defeat by German armies was followed by the proclamation of the Third Republic in Paris, and France entered the 1870s facing the twin problems of ending a losing war and launching a new government. After the surrender of Paris, the Germans permitted national elections to be held so that the peace would be made by a representative government and could not be repudiated easily; consequently, a new national assembly met in Bordeaux in February of 1871. The first task of this new government clearly was to make peace with the Germans, and in May it signed a treaty that provided for cession of Alsace and part of Lorraine, payment of a heavy indemnity and acceptance of an army of occupation; it was a harsh peace, but in the face of military collapse the government had no choice.

At the same time that it was dealing with the Germans, the new republic had to confront an insurrection, for Parisian radicals, recognizing that the national assembly was hostile to the radical republic that they demanded, formed a commune, seized the weapons available in the capital and prepared for conflict. Adolphe Thiers, whom the Bordeaux Assembly had elected as its chief executive, used regular troops to suppress the Parisian revolt, and the affair ended in bloody street fighting, but Thiers' action demonstrated to all of France that the government could maintain stability and that republicanism did not necessarily mean radicalism and the Jacobin terror of 1792.

The Bordeaux Assembly was divided quite seriously in its political aspirations; of the six hundred deputies, about four hundred were monarchists, but this majority was divided about equally between Bourbonists and Orléanists. Unable to resolve their differences, in February of 1871 they agreed to the Pact of Bordeaux, by which political quarrels were suspended temporarily so as to allow cooperation in the task of national recovery, and the monarchists left to the republicans the unpopular chores of signing a harsh peace with the Germans and crushing the Paris commune. Monarchical strength was shown, however, in a decision to settle the government at Versailles, the traditional royalist capital, rather than at Paris.

In 1873, fearful that Thiers' government was winning too much credit, the monarchists hurried him out of office as soon as he had finished paying the indemnity to the Germans and had secured the withdrawal of German occupation troops; then they chose the conservative monarchist, Marshal MacMahon, as president of the Republic for a seven year term. Since the division between Bourbonists and Orléanists was still unresolved, and some sort of regular arrangements had to be made, in 1875 the monarchists enacted a rudimentary republican constitution that they hoped could be converted easily to monarchy. The new constitution simply provided for a strong president, with the powers of a constitutional monarch, and for a legislature consisting of a Senate and a Chamber of Deputies. In 1876 general elections were held under the new constitution, and monarchical fears that the republicans had been too successful proved justified. In the Senate, where the monarchists had tried to perpetuate themselves by providing for some members to be appointed and for the rest to be chosen indirectly, the elections left the republicans just two seats short of a plurality; in the Chamber, which was elected by direct universal manhood suffrage, republicans outnumbered monarchists more than two to one.

During the late 1870s, the government of the Third Republic was dominated by a legislative-executive struggle which ended with MacMahon's resignation and the Chamber's success in establishing the principle of ministerial responsibility. This republican triumph was followed in the early 1880s by amnesty for surviving communards, the legalization of trade unions and the enactment of a number of anticlerical measures designed to exclude religious influences from French education while making primary education compulsory. By the middle of the 1880s, however, the conservative republican government was being attacked from both the right and the left. Monarchists gained strength significantly in the elections of 1885, while radical republicans and socialists formed new parties committed to further social reform and the defense of the working classes.

Among supporters of the radical left, where the traditions of the French revolution of 1789 lived on, nationalism was very strong. They never had become resigned to the cession of Alsace-Lorraine, forced upon France in 1871, and their desire for a war of revenge against Germany precipitated a crisis in the late 1880s when they forced the government to appoint General Boulanger as Minister of War. Though favored by the radical left for reasons of foreign policy, Boulanger was rather authoritarian in his views on domestic affairs, and the monarchists, their divisions ended by the death of the last Bourbon, soon rallied to him, hoping that he would support a monarchical restoration. At the same time, the government was shaken by scandals which further increased Boulanger's popularity as a strong political figure who might clean out corruption. The climax of the Boulangist movement came in January of 1889, when having won an election in Paris he was expected to lead a march on the government buildings, demanding extraordinary powers to reform the government and to revise the constitution, but at the critical moment Boulanger proved indecisive, missed his chance for dictatorial power and quickly went into eclipse. The government considered trying him for treason, and he fled abroad, where he committed suicide two years later. The short-lived but powerful Boulangist movement appears to have been a sort of Bonapartist revival, a popular reaction against the constant bickering of the parties in favor of personal leadership by a strong, magnetic individual.

In the aftermath of the Boulanger affair the republic appeared much strengthened as general elections in 1889 produced large republican majorities, but new crises soon arose. Early in the 1890s the speculative company that was attempting to dig a canal across the Isthmus of Panama collapsed, wiping out massive investments, and subsequent investigations showed that a number of senators and deputies had accepted money from the company—had allowed their influence to be bought. And hardly had this scandal subsided when another crisis broke over charges of treason against a French army officer, Captain Alfred Dreyfus.

In 1894 French army intelligence obtained evidence indicating that someone on the general staff was selling information to the Germans, and though the evidence was very vague, a culprit had to be produced quickly since the story had reached the newspapers. Dreyfus had the misfortune to be a middle-class Alsatian Jew in an officer corps that was overwhelmingly aristocratic, Catholic and anti-Semitic, and he had had access to the documents in question; he was accused, tried quickly in a closed court martial, condemned and sent to Devil's Island. The case appeared to be closed, and the public was satisfied.

The Dreyfus case was hardly more than begun, however, for both the new head of French intelligence and Dreyfus' brother soon discovered the identity of the real culprit. The intelligence officer was transferred to a frontier post in Africa, for the army did not wish to reopen the question and perhaps have to admit that it had been wrong. In 1898 Dreyfus' brother finally obtained trial of the other suspect, Major Esterhazy, but a military tribunal found him not guilty, and again the army tried to close the case, and again it failed. The journalist and novelist Emile Zola lent his talent to Dreyfus' defense, and it was discovered that some of the evidence against Dreyfus had been forged by a member of the general staff, who admitted forgery and then committed suicide. By this time, however, the army considered itself committed, and in 1899 a retrial of Dreyfus by another military court again found him guilty, though he was spared further imprisonment by a presidential pardon.

What made the Dreyfus affair a great political issue was that the case crystallized opinion for and against the republic. Generally the left had rallied to Dreyfus' defense in the name of simple justice and the primacy of the individual in society, while under the cloak of patriotism the right had tried to insist that the army must be above criticism and immune to civilian review. A number of factors had complicated the affair. On the one hand, antagonism between France and Germany continued strong, while imperial rivalry in Africa almost led to war between France and Britain in 1898; many felt that in this situation the army, France's only shield, must not be questioned in any way, and they were willing to sacrifice one man to it. Moreover, the officer corps was the stronghold of the aristocratic Catholic families who hoped for a monarchical restoration, and if the conviction of Dreyfus could be upheld, it would help them to maintain the corps as a preserve for their own kind. On the other side, in addition to their commitment to the social principles of the great revolution, the radicals saw the case as an opportunity to bend the army to obedience to the civilian government of the republic and to break one of the important strongholds of the political opposition. Thus, to almost everyone except his family Dreyfus became a symbol of something: of the army embattled, of the republic threatened, of the church endangered, of monarchism resurgent. For a decade French politics were dominated almost wholly by what was called simply "the affair." It broke governments, caused suicides and destroyed careers. Ultimately, it affirmed the republic, ruined the monarchical party and reduced the church greatly. In the aftermath of Dreyfus' pardon, the left enjoyed a considerable electoral victory, and it consolidated its position by moving quickly to complete the disestablishment of the French church. Between 1901 and 1905 a number of laws were enacted dissolving Catholic orders, closing remaining church schools, guaranteeing absolute liberty of conscience and establishing complete separation of church and state. Appropriately, in 1906 the republic finally rendered justice to Dreyfus, who had been the instrument of its victory; the high court of appeals cleared his name, and he was reinstated in the army, promoted and decorated.

As the Dreyfus case faded into the past, France experienced a notable resurgence of aggressive nationalism, partly a reaction to imperial rivalries and partly a desire to reunite the nation in the face of a deteriorating international situation, but this movement had strong Catholic and monarchical sympathies and represented also the desire of authoritarian elements of the society to regain the position lost in the fight over Dreyfus. By contrast, there also was labor unrest as the socialists became more demanding, and after 1906 a whole series of strikes swept the country. Thus, France entered the first world war with many of the quarrels inherited from the revolution of 1789 still unresolved.

Hardly was the new German Empire proclaimed in 1871 than the government became involved in a serious struggle with the Catholic Church, known as the *Kulturkampf*. There were two major bases to the quarrel, the resurgence of papal power and the political activity of German Catholics. The reconsolidation of the papacy after the revolutions of 1848 culminated in the promulgation of the dogma of papal infallibility in 1870; to Bismarck, this appeared as preparation for papal support of the German church against the government, and he was antagonized. The tension was increased in March of 1871 by the organization of a Catholic Center Party to campaign in the first general elections of the German Empire; since the preponderance of German Catholic strength lay in the south, the Center Party tended to represent southern particularism as well as Catholicism, and on both grounds it was hostile to the imperial government dominated by Protestant Prussia. During the early 1870s these tensions developed rapidly into a serious struggle as the government expelled the Jesuits and extended governmental control of ecclesiastical education and discipline; then in 1875 it made civil marriage obligatory, suspended governmental financial aid to the church and dissolved all religious orders except those involved in nursing. The church in Germany suffered severely, and improvement came only at the end of the 1870s when Bismarck decided that the state was in no danger from the church and that the support of the Center Party would be useful to new tariff policies that he wished to adopt. After 1879 the repression was eased, and by the mid-1880s the *Kulturkampf* had died out, but the state's supremacy over the church in the new German Empire had been established clearly.

During the *Kulturkampf,* a new problem for the government developed with the considerable growth of German socialism and the foundation in 1875 of the Socialist Workingmen's Party. These early socialists were hampered at first by internal divisions between revolutionary Marxists and those who followed the evolutionary programs of Ferdinand Lassalle, a social-democratic thinker of the 1860s, but despite divisions they recruited very rapidly. At first Bismarck was inclined to repression, especially when two attempted assassinations of the emperor suggested a mood of violence in the country, and in 1878 an Anti-Socialist Law was passed prohibiting meetings, publication and fund-raising by socialists.

As German industry expanded, however, Bismarck appears to have recognized that socialist complaints about working conditions were well founded, and he undertook a series of state-sponsored reform measures which he hoped would undermine the socialists' appeal. Sickness insurance for workers in 1883 was followed a year later by accident insurance, and then in 1889 came old age and invalids' insurance. In the early 1890s, the Anti-Socialist Law was allowed to lapse, and the program of state socialism was extended by the establishment of industrial courts and a Department of Labor, which further protected workers against exploitation. These programs did not destroy socialism, but they improved greatly the condition of German workers, and they may have been an important factor in the development of revisionism in the early twentieth century—the weakening of Marxian revolutionary ideas in favor of parliamentary reforms and evolutionary betterment.

Bismarck's retirement in 1890 marked the end of an era politically and had significant repercussions on foreign policy, but economic development continued from foundations he had established. German industry expanded rapidly, for unification of the separate German states had brought together large reserves of coal and iron ore, the bases of heavy industrialization. To develop these resources, an Imperial Bank was founded in 1876 to provide capital, and protective tariffs were established in 1879 to shield infant industry from foreign competition. On the eve of the first world war Germany had passed both England and France in the production of iron and steel and was second only to the United States. The economic and military power of the new state kept it relatively stable internally, but under the personal direction of the emperor new foreign policies after 1890 took dangerous courses that led finally to disaster.

By contrast, the new kingdom of Italy failed to develop rapidly after unification. The mountainous spine of the Appenines divided it geographically; it lacked the vast natural resources of Germany; and no statesman of the first rank appeared to lead the government after Cavour's death in 1861. Moreover, Italy faced a critical and unique problem in its relations with the papacy.

Shortly after Rome was annexed by force, the Italian parliament passed the Law of Guarantees, which granted the pope royal dignities, free communications with Catholics all over the world, the right to receive foreign embassies, possession of the Vatican palace and other properties and a subsidy from the state treasury equivalent to his former income from his lands. The pope insisted he must retain some part of Rome, however, and when the government would not agree, he refused to accept the settlement and denied recognition to the new Italian state, forbidding Catholics to participate in its affairs. Thereafter, the pope styled himself, somewhat fancifully, the prisoner of the Vatican, and the issue remained unresolved as all attempts at compromise foundered on the Roman question. A major result of this quarrel was that many Italian Catholics refused to vote or stand for office, so that politics were left largely to the anticlerical parties that simply ignored the papal ban. In 1904 the papal position was modified somewhat by Pope Pius X who allowed Catholics to vote to preserve the social order, but relations between the papacy and the kingdom of Italy were not regularized until 1929, when the Mussolini government established the independent Vatican State (a bit more than one hundred acres) and a new indemnification.

Moderately conservative governments in the tradition of Cavour ruled the kingdom of Italy until 1876, when the first leftist ministry took office, but thereafter the government tended to nationalist ventures and doctrinaire radical measures that Italy could ill afford. A movement called *Irredentism*, agitation to secure from Austria the areas north and northeast of the Venetia, was encouraged, anticlerical policies were pursued without very specific goals and a haphazard imperialist venture was undertaken in Ethiopia.

Some economic expansion took place, particularly in shipping, but banking scandals inhibited the growth of confidence in the capital market, and just after the turn of the century growing socialist activism among workers led to a series of widespread strikes. On the eve of the first world war Italy still was basically a poor country, and she remained divided over the state-church issue and shaken by labor unrest.

The Habsburg empire, reorganized as the Dual Monarchy of Austria-Hungary in 1867, faced many serious problems in the late nineteenth century, but the most disruptive of them was Slavic pressure for some form of autonomy. Mostly the agitation took the form of a federalist movement seeking a position for Bohemia comparable to that granted to Hungary, but both Austrian Germans and Hungarian Magyars were opposed to this, and several governments fell without finding a compromise. Austria experienced some labor unrest, but the government that ruled all through the 1880s responded with a program much like Bismarck's, with the result that the issue did not become too serious. Toward the end of the nineteenth century Slavic agitation was intensified, as symbolized by the foundation of the radical Young Czechs, and again it toppled ministries and paralyzed parliamentary government. In the last half-dozen years before the first world war Austrian governments lacked parliamentary majorities and ruled by decree, so Austria entered the war amid political crisis.

Hungary faced problems quite as serious, for on the one hand there was a strong group that wanted full independence and objected to the compromise arrangements of the Dual Monarchy, while on the other, subject nationalities, especially Slavs, objected to education and language regulations designed to make Hungary wholly a Magyar state. Because the subject nationalities constituted more than half of the population, every Hungarian government refused to consider universal suffrage, and a Magyar aristocracy still ruled Hungary as a semi-feudal state when the first world war broke out.

The foundation of most of the troubles of Austria-Hungary was nationalism in one form or another, for the Dual Monarchy contained many peoples, and it was surrounded by states with which its minorities felt ties. Austrian Germans reluctantly had admitted the Magyars to equality with themselves, but both of these dominant peoples felt proudly superior to the other races of the empire. Slavs formed a major element in the population of the Dual Monarchy, but they had no institutions to express their national feeling, and inevitably they were attracted by the great Slavic state of Russia. Austria ruled Italian speaking peoples, and *Irredentists* from the kingdom of Italy constantly encouraged them to resent Austrian rule, while in Hungary's Transylvanian districts there was a large Rumanian population and a comparable *Irredentist* movement looking toward Rumania. The Italian and German achievements of unification inspired the nationalist ambitions of other peoples, and once the first world war weakened the central government, it is not surprising that the centrifugal forces of conflicting nationalities pulled the Dual Monarchy apart; what is astonishing is that the Habsburg empire managed to govern so long and generally so well over such a heterogeneous and often resentful collection of subjects.

In Russia the late nineteenth century saw growing opposition to czarist autocracy. Radicals and socalists advocated revolutionary overthrow of the whole social structure, claiming that the reforms of Czar Alexander II had not gone far enough. Liberals, influenced by western ideas, wanted a constitution, a demand that had been voiced in Russia as early as 1825. Secret societies developed a broad populist movement aimed at further agrarian reform; the emancipation of serfs, for instance, had included generous long-term compensation to landowners for lands transferred to peasants, which burdened the peasantry terribly. Advocates of the Pan-Slav movement blamed the government for not doing more to help Slavs under Turkish and Austrian rule. And, finally, a terrorist group known as Will of the People undertook a series of assassinations, culminating in the murder of the czar in 1881.

Czar Alexander II had been prepared to make some concessions just before his death, but his successor, Alexander III (1881–1894), reaffirmed the autocratic system and established a violent repression which included persecution of religious dissenters and subject nationalities. At the same time, however, he attempted a costly program of rapid industrialization, and while great progress was made in railway construction and iron production, an industrial working class was developed which lived in miserable conditions, and a staggering burden of taxation was imposed upon the peasantry. The end of Alexander III's reign was marked by growing unrest in the cities and famine in the countryside.

The new czar, Nicolas II (1894–1917) continued the policy of repression, but it failed to check the growing opposition. Socialists, though forced to live and write in exile, won a wide following among industrial workers, and shortly after the turn of the century one wing of the Social Democratic Party became frankly revolutionary. A Social Revolutionary Party, terrorist and peasant oriented, also developed. And liberal intellectuals formed a Union of Liberation to work for a constitution. All of these opposition groups were strengthened when crushing defeat in the Russo-Japanese War of 1904–1905 discredited the government utterly, and violence erupted all across the country.

At last the czar recognized the necessity of concessions, and he relaxed the efforts at Russification of minorities, eased the financial burdens on the peasants and announced the creation of a national assembly, the Duma, to have a consultative role in government. These measures were too little and too late, however, and in October of 1905 a great general strike occurred which quickly paralyzed the government. Czar Nicolas finally realized that real reforms were needed to pacify the country, and he dismissed his reactionary ministers and issued the October Manifesto which established a constitution, granted legislative powers to the Duma and protected civil liberties.

This program satisfied the more moderate liberals, but a progressive group established the Constitutional Democratic Party to press for further reforms, and the radicals and socialists continued to advocate revolutionary social change. The arrest of members of one of the more active socialist groups, the St. Petersburg Soviet (workers' council) led to a great workers' insurrection in December of 1905, but the government succeeded in suppressing it with regular troops, and 1906 opened with apparent stability. The violence had died down, a very large foreign loan had improved the financial outlook and the government appeared to have the situation firmly under control. Consequently, just before the meeting of the first Duma, new fundamental laws were promulgated which limited seriously the powers that the assembly had expected to exercise, and a year later a new electoral law weakened it further, with the result that the Duma did not develop into the effective parliamentary body that liberals had hoped it would become, and extremists were justified in their often-voiced distrust of the czar's reforms. Opposition continued widespread, terrorism remained endemic and the czarist government was far from secure in 1914 when it plunged into the war that was to destroy it.

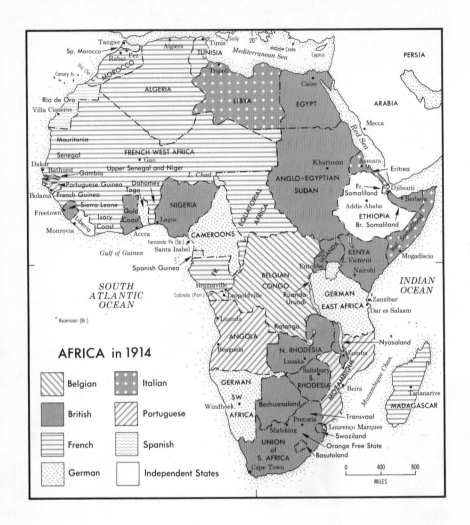

AFRICA in 1914

Legend:
- Belgian
- British
- French
- German
- Italian
- Portuguese
- Spanish
- Independent States

Map labels:

Tangier, Sp. Morocco, Algiers, Tunis, Sicily, 20°, Crete, Cyprus, PERSIA
Rabat, Fez, TUNISIA, Mediterranean Sea
Canary Is., Ifni (Sp.), MOROCCO, Tripoli, Cairo, ARABIA
Rio de Oro, ALGERIA, LIBYA, EGYPT, Mecca
Villa Cisneros
Mauritania, Red Sea
Senegal, FRENCH WEST AFRICA, Khartoum, Asmara, Eritrea
Dakar, Gão, Upper Senegal and Niger, ANGLO-EGYPTIAN, Fr. Somaliland, Djibouti
Bathurst, Gambia, L. Chad, SUDAN, Berbera
Portuguese Guinea, Dahomey, Addis Ababa
Bolama, French Guinea, Togo, NIGERIA, ETHIOPIA, Br. Somaliland
Freetown, Sierra Leone, Gold, Lagos, EQUATORIAL AFRICA
Liberia, Ivory, Coast
Monrovia, Coast, Accra, CAMEROONS, UGANDA, KENYA, Mogadiscio
Fernando Po (Sp.), Santa Isabel, L. Victoria, Nairobi
Gulf of Guinea, Entebbe
Spanish Guinea, FR., BELGIAN CONGO, INDIAN OCEAN
SOUTH ATLANTIC OCEAN, Brazzaville, GERMAN EAST AFRICA, Zanzibar
Cabinda (Port.), Leopoldville, Ruanda Urundi, Dar es Salaam
Ascension (Br.), Luanda, Katanga, Nyasaland
ANGOLA, Benguela, N. RHODESIA, Zomba
Lusaka, Salisbury, S. RHODESIA, Beira
GERMAN SW AFRICA, Tananarive
Windhoek, Bechuanaland, MADAGASCAR
Pretoria, Transvaal, Lourenço Marques
Mafeking, Swaziland, Orange Free State, Basutoland
UNION of S. AFRICA, Cape Town
Mozambique Chan., MOZAMBIQUE

0   400   800
MILES

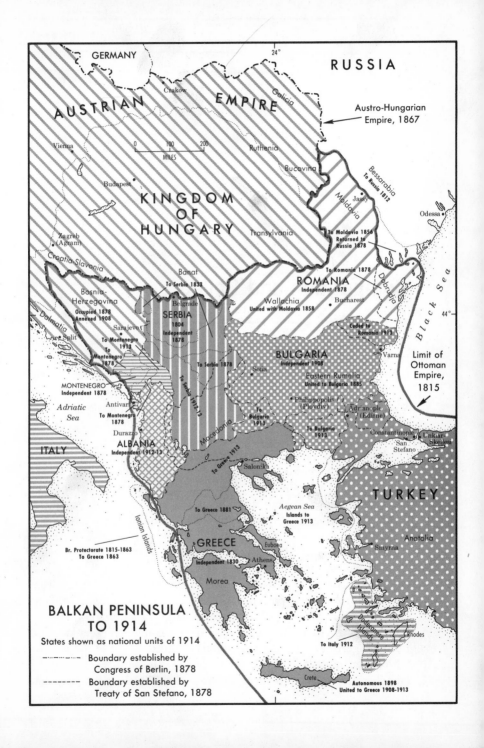

GERMANY

24°

RUSSIA

AUSTRIAN EMPIRE

Crakow

Galicia

Austro-Hungarian
Empire, 1867

Vienna

0   100   200
MILES

Ruthenia

Bucovina

Bessarabia
To Russia 1812

Budapest

KINGDOM
OF
HUNGARY

Jassy

Moldavia

Odessa

Zagreb
(Agram)

Transylvania

To Moldavia 1856
Returned to
Russia 1878

Croatia-Slavonia

Banat
To Serbia 1833

To Romania 1878

Black Sea

44°

Bosnia-
Herzegovina
Occupied 1878
Annexed 1908

Dalmatia

Belgrade

SERBIA
1804
Independent
1878

ROMANIA
Independent 1878

Wallachia
United with Moldavia 1858

Bucharest

Dobrudja

Split

Sarajevo

To Montenegro
1913
To
Montenegro
1878

To Serbia 1878

BULGARIA
Independent 1908

Sofia

Eastern Rumelia
United to Bulgaria 1885

Varna

Ceded to
Romania 1913

Limit of
Ottoman
Empire,
1815

MONTENEGRO
Independent 1878

Adriatic
Sea

Antivari
To Montenegro
1878

To Serbia 1912-13

Macedonia

To
Bulgaria
1913

Philippopolis
(Plovdiv)

To Bulgaria
1913

Adrianople
(Edirne)

Constantinople

San
Stefano

Unkiar-
Skelessi

Durazzo

ALBANIA
Independent 1912-13

To Greece 1913

Salonika

ITALY

Ionian Islands

To Greece 1881

Aegean Sea
Islands to
Greece 1913

TURKEY

Br. Protectorate 1815-1863
To Greece 1863

GREECE

Euboea

Athens

Anatolia

Smyrna

Independent 1830

Morea

Dodecanese Islands

Rhodes

BALKAN PENINSULA
TO 1914

States shown as national units of 1914

To Italy 1912

Crete

Autonomous 1898
United to Greece 1908-1913

— · · — · · — Boundary established by
Congress of Berlin, 1878

— — — — — Boundary established by
Treaty of San Stefano, 1878

Chapter 13

Competition and Collapse

During the late nineteenth and early twentieth centuries industrialization provided the power and nationalism the motive for the European states to impose themselves upon most of the rest of the world. Earlier empires had consisted of little more than forts and trading posts aimed at the control of precious metals and high priced luxury goods such as tobacco, sugar and furs, but nineteenth century imperialism sought possession of raw materials, domination of sheltered markets and gratification of national pride. Prior to the nineteenth century, India was the only highly developed old culture over which the Europeans had established domination, but the new imperialism with its colonial administrations, its protectorates and its spheres of influence tended to divide the whole world among it.

About the middle of the nineteenth century both France and Britain evinced new interest in imperialism. France long had held trading posts in Senegal, on the west coast of Africa, and Charles X had acquired a small position in Algeria, which Louis Philippe and Napoleon III subsequently expanded. The west African holdings remained little more than opportunities for commercial exploitation, but in Algeria France made determined efforts to settle the country with French colonists. Comparably, in the 1830s the British launched planned settlement in Australia, which previously had been regarded primarily as a convenient penal colony, and in the 1840s representative and ultimately responsible government was established in both Australia and Canada, which settled these colonial areas more securely into the British empire. Then in the 1850s a great mutiny in India led to the abolition of the private British East India Company and the reform of Indian administration under direct governmental control. Thus, by the 1860s both Britain and France had extensive commitments to growing empires.

Steamships also accelerated the growth of imperialism, for they made possible cheaper and more reliable long distance commerce, and it became economically feasible to ship coal from England to Italy, returning with cotton from Egypt or Indian goods brought up the Red Sea and transshipped via Egypt. Another stimulant to imperialism was the opening of the Suez Canal in 1869. The canal was built by a private company, but in 1875 the financially hard-pressed ruler of Egypt offered to sell his shares, and Disraeli bought them for the British government, which made it the major stockholder. The canal cut the passage from England to India from six months to three weeks, and voyages to the Far East were reduced comparably. One effect was to tighten Britain's control of India, and another was to expand tremendously Europe's trade with the Orient, increasing proportionately Europe's influence upon the non-European world.

In Egypt continued extravagance endangered large loans that had been contracted in England and France, with the result that the Egyptians were forced to accept a change of government and the appointment of English and French advisors. Resentment of this foreign intrusion led to a revolt of the army in 1881, in the course of which some Europeans were killed, and despite the fact that he was personally hostile to imperialism, Gladstone, then prime minister of Britain, had to send troops. The British soon controlled the whole country, and they reorganized it completely, governing through a British resident. Then, in the mid-1880s, a British force attempting to evacuate Egyptian garrisons from the rebellious Sudan, just south of Egypt, was massacred at Khartoum; a decade passed before Britain sent another expedition, but in the 1890s an army under General Lord Kitchener was totally successful, and the area became known as the Anglo-Egyptian Sudan. Government by British residents continued until the outbreak of the first world war, when British control was tightened through the establishment of a protectorate.

The situation in the extreme south of Africa was equally as complicated. Britain had captured the Cape during the Napoleonic wars, but most of the white inhabitants of the area were Boers, of Dutch extraction, and they resented British rule. In 1834 the abolition of slavery throughout the British empire created acute labor problems in south Africa, further antagonizing the Boers, and in the late 1830s several thousand of them trekked northward and resettled beyond British authority. As the British colony expanded, however, many of the Boers were absorbed again, despite resistance, and by the mid-1850s only the Transvaal and the Orange Free State remained independent; the rest of south Africa consisted either of the British colony or of native states under British protectorates.

In the mid-1880s, the discovery of gold brought a flood of people into the Boer territories—developers, miners and hangers-on, who aggravated further the political situation. The Boers were old-fashioned farmers, rural in their tastes, conservative in their social views and fundamentalist in their Christianity. The roaring boom towns that grew up around the mining industry negated most of their values, and they resisted stubbornly the influence of the new settlers, who soon outnumbered them. Led by Paul Kruger, the president of the Transvaal, they followed a policy that taxed mining interests heavily while excluding those interests from any voice in the government. Adding to the tension was the fact that the development companies were controlled largely by British financiers, most notably Cecil Rhodes, who became prime minister of the Cape Colony in 1890. Rhodes was an avid imperialist who wished to expand the British position in south Africa, and he was disturbed by mounting evidence of German interest in the area; to forestall such an intrusion, he launched privately the British South African Company to develop the large territory later called Rhodesia, northward of the south African settlements, which both extended British claims and hemmed in the Transvaal.

In 1895 Rhodes supported subversive projects intended to overthrow Kruger's government; the mining interests were to mount a revolution, and Dr. Jameson of the South Africa Company's forces was to invade the Transvaal in support of it. The revolt was postponed, but the "Jameson Raid" proceeded anyway and resulted in a fiasco. The invading forces were defeated and captured easily, Rhodes was forced to resign as prime minister of the Cape Colony, and the German emperor seized the opportunity to express solidarity with the Boers through a congratulatory telegram.

Convinced by the Jameson Raid that only war could save the Transvaal, Kruger triggered a conflict in the autumn of 1899. At first the Boers were notably successful, but ultimately the vastly superior resources of the British turned the tide. In the spring of 1900 the Orange Free State was overrun and annexed, and a few months later the Transvaal suffered the same fate. The Boers then went over to guerilla fighting, which prolonged the war until the spring of 1902, and Britain resorted to massive destruction of property and the establishment of concentration camps for civilians; before the fighting was ended she employed 300,000 troops to crush fewer than 75,000 Boers and force them to accept British sovereignty. In 1906 and 1907 responsible government was granted in the Transvaal and the Orange River Colony, so workable compromises appeared to be developing, but these decisions were reversed in 1908 by the creation of the heavily centralized Union of South Africa. The struggle between British and Boer interests was still bitter in 1914 and produced considerable unrest and some violence in the new union while Britain was distracted by the war in Europe.

In the late nineteenth century France also expanded in Africa from Algeria and her positions on the west coast. The French followed the caravan routes across the Sahara, occupying key oases, and established claims to an enormous area by 1900. This growth almost led to war with England in 1898 over a conflict known as the Fashoda crisis, the basic issue of which was control of the upper Nile, but by the early twentieth century a French sphere of influence was delineated rather clearly and was accepted by most of the other powers. Britain held the upper Nile, and Italy was conceded primacy in Tripoli, but west of the Sudan France's position was recognized through most of the hinterland, and she had protectorates in Tunis and Morocco; meanwhile, this expansion in the north was supplemented by the growth of French control over the large island of Madagascar off the southeast coast, which became a French protectorate in 1890 and a colony in 1896.

Unique among the imperial efforts of the late nineteenth century was the development of the Congo Basin in central Africa. In the 1870s King Leopold of Belgium took an interest in the area and founded the International Association for the Exploration and Civilization of Central Africa, which was transformed rapidly into a company for development and exploitation. This activity galvanized the French into founding a protectorate on the north bank of the Congo River, but most of the great basin was claimed by King Leopold's association, and the Independent State of the Congo was recognized by the European powers at an international conference in Berlin in 1884–85, with the king assuming sovereignty over it as a personal possession.

This recognition left the Congo in the possession of a private development company unrestrained by the laws of any of the European states, and conditions soon deteriorated unbelievably. King Leopold had agreed at the Berlin conference to abolish slavery in the Congo, but the establishment of taxes in goods and labor in 1892 reintroduced it covertly as a government program; natural resources such as rubber and ivory were exploited ruthlessly; and frequent rebellions were crushed brutally. Congolese government was an international scandal until the Belgian government annexed the Congo State in 1908 and began a series of reforms.

The central European powers also tried to carve out bits of African territory. In the 1880s the new Italian kingdom secured an uncertain position in Ethiopia, but most of this was lost in an Ethiopian uprising in the mid-1890s. The Italians then turned their interests to Tripoli, just across the Mediterranean from south Italy, and shortly before the first world war they were recognized there in return for acceptance of the French position in Tunis. Generally Germany tried to stay out of the imperialist race so long as Bismarck dominated her policy, for he wanted to avoid the rivalries that imperialism produced, and he believed that imperial ventures would necessitate the construction of a large navy that unavoidably would lead to clashes with Britain. Even the old chancellor could not restrain the expansive enthusiasm of German merchants and missionaries, however, and in the middle and late 1880s protectorates were established in Togoland, the Cameroons, German Southwest Africa and German East Africa, positions over which German control was tightened after 1890, when Bismarck was dismissed.

While Africa was being parcelled out among the European powers, imperial rivalries also were developing in Asia. To guard India against growing Russian strength in Turkestan, the British fought two wars in Afghanistan in 1839–42 and 1878–81, which left Afghanistan a semidependent state. In southeast Asia a series of clashes between the Burmese and the British culminated in British occupation of the whole country by the mid-1880s, and during the late nineteenth and early twentieth centuries British rule was established throughout Malaya. Meanwhile, between the early 1860s and the middle 1890s the French acquired control of all of Indo-China, and Siam retained its independence, though it lost some territory, chiefly because Britain and France found it advantageous to maintain a buffer between their respective colonies. East and southeast of Malaya, Indonesia remained in Dutch hands, as it had been since the sixteenth century, while to the north the Americans, late starters in the imperial race, took advantage of a war with Spain in 1898 to establish a colonial position in the Philippines.

An exception to the general pattern of spreading European control occurred in Japan, where contact with imperialism stimulated an unparalleled national effort at modernization and industrialization that soon made Japan one of the imperial powers rather than one of their victims. In the mid-ninteenth century Japan was still a feudal and agrarian state little known to the west, for her government had followed an isolationist policy for over two hundred years; then the United States sought to break this isolationist policy so as to secure better treatment for shipwrecked American whalers and coaling stations for American ships engaged in the China trade. An American naval mission that attempted to open official contacts in the mid-1840s was rejected and some of its personnel were handled roughly, so in the early 1850s a second mission was sent in greater strength, and Commodore Perry, who commanded it, insisted on delivery of his letter to the emperor.

For more than two centuries the emperor's power in Japan had been exercised by an officer called the *shogun,* but delivery of Perry's letter brought the emperor back into governmental affairs, toppled the *shogun* and triggered a political revolution called the Meiji Restoration. Then followed social and economic revolutions of incredible rapidity. Feudalism was abolished, a program of industralization was launched and modern military and naval forces were begun. Probably no nation that lacked Japan's long tradition of national unity and social cooperation could have achieved so much in so short a time; not only did Japan avoid partition by the western powers, but twenty-five years after the Meiji Restoration she was seeking for herself a share of the partition of China.

A major focus of imperialism in Asia was, of course, China. Europe had had some regular contact and trade with China since the sixteenth century, but the modern imperial experience began with the Opium War with Britain in the 1840s, which gave Britain Hong Kong and opened several ports to normal commerce. This forcible European intrusion discredited an already shaky government in Peking, and in 1850 a great insurrection known as the T'ai P'ing Rebellion broke out and soon engulfed the entire southern half of China. The overt revolution lasted for a decade and a half, but in fact the imperial government never reestablished effective control of the south before its demise in 1912, a major factor in China's impotence in the face of European pressure.

From the 1850s to the 1880s China slowly lost to the western powers more and more control of her own affairs, and while the westerners were pressing in from the ports the Russians advanced from the north, forced the cession in 1860 of the whole Manchurian coast and founded Vladivostok. The 1880s saw some attempts at modernization—a railway line, coal and iron mines and a steel plant—but the same decade witnessed the loss of two former client states, Indochina and Burma, and serious Japanese penetration into another, Korea. The Chinese government was weakened still further by the Sino-Japanese War of 1894–95, for the Japanese defeated Chinese forces easily, winning primacy in the development of Korea, a large cash indemnity and enormous prestige. After the war secret societies seeking the overthrow of the discredited regime in Peking became a problem which grew ever more severe as the imperialist powers wrested more and more concessions from that regime, including leases of large areas.

By the early twentieth century most of China had been divided into spheres of influence under foreign domination. The southwest was controlled by France, who had pushed northward out of Indochina; most of the coast and a large part of central China was in British hands; the Germans held an important position in the north; Korea was in Japanese hands; and Russia dominated northern Manchuria while Japan was expanding from Korea into southern Manchuria. Beset on every side, the tottering government collapsed. A revolution erupted in 1911, resulting in the abdication of the last emperor in 1912, and China fell into chaos and anarchy which remained still unresolved when the first world war altered drastically the relative positions of the imperialist powers.

While Europeans were competing all over the world for the prizes of successful imperialism, they also were involved in a search for security in Europe, where the most explosive issue immediately after the Franco-Prussian war was the bitter resentment in France. Since Bismarck feared that a new European conflict might rip apart the still fragile German state, the major purposes of his foreign policy during the next twenty years were to encourage France in any projects that might distract her from Alsace-Lorraine and to deny her the means of starting a war of revenge. Not only did he keep Germany out of the imperial scramble, as noted already, but also he made considerable efforts to support France's imperial ambitions and to help other powers find peaceful solutions to their conflicts. Thus, in the summer of 1878 he convened an international congress in Berlin, and patterns of development were worked out for the Balkans, where progressive disintegration of Turkish rule threatened to involve Austria and Russia; and he managed another on African affairs in 1884–85 which provided for recognition of imperial claims. Bismarck's role was that of mediator, or honest broker, as Germany's major interest at this time was maintenance of the peace rather than acquisition of new territory.

Beyond a doubt, Bismarck's greatest single effort to avoid a conflict was his development of a complicated alliance system that isolated France diplomatically. The Franco-Prussian War had demonstrated that Germany was stronger than France, and rapid industrialization was increasing German strength, so France would not dare to begin a new war unless she could find allies. Germany's complex alliances in the late nineteenth century are comprehensible only if their underlying purpose is understood; they did not constitute a power bloc to oppose France but a web of commitments and obligations to isolate the French government.

The first of the new German alliances, called the Three Emperors' League, was a loose association of the heads of state of Germany, Austria and Russia, negotiated in the early 1870s. In this pact, the emperors agreed to cooperate to preserve monarchy, and the two eastern rulers pledged support to Germany should trouble arise with France. The German and Russian governments also negotiated a reciprocal military defensive alliance in 1873, and in the same year Italy associated herself loosely with the Three Emperors' League in hopes of support if France should seek to intervene in the Roman question on the pope's behalf. Then in 1876 Bismarck attempted to interest Britain in an alliance that would have joined the greatest land power and the greatest sea power in Europe, but the British rejected his advances; confident of her growing strength and secure in her expanding empire, Britain preferred an isolationist policy at this time, free of commitments to any other state.

During the mid-1870s the situation in the Balkans grew ever more critical as the Russian government was supporting national uprisings against the Turks. The threat of Russian influence extending more strongly across Austria's southern flank brought Russia and Austria near to open hostilities, for by 1878 Russia had created a satellite, Serbia. Since this advance threatened an early Russian presence on the Mediterranean, British pressure forced the creation of an independent Bulgaria, too, as a counterpoise, but the Russian achievement remained important. Desperately concerned that Austria might precipitate a war and fearful of Russian aggressiveness, Bismarck then negotiated the Dual Alliance between Germany and Austria in 1879, a reciprocal agreement to full support in the event of an attack by Russia; the alliance both checked Russia and gave Germany the opportunity to impose some restraint upon Austria. In mid-1881 a worried Russia secured renewal of the Three

Emperors' League, and while the Balkans remained turbulent, the likelihood of hostilities among the great powers diminished. Bismarck had achieved a system that held both Austria and Russia in alliance with his government despite conflicts between them, and to stabilize the situation further, in 1882 Italy was admitted to the Austro-German agreements, forming a Triple Alliance. In 1887 tension between Austria and Russia had become so great that the Three Emperors' League no longer could be maintained, but Bismarck renewed the Reinsurance Treaty, and in the same year France was isolated further by a Mediterranean agreement first arranged between England and Italy and then adhered to by Austria and Spain. Thus, Bismarck's system remained intact until his retirement in 1890, with France isolated and Austria and Russia restrained in their Balkan rivalries.

Even before 1890, however, serious dangers to Bismarck's Germany were becoming apparent. French resentment was intensifying, as evidenced by the Boulanger affair in the late 1880s, while in Russia there was violent objection to the German policy of restraint from nationalist groups that favored Russian solidarity with other Slavs and Russian expansion to the Mediterranean. These problems came to a crisis after 1890 when the aggressive German Emperor William II refused to renew the Reinsurance Treaty with Russia. Apparently he felt that the bitterness between Austria and Russia made it impossible to retain both as allies, and he hoped for some closer agreement with England, which opposed Russia's Mediterranean ambitions. This decision left Russia as isolated as France, and not surprisingly the two powers quickly gravitated toward one another, in 1893 signing a military convention that provided for joint action in the event that either were attacked by Germany or by another power with Germany's support. Thus, within three years of Bismarck's retirement the alliance system aimed at restraint had been transformed into two power blocs in confrontation.

During the 1890s Britain began to seek understandings with other powers, for splendid isolation appeared less attractive when she was embroiled in dangerous rivalries all over the world, and although she was not willing to commit herself to firm alliances, the Mediterranean Agreements of the 1880s constituted a precedent for loose accords. At first Britain seemed to incline toward the Triple

Alliance; on the one hand the Mediterranean Agreements had provided the basis for friendly relations with Italy and Austria, and the
German emperor was seeking closer relations, while on the other,
serious conflicts of interest in Africa and Asia divided Britain from
both France and Russia. Through the late 1890s, however, a number of events, mostly related to the aggressiveness of Emperor William II, moved Britain toward the Franco-Russian orbit.

In January of 1896 the congratulatory telegram sent by the German emperor to President Kruger of the Transvaal, after the Jameson Raid, offended the British deeply and aggravated their fears of
a close link between German Southwest Africa and the Boers. Then
in the spring of 1898 Germany enacted a new naval law providing
for the construction of a powerful high seas battle fleet, which was
a challenge to what Britain felt to be her most vital interest. Growing Anglo-German tension was paralleled briefly by the Anglo-
French clash at Fashoda late in 1898, but this was resolved by nego-
tiation, and toward the end of 1899 another German project, a Berlin
to Baghdad railway, threatened Near Eastern interests of Britain,
France and Russia. Despite efforts by the Berlin government, Anglo-
German relations continued to deteriorate at the turn of the century,
for during the Boer War the press and public opinion in Germany
were violently hostile to Britain, while the British resented Germany's overt sympathy for the Boers. Thus, in the early twentieth
century, though Britain still was far from close understandings with
France and Russia, Germany's belligerence and particularly Germany's naval construction program had cooled Anglo-German relations considerably. At the same time adverse international press
reactions to Britain's war with the Boers made the British very conscious of the fact that they were friendless.

A major transformation of international patterns took place in
1902. In January Britain abandoned her isolationism definitively by
signing an alliance with Japan. For Japan the agreement meant that
in the very likely event of war with Russia, Britain would neutralize
the fleet of Russia's ally, France; for Britain it meant that Japan
would take over policing of some common interests in east Asian
waters, allowing reassignment of British naval units so as to
strengthen the home fleet against the rising threat of German naval
power. Late in the same year France and Italy achieved an understanding over most of the issues dividing them, while Italy's partici-

pation in the Triple Alliance became almost meaningless due to new trouble with Austria over Italian irredentist ambitions for southern Austrian lands. Then a series of conversations in 1903 and 1904 resulted in an Anglo-French Entente, not a firm alliance but a settlement of outstanding colonial issues and the basis for joint action in the face of the common danger from Germany. The Entente was strengthened in 1905 by the first Moroccan crisis, a German attempt to intrude upon a French sphere of influence, and in 1906 Anglo-German naval rivalry was intensified by Britain's launching of the *Dreadnought*, a capital ship mounting only very heavy guns, and by Germany's decision to build ships of the same class.

In 1907 the reorientation of British policy was completed by the conclusion of an Anglo-Russian Entente. Ever since her humiliation in the Russo-Japanese War of 1904-5, Russia had been amenable to an agreement that would reduce the dangers she faced, and France had exercised her good offices in hopes of strengthening the anti-German bloc. As in the entente with France, Britain undertook no firm commitments, but outstanding imperial issues were resolved, especially in Persia and Afghanistan. By the end of 1907, Bismarck's diplomatic arrangements had been reversed; Germany had a firm alliance with Austria, but she faced a hostile Triple Entente of France, Russia and Britain, and Italy had moved so far toward agreement with the entente powers that she was a very dubious member of the Triple Alliance.

Continuing German ambitions sparked new Moroccan crises in 1909 and 1911, and though these were settled peaceably, like earlier colonial conflicts, in conjunction with the growing German naval challenge they contributed to rising animosity between Germany on the one hand and France and England on the other. Even more serious were clashes of interest in the Balkans as both Austria and Russia sought to expand into the vacuum created by the decline of Ottoman power. For Russia the issues had grown far beyond the simple question of access to the Mediterranean. Nationalist elements were too strong to be ignored after the 1905 revolution, and they rallied to the pan-Slav movement to such an extent that the government had little choice but to support Slav nationalism, and particularly Serbia, in the Balkans; thus, taking into account the humiliation of the Russo-Japanese War, the Russian government found both its international prestige and its domestic stability deeply involved in the

Balkan crises. To Austria Balkan affairs were no less critical. Since the creation of the Dual Monarchy in 1867, the greatest single problem of the Habsburg government had been Slavic aspirations for arrangements at least comparable to those achieved by the Magyars, and the emergence of the Slavic state of Serbia, with Russian support, had aggravated Slavic nationalism in the Habsburg domains seriously. Hence, to the Austrians as to the Russians, Balkan affairs seemed to involve not only territorial aspirations and international prestige but also questions of domestic security.

Russia had been forced to accept unfavorable settlements in the Balkans several times: in 1878 when an independent Serbia was created but with very limited frontiers, in 1908 when Austria annexed Bosnia-Herzegovina, and in 1913 when the state of Albania was created to deny the Serbs and their Russian backers an outlet to the sea. Thus, by 1914 Russia felt that she had been pushed to a point of no return; any further concessions to Austria likely would have meant further diminution of Russian prestige, total loss of Russian influence in the Balkans and charges of abandonment of pan-Slavism by domestic nationalists.

Unfortunately a new crisis was precipitated in June of 1914 when the Austrian Archduke Franz Ferdinand was assassinated by a Bosnian revolutionary who hoped by terrorism to promote Bosnian independence of Austria and incorporation with Serbia. Then the dangers of the interlocking alliances and inflexible military plans quickly became evident.

The assassination brought to a head the long-standing hostility between Austria and Serbia, for though the Serbian government had not supported the plot officially, it was demonstrated beyond reasonable doubt that high Serbian officials had known of it and had done nothing either to stop it or to warn Vienna. Consequently the Austrians resolved to act boldly, while they enjoyed the sympathy of world opinion, and to crush Serbia's aggressive ambitions definitively. In the first week of July Austrian inquiries elicited promises of German support, the first of the famous "blank cheques"; then the Vienna government, though unwilling to declare war immediately, decided to proceed strongly despite the risks.

Apparently the Austrians thought they could deal with the Serbs without Russian intervention, as in the past, but this time they were proved wrong. President Poincaré of France was visiting in St.

Petersburg, and he reaffirmed the Franco-Russian entente, which encouraged the Russians to take a firm stand. Thus both Germany and France failed to restrain their allies, and, confident of support, Austria demanded satisfaction of Serbia while Russia determined to uphold the Serbs at all costs. On July 23, the Vienna government sent to Belgrade an ultimatum so far-reaching that it would have compromised Serbian sovereignty, and the next day Russia warned Austria that the Serbs must not be attacked. Then, as the crisis deepened, France assured Russia of support, another blank check. In effect, both Germany and France had transferred control of policy to their allies.

When the predictable Serbian rejection of Austria's ultimatum was delivered on July 25, both Serbia and Austria mobilized; then on July 28, Austria declared war on Serbia, and all Europe teetered on the brink of war, though another week of frantic discussions took place before the great powers committed themselves. There was something almost pathetic about the last days of peace, as governments that had committed themselves too far tried to find a road back without sacrificing their alliances or their popular support; if peace could not be maintained, they sought at least to localize the impending conflict. Massive forces were working against them by this time, however, for military planning in most countries had not foreseen limited war, and everyone's plan anticipated full mobilization. The tragic element began to appear when it was discovered that the Russian army literally was incapable of mobilizing forces only against Austria and not against Germany, for the subsequent decision to order general mobilization on July 29 and 30 forced Germany's hand.

German war plans, which assumed Franco-Russian partnership, were equally inflexible and were based on rigid timetables. When last minute negotiations aimed at limiting Russian efforts, at neutralizing France or at finding a private Franco-German accommodation all failed, both France and Germany mobilized on August 1, and Germany began the invasion of Luxemburg. Then on August 3 Germany declared war on France, and within a few days all of the great powers had committed themselves to an attempt at a military solution of their rivalries. All were convinced of the justice of their causes, and all expected a short, victorious struggle; none suspected that they had embarked upon the first world war, four years of the most costly conflict Europe yet had experienced.

Chapter 14

The Retreat of
Liberal Democracy

Ever since the signature of the Franco-Russian alliance in the 1890s, German military planning had had to assume the likelihood of a war on two fronts, and in 1905 the general staff had produced a strategic project called the Schlieffen Plan to deal with this situation. This plan projected a massive invasion of France intended to encircle Paris and force a quick decision that would free Germany's forces for concentration against the Russians. In August of 1914 it appeared that the Schlieffen Plan might succeed, for the French focussed their efforts on an unsuccessful attempt to reoccupy Alsace-Lorraine, and German armies swept southward into France almost unchecked. Early in September, however, the French commander-in-chief, General Joffre, threw his forces into the path of the German advance and halted it at the Battle of the Marne. By mid-October a line of trenchworks extended six hundred miles from the Swiss border to the sea, and despite massive commitments by both armies, the lines hardly moved until the last year of the war.

On the eastern front a comparable situation developed. The Russians attempted to invade East Prussia almost immediately that war was declared, but in two battles at the end of August and beginning of September the Germans defeated them utterly. In the winter a Russian advance in Poland was halted, and in 1915 a combined Austro-German force occupied most of that country; then lines began to stabilize, developing into thirteen hundred miles of trenches from the Black Sea to the Baltic.

When war first broke out, Italy refused to join the Central Powers, and despite the Triple Alliance she declared her neutrality; then influenced by her territorial ambitions, she declared war on Austria-Hungary in the spring of 1915. The Austrians managed to contain the Italian attack, however, and late in the war they counterattacked with German reinforcements and broke the Italian army completely, so the Austro-Italian front never acquired major significance to the general course of the war.

At sea the British caught a small German fleet homeward bound from the Pacific in December of 1914 and destroyed it in the Battle of the Falkland Islands. More significant was the growth of German submarine warfare, which almost brought the United States into the war in the spring of 1915 when the passenger liner Lusitania was sunk with the loss of many American lives. The diplomats managed to smooth over this crisis, however, when the German government agreed to restrict attacks upon passenger vessels. Then in the spring of 1916 the major battle fleets of Germany and Britain met in the Battle of Jutland, and British superiority in capital ships forced the Germans to retire, though they inflicted more damage than they suffered. Thereafter, German naval effort concentrated upon commerce raiding, and in January of 1917 unrestricted submarine warfare was resumed. The submarine campaign destroyed eight million tons of shipping by the autumn of 1917, but eventually it was countered effectively by the development of the convoy system, and it proved costly, for it provoked a U.S. declaration of war against Germany in April of 1917.

The Russian Revolution of 1917 ended the fighting on the eastern front, but in the west casualties climbed rapidly as each side sought to break the stalemate. In July of 1918 the Germans made a final effort with a great offensive on the Marne, but it was repulsed, and as allied armies were reinforced by the daily arrival of ten thousand fresh American troops, they turned the German retreat into a rout. On November 11, a general armistice was signed, and at last the war ended, having killed about ten million men and wounded twice that number.

In Austria-Hungary and Germany as well as in Russia the war triggered political revolutions. Subject nationalities in the Habsburg lands staged several uprisings during the summer of 1918, and in late October both Czechoslovakia and Yugoslavia declared their independence. A few days later naval crews in the north German ports mutinied, and revolution broke out in Munich; in the face of these disturbances, the German chancellor announced the abdication of the Kaiser on November 9, and the leader of the German socialists promptly proclaimed a republic. Then on November 12, the Habsburg emperor abdicated, and republics were proclaimed in both Austria and Hungary.

In January of 1919 a peace conference convened in Paris, the city where animosities toward Germany were most inflamed. The Germans thought they had surrendered on the basis of President Wilson's Fourteen Points, an idealistic program aimed at justice and stability, but it quickly became obvious that Britain and France sought indemnification and retribution above all else. Under the terms of the harsh Treaty of Versailles submitted to the Germans in May of 1919, Germany accepted full responsibility for the war and agreed to pay reparations, the amount to be decided later (eventually the impossible sum of thirty-two billion dollars); she agreed to cede territory to France, Belgium and Poland and to give up her colonies; she accepted international administration of the Saar coal region for fifteen years; the German army, navy and merchant marine were to be reduced sharply; and the Rhineland was to be demilitarized. Having no choice, the German government ratified the treaty on July 7, 1919. Austria signed the comparable Treaty of St. Germain and Hungary the Treaty of Neuilly, which provided territorial cessions to Italy, Yugoslavia, Rumania, Czechoslovakia and Poland, reparations payments and limitations of armed forces; in addition the union of Austria and Germany was forbidden. Subsequent treaties then arranged settlements in the Balkans.

The Paris peace settlements were full of contradictions, for once the pressure of the war ended, President Wilson's idealistic influence waned rapidly, especially when his own government refused to participate in the League of Nations. After proclaiming "open covenants openly arrived at," the major allied powers wrote the settlements in closed sessions. After endorsing national self-determination, the victors transferred large blocs of Germans to foreign governments and drew arbitrary boundaries in the Balkans, where the mix of nationalities made minority problems inevitable. After offering France international guarantees of her security so as to dissuade her from even harsher demands upon Germany, the United States and Britain proved unable to fulfil their undertaking; the United States Senate refused to ratify the alliances, and France was left to confront a still united Germany with no firm commitments from her erstwhile allies. And a major European power, Russia, was excluded from the conference entirely although the question of Russia's western borders was critical to an eastern European settlement.

In the early twentieth century intellectuals generally considered the nineteenth century a period of peace. In fact it was far from that if one considers the Greek revolt, the Crimean War and the Austro-Prussian and Franco-Prussian Wars or if one counts domestic strife, the revolutions of 1830 and 1848 and the bloody Commune of 1871; moreover, through much of the latter part of the century Europeans were fighting in Egypt, South Africa, India and China. But though the century of peace was an illusion, it is true that Europe had been spared great holocausts such as the Napoleonic Wars during the century between 1815 and 1914, and intellectuals had begun to assume that European nations had outgrown war, had passed to a higher stage of civilization where war was anachronistic. Thus, the outbreak of a new general war in 1914 shook them badly.

It also had been believed widely that social change generally resulted in progress, some desirable transformation, despite occasional setbacks. Human society was assumed to pass through natural stages from tribal life to aristocratic feudalism to royal absolutism to some sort of participatory democracy governed by the liberal-democratic compromise, majority will restrained by constitutional guarantees for the rights of individuals and minorities. In the early twentieth century there were grounds to believe that this liberal-democratic compromise was a natural result of social evolution. Democratic systems based on the British model had developed in Canada, Australia and the Union of South Africa, and the American system of congressional federalism showed every likelihood of proving both flexible and strong. The unifications of Italy and Germany had resulted in the establishment of parliamentary monarchies in central Europe, and something comparable had developed in Japan by the 1880s. Austria-Hungary appeared to be moving toward responsible parliamentary government; the establishment of a duma in Russia in 1905 was interpreted as a first step in the same direction; and even in China the revolution that broke out in 1911 seemed to be fumbling toward parliamentarianism.

Obviously World War I was a bewildering shock to western intellectuals. Convinced that war was barbaric, and hence unwilling to believe that it remained an important tool of statecraft for European governments, they ignored the chauvinistic and bellicose clamor of the decades that preceded the war and decided that it had been a great mistake, that because of some sort of failure of diplomacy Europe had fallen into a war that no responsible person had wanted. This self-deception, which distorted facts to fit a theory, spawned a number of studies which sought to identify the great mistake or mistakes that had brought on this conflict, but while the intellectuals thus were explaining away the great war, new challenges to their theories of inevitable liberal-democratic progress appeared in the postwar era, most especially the depression of the 1930s.

An analysis of the origin and spread of the great depression belongs to later considerations of international developments in post-war Europe, but the experience of the separate European states cannot be set in proper perspective without some estimate of the general impact of the economic collapse. The late 1920s were characterized by prosperity and optimism, but between 1929 and 1931 financial crises and bank failures all over the world restricted the availability of investment capital, limited market opportunities and brought on industrial failures. Through the greater part of the 1930s there was massive unemployment, and the hardship and despair that resulted must be counted one of the major sociopolitical forces of the two decades following the end of the first world war. Men who were jobless, hungry and hopeless were vulnerable to arguments of social and racial exploitation and were attracted by proposals for extremist solutions, which undermined the liberal-democratic development that the peacemakers had hoped to see. As early as the relatively prosperous 1920s, there were signs that the liberal democrats had been too optimistic, and the profound socioeconomic impact of the depression of the 1930s completed the ruin of their hopes.

Among the least stable areas of post-war Europe were the new states recognized by the peace treaties of 1919—Austria, Poland, Hungary, Czechoslovakia and Yugoslavia. In the new republic of Austria about twenty-five per cent of the population was in Vienna, an industrial city cut off from its former resources and markets by high tariff walls. Some of the other new states were in a better economic position but faced serious minority problems: Slovaks, Ruthenians and Sudeten Germans in Czechoslovakia; Ukrainians, Germans and Jews in Poland; Slavs and Jews in Hungary; and Croats and Slovenes in Yugoslavia. In addition, there was almost constant fighting over the new borders, and these varied troubles produced political chaos, especially when they were aggravated by the depression. In the 1930s Austria experienced suspension of parliamentary government, bloody repression of socialist dissent, dictatorship and finally union with Nazi Germany. Czech government foundered on the problems of minorities, especially the three million Sudeten Germans, and in 1938 Germany seized a third of Czechoslovakia, occupying the remaining fragment the following year. In Poland a military coup established an authoritarian government in the mid-1920s, and the regime became a dictatorship through constitutional revisions in 1935. Hungary remained a semifeudal state of great seigneurs and peasants with a very restricted parliamentary assembly, and it was drawn more and more into the German orbit. And Yugoslavia's parliamentary monarchy collapsed in 1929 when the king proclaimed a dictatorship. Thus the new states did not evolve along the lines expected by western liberal democrats.

Developments farther east, in Russia, were still more discouraging. Except in her western cities, Russia had entered the twentieth century a land of backward and illiterate peasants and equally backward country nobility, and except for some state-owned factories, mostly in St. Petersburg and Moscow, society was still preindustrial. The Russian army, which had been a decisive factor in the defeat of Napoleon, had been humiliated later in the nineteenth century, and its position had worsened by the twentieth century. After the revolution of 1905 Russia's situation appeared to be improving as industrial expansion strengthened the economy and the convocation of four dumas seemed to promise development of peaceful channels of protest. At the same time, however, terrorism continued, industrial growth swelled the urban proletariat and national minorities, especially Poles and Finns, grew more restive. The czar attempted limited conciliation, but he refused to concede ministerial responsibility to the duma, and in the autumn of 1915 he compounded his unpopularity by dismissing a highly regarded commander-in-chief and assuming command of the armies himself, an ill-advised move that linked him directly with Russia's military fortunes in the war. Military priorities and repeated mobilizations resulted in labor shortages, the breakdown of the transportation system and serious shortages of food and fuel in the cities, and violence erupted in March of 1917. Strikes and riots turned to revolution when troops in the capital mutinied, and the duma resolved to form a provisional government. In mid-March the czar abdicated, and the first step of the revolution had been accomplished.

The moderate liberals who dominated the provisional government were prowestern, however, and while they announced better treatment for minorities and eventual land reform, they were committed to the alliance with the western powers. The leaders of the workers' soviets disagreed, and they were strengthened when a number of exiled radicals led by Lenin returned to Russia. Lenin advocated the supremacy of the soviets over the provisional government, immediate peace without regard for western war aims, unconditional transfer of land to the peasants and control of industry by the workers. With slogans such as "all power to the soviets" and "peace, land and bread," Lenin's group, called Bolsheviks, found considerable support from a war-weary and deprived population. A premature coup failed in July of 1917, but another succeeded in the autumn, and control passed to the Bolshevik wing of the socialist movement, soon called the Communist Party.

Czarists, liberals, moderate socialists and minority independence movements resisted for three years, and the Bolsheviks quickly resorted to authoritarian measures. A secret police was organized, land and industry were nationalized, foreign debts were repudiated, private bank accounts were confiscated, and forced labor and requisitions of food were inaugurated. In March of 1918 the Bolshevik government concluded the Treaty of Brest-Litovsk with Germany, giving up Poland, the Ukraine and several western border regions, and partly because St. Petersburg (renamed Leningrad) thus became dangerously exposed, the new government then moved the capital to Moscow.

The western powers, regarding the Bolsheviks as pro-German as well as radically socialist after the Treaty of Brest-Litovsk, put troops into Russia to support counter-revolutionary movements, and though ultimately all such opposition was defeated, devastating civil wars raged from 1918 to 1920. In March of 1921, to stimulate national recovery, the government was forced to accept a temporary retreat from communism, the New Economic Policy, which permitted some revival of private ownership and profit incentive. This proved largely successful, and toward the end of 1922 the victory of the revolution was consolidated by the organization of the Union of Soviet Socialist Republics. This victory was a great disillusionment to western liberal intellectuals, for the Bolshevik government's birth in revolutionary violence, its authoritarian suppression of dissent with secret police and political executions and its one-party political system set the U.S.S.R. well outside the liberal-democratic tradition.

In 1924 Lenin died, and in the ensuing struggle for power victory fell to Josef Stalin, who added a decidedly nationalistic note to a revived socialist drive. Proclaiming a New Socialist Offensive, Stalin's government undertook rapid industrialization and renewed collectivization of agriculture in a series of five-year plans, turning ever more industrial output to armaments and consolidating control of the party through purges of rivals. Russia had moved from the absolutism of the czar to the dictatorship of Stalin, and whatever the material benefits, the new authoritarianism was more frightening than the old because it was so much more efficient.

In east Asia as in Europe, liberal democrats were disillusioned in the 1920s and 1930s. China fell into chaos after the revolution of 1911; despotic warlords controlled several provinces, civil war was endemic and the government in Peking was paralyzed by personal rivalries. The leader of the revolutionary Kuomintang Party, Dr. Sun Yat-sen, was influenced profoundly by western liberal and democratic ideas, expressed in his Three Peoples' Principles of national-

ism, democracy and social progress, but he died early in 1925, and
the promise implicit in his program died with him as rightist and
leftist elements in the Kuomintang engaged in a struggle for power.
On the left was the Chinese Communist Party, supported by Russian
advisors; on the right was the creator of the Kuomintang's military
organization, Chiang Kai-shek, a conservative reformer from an old
gentry family. By the spring of 1927 Chiang's forces, known as the
Nationalists, controlled the Kuomintang, and the Communists had
been driven into the desolate north. By late 1928 some warlords had
been suppressed, and others had adhered to the Nationalist movement, but under the pressure of civil conflict and new foreign problems, Chiang's thought had drifted farther to the right. The Kuomintang assumed absolute control of the new government, explaining
that "political tutelage" was a necessary forerunner of constitutional democracy, and when a crisis developed in 1931 over Japan's
seizure of Manchuria, discipline gained ascendency over democracy.

In 1937 the Japanese seized Shanghai, then followed up with
the occupation of much of the Chinese coast, and Chiang had to
move the capital to Chungking, deep inland. This cut the Kuomintang off from the revenues of the coastal cities, making it dependent
upon the conservative country gentry and upon foreign aid, and resistance to the Japanese became almost the only policy of the government. Political tutelage, social welfare programs, industrialization and land reform had to be suspended, and the Kuomintang,
which had raised hopes of liberal democratic evolution in the mid-
1920s, evolved into just another military government.

Japan's experience was even more tragic, for by the 1920s a
viable parliamentary system had been functioning for three decades,
but unfortunately for liberal democracy in Japan, the civilian elements of the government had proved far less effective than the military in advancing the nation's interests. In the mid-1890s, after the
new Japanese army defeated China, the European powers refused
to allow Japan to impose upon China the sorts of terms that Europeans had been imposing for years, and the generals said that what
they had won on the battlefield was lost at the conference table. A
decade later, when Japan fought Russia, her successes were astonishing, and again her gains seemed to slip through the fingers of her
diplomats.

Russia was humiliated, but Japan did not gain a clear sphere of influence in Manchuria, and she did not obtain an indemnity to relieve the economic strain resulting from the war. In truth, these disappointments resulted largely from the fact that the army lacked the resources to pursue the enemy and impose terms, but once again the diplomats were criticized. The end of World War I saw the same sorry pattern repeated; although Japan stood firmly with the victorious allies, the Versailles Peace Conference refused to grant her Germany's Asian possessions and failed to recognize Japan's special position in Asia, further discrediting the civilian elements of Japanese government.

The result of these disappointments was considerable instability: in 1921 a premier was assassinated; in 1922 there were riots; in 1923 there was an attempt on the life of the prince regent. Natural catastrophes and foreign governments aggravated the difficulties. A great earthquake hit Tokyo in 1923, followed by fires and tidal waves, with losses estimated at nearly a quarter of a million lives and a billion dollars worth of property. In 1924 a new U.S. immigration act excluded all Japanese, and resentment was widespread. The situation worsened with a bank crisis, labor troubles, the depression and a rash of assassinations. Finally, in the spring of 1932, affirming the triumph of authoritarian influences over earlier liberal democratic trends, a military cabinet took office and inaugurated a policy of aggressive military imperialism that was to lead to total war and disaster.

One of the most serious failures of liberal democracy occurred in Italy in the 1920s. The end of the great war left Italy resentful, disillusioned and loaded with debt. Though part of the victorious alliance, her armies had performed with no great distinction, and at the peace conference she failed to acquire either control of the Adriatic Sea or possession of German colonies, her two prime goals. Moreover, an already strained labor market was flooded with two million demobilized troops. The strongest popular force in Italian politics was the violently anti-clerical Socialist Party, for Catholics generally held themselves aloof because of the Roman question, and after the war the socialists were influenced strongly by the revolutionary tactics that had succeeded in Russia. In the face of massive unemployment and economic stagnation, they secured the largest single bloc of seats in the parliamentary elections of 1919, about one third of the total, as well as control of many local governments.

The conservative reaction focussed around Benito Mussolini, a former socialist turned vehement nationalist. In postwar Italy demobilized soldiers were jeered instead of cheered, and there were no jobs for them. Mussolini organized them for self-protection and political action into bands called *fasci,* and his followers soon were called fascists. The Fascist Party never developed very coherent doctrines, but a few basic principles emerged. Mussolini was an unquestioning supporter of nationalism and imperialism, and he believed that war had great moral values, bringing out the best of courage and dedication in men. Though convinced that Italy could not afford the economic wastage implicit in competitive enterprise, he had no use for the socialists who wanted to control industry for the benefit of the workers; his goal was national strength, not individual welfare, so he advocated great corporations or cartels under government supervision. This combination of pragmatic programs and romantic idealism exercised a sort of magnetism upon Italian veterans who were humiliated, impoverished and angry.

At first the Fascist Party did not do well politically, winning no parliamentary seats in 1919 and only thirty-five in 1921, so the fascists turned to intimidation and violence. Fearful of turning popular discontent into revolution, the national government normally stood aloof from local disorders, and Mussolini's fascist squads were able to take over local governments through intimidation of voters or simply by seizing government buildings. The patronage jobs thus secured won some popular support, and the ouster of the normally socialist local governments won covert financial aid from wealthy conservatives. Then at a party congress in 1922, Mussolini endorsed limited monarchy and an appeal for army support, and the fascists marched on Rome. As the king refused to declare martial law, the government resigned.

Mussolini, though leader of only a splinter party in the parliament, was asked to form a new cabinet, and the parliament gave him dictatorial powers for a year in order that he might reestablish order and introduce reforms. He used this authority to tighten his control of the apparatus of government, appointing fascists to key posts and enacting a new electoral law. Elections in the spring of 1924 left the parliamentary opposition impotent, and during the next two years political arrests, laws censoring newspapers and decrees suspending local elections assured that the opposition would find no extra-parliamentary support such as had raised the fascists to power. Absolute fascist control was achieved in January of 1926 when parliament authorized the prime minister to govern by decree, and the last potentially dangerous opposition was neutralized early in 1929 when a concordat won papal recognition of the fascist government at the price of independence for the Vatican City. Thus in the 1920s, a troubled but operative parliamentary system passed under the control of an authoritarian party, and Italy became a dictatorship.

There also was great discontent in Germany following World War I, for many Germans refused to believe that their nation had been defeated. They asserted that the new government had made a shameful peace in order to win recognition from the western powers, and had stabbed the army in the back. This stab in the back theory, which the Nazis later exploited profitably, was wholly wishful thinking, for in the summer of 1918 the German commander-in-chief, Ludendorff, had informed Berlin that he no longer could hold back the enemy. But German discontent also had more solid foundations, for the Versailles Peace Treaties had held Germany solely responsible for the war, and consequently Germany had had to agree to pay enormous indemnities and reparations, to give up the territory won from Russia at Brest-Litovsk and to allow Germans to fall under the rule of France, Czechoslovakia, Poland and Belgium. Moreover, she had to accept the isolation of Austria and agree to maintain an army of no more than one-hundred thousand men and to equip them with no heavy weapons. The new German government had signed such a treaty not so much from ambition as from resignation; the alternative was allied occupation.

Violence erupted in Germany almost immediately the war was over as coups were attempted from both the communist left and the monarchical right, but the army's tradition of obedience to the government kept the military loyal, and the center moderates managed to restore order. In 1922 and 1923 the currency began to collapse due to the weight of reparations payments, and then the French, fearful of German recovery, seized a pretext of default on reparations to occupy the industrial Ruhr area, triggering a first grasp for power by Adolph Hitler and the Nazi Party.

Hitler, an Austrian by birth, had settled in Bavaria after the war and involved himself in the shadowy world of ultranationalist politics and paramilitary societies, becoming the leading figure of the minor group named the National Socialist German Workers Party, usually called the Nazis. Largely a hate group that preached antibolshevism, anticapitalism, anti-Semitism and national power, the Nazis nonetheless attracted both a popular following and the support of some army officers and ex-officers whose careers had been blighted by the military limitations of the peace treaty, including Ludendorff, the immensely prestigious former commander-in-chief.

In the confusion following the French intervention and the financial collapse of 1923, the Nazis tried to seize the Bavarian state government, in emulation of the tactics of the Italian fascists, but the German authorities were willing to use police and military forces to maintain order; the *putsch* was broken easily, and Hitler and his colleagues served short jail terms. After their release, they turned to legal tactics as a political party seeking parliamentary seats, but during the economic recovery of the late 1920s, the situation was unfavorable to extremist parties, and neither the Nazis nor the Communists enjoyed much electoral success. Nonetheless, Hitler kept the party intact, developing a paramilitary troop, the S.A. or brownshirts, and a personal bodyguard, the S.S., and when the beginnings of the depression shook Germany, the Nazis were ready to profit from the public impulse to seek extremist solutions. In the elections of 1930 the party's parliamentary bloc jumped from a dozen to over a hundred seats, though in the same elections the Communists increased their strength from twenty-three to seventy-seven seats, and all the moderate parties lost heavily.

In 1931, as the depression settled fully upon central Europe, unemployment figures in Germany rose to six million, and disorders multiplied, with numerous clashes between Nazi and communist street gangs. In 1932 Hitler ran for the presidency and lost to old general von Hindenburg, but in parliamentary elections in the same year the Nazis secured about half the seats, not a working majority but enough to paralyze Germany's political machinery for the next several months, and in January of 1933 von Hindenburg was forced to offer Hitler the chancellorship. The Nazis secured a majority in new elections in March, and the Reichstag then passed the momentous Enabling Act, which gave Hitler's government dictatorial power for five years.

While the Nazis by no means enjoyed the unqualified confidence of the whole country, it is clear that their support was broad. The brownshirts both intimidated opposition and evoked emotional chauvinistic responses; the party's anticommunism appealed to conservative and business interests; anti-Semitism appealed to middle classes ruined by the depression and eager for the elimination of Jewish competition; and Hitler's denunciation of the Versailles Treaties and his promises to restore Germany's self-sufficiency and self-respect exercised a broad appeal that cut across class lines. Party strife and a depression had destroyed another liberal democracy.

A whole structure of western intellectual assumptions was collapsing like a house of cards. In the Austrian domains, in Russia and in China bright promises proved illusory and melted in the heat of material problems. In Italy, Japan and Germany, established parliamentary systems proved unable to survive the strains of the post-war era. Even the west appeared endangered, for the post-war period saw the growth of leftist radical parties in France, while a comparable popular awakening in England resulted in the growth of the Labour Party. In both countries conservatives overreacted, and there was talk of Bolshevism and wildly exaggerated fears of imminent communist revolution, which the depression heightened. A sort of paralysis developed in which both left and right watched one another suspiciously and neither dared attempt more than a caretaker government. The dangers of this irresolution were shown during a Spanish civil war in the mid-1930s.

By 1931 the many opposition groups in Spain had developed into a strong republican movement, and the king fled abroad. A republic was proclaimed, but the new government was unable to achieve stability because of internal rivalries between moderates and radicals, and by 1936 the situation had degenerated into civil war between a leftist republican government and a large part of the army led by General Francisco Franco. Italy and Germany quickly recognized Franco and sent aid, seeing the civil war as an opportunity to test their new military forces and a fascist Spain as a potentially valuable ally. At the same time, Russia sent help and advisors to the republican forces, hoping thus to strengthen the republic's leftist elements and to turn the civil war into a communist revolution. Meanwhile, England and France were paralyzed by their internal political situations and their reluctance to undertake foreign spending during the depression. The result was that the republican moderates were boycotted by their friends while the authoritarian extremists of both right and left got foreign aid.

By early 1939 Franco's forces controlled so much of the country, and the republican forces were so deeply influenced by the Russians, that Britain and France recognized the Franco government, and the United States followed suit a few months later; Madrid surrendered to Franco in March, and the civil war was over. The first direct confrontation between the new authoritarian governments and the old liberal democracies showed the contrast between the ruthless pragmatism of the former and the hesitancy and paralysis of the latter. Given the aggressive ambitions of Mussolini and Hitler, the implications were chilling.

Chapter 15

The End of
European Hegemony

Despite the shortcomings of the Versailles Peace and the wide-spread dissatisfaction with it, especially in Germany, Italy and Japan, for a brief time it appeared that the settlement might endure and be strengthened. The many disputes immediately consequent upon the peace tapered off in the mid-1920s, and new developments held forth some hope of stability.

Recognizing that the original reparations schedules were unrealistic, especially after the German economic collapse that followed French occupation of the Ruhr, in 1924 the allies accepted a committee report called the Dawes Plan; this plan revised payment schedules and provided for massive loans to Germany to restabilize her economy. Then in 1925 international discussions resulted in the Locarno Treaties; the most important aspect of these was Franco-Belgian-German acceptance of existing borders, with Great Britain and Italy serving as guarantors, but there also were a number of arbitration agreements, chiefly concerning Germany and her neighbors, and a Franco-Czech mutual assistance pact. For several years the "spirit of Locarno" suggested growing security and the reacceptance of Germany into the European community.

In 1926 Germany was admitted to the League of Nations; the next year saw the first of several disarmament conferences; in 1928 most of the major powers signed the Kellogg-Briand Pact renouncing aggressive war; and in 1929 diminishing hostility toward Germany led to another revision and reduction of reparations under the Young Plan.

The progress toward international stability that seemed so apparent in the late 1920s evaporated rapidly under the pressure of the international depression of the 1930s, but actually economic affairs long had been the weak point in international cooperation. Nationalism, one of the prime causes of World War I, had emerged from the war stronger than ever, and many governments were striving for national self-sufficiency. This desire and the drive for rapid industrialization by most of the new states resulted in high tariff barriers and other artificial impediments to the redevelopment of international commerce in Europe. Moreover, much prewar trade could not be recovered, for while Europe had been locked in a grim struggle, industrialization had proceeded rapidly in the United States, Canada and Japan, and these nations had secured a large share of the world's non-European markets. Ironically, however, behind the facade of national effort, the economies of all nations were linked closely in a great web of international finance to which the United States and Germany were the keys. During the war, Britain and France had contracted enormous debts for munitions bought in the United States, and the Washington government insisted on repayment, but the only way the western European powers could manage this was to collect reparations. Since a major source of the funds with which Germany and Austria paid reparations was loans from the United States, the cumulative effect was that dislocations in any one economy, but especially that of the United States, would have repercussions all through the loans-reparations-war debts cycle.

Such a dislocation of major proportions occurred in October of 1929 when the American stock market collapsed as a result of unrestrained speculation, limiting the flow of funds to Germany. Compounding the problem was the American government's shortsighted response to its own crisis, the Smoot-Hawley Tariff Act, which raised import duties fifty to one hundred per cent in an effort to protect the American economy from foreign competition. Thus, at the same time that the flow of American money to central Europe diminished, impeding the collection of reparations, increased American tariffs made it impossible for Britain and France to repay war debts through expanded trade with the United States. Moreover, by late 1931 some two dozen other nations had retaliated by increasing their tariffs, further impeding international trade.

As the problems multiplied, the pressure on international credit increased enormously. In the spring of 1931 the Austrian State Bank failed, and though guarantees from the Austrian government and from other large European central banks staved off disaster, a panic ensued, and quantities of foreign funds were withdrawn from central Europe. In the face of the spreading crisis, President Hoover arranged a moratorium on all intergovernmental debts in the summer of 1931, but the panic continued. A few months later the Bank of England was forced to abandon the gold standard, a covert form of devaluation which lowered the price of British goods on the world market in an attempt to salvage British trade. All over Europe and North America industrial enterprises failed and unemployment soared. Overall European production fell to less than seventy-five per cent of 1929 levels by 1932, and the value of world trade fell to less than half of 1929 levels during the 1930s. To ease the economic crisis a few nations turned to government spending—public works in the United States and a combination of public works and military projects in Germany and Italy—but most governments simply tried to balance budgets, to protect the national economy against further shocks from abroad and to maintain order while hordes of the unemployed roamed around in search of work.

In Germany the depression of the early 1930s finished what the inflation of the mid-1920s had begun, the ruin of the middle class, and in such troubled conditions Nazi support continued to grow. Hitler had promised that he would secure revision of the clauses of the Versailles Treaty which were humiliating and economically ruinous, and he began quite early to dissolve Germany's international commitments. Late in 1933 he announced withdrawal from both the disarmament conferences and the League of Nations; early in 1935 he denounced the arms limitations provisions of the treaty and reintroduced universal military training in Germany; early in 1936 he reoccupied the demilitarized Rhineland. These last moves were clear violations of the World War I peace settlements, and undoubtedly Hitler was testing the willingness of the allies to defend those settlements. The answer was clear; confronted by determined action, none of Germany's former enemies was willing to act.

Meanwhile, other governments had been making the same discovery. Late in 1931, acting on very dubious provocation, the Japanese had occupied Manchuria, and while a League of Nations report a year later generally condemned the action, it accepted the result. Then, in 1935, Italy began a full scale occupation of Ethiopia, which was completed successfully in 1936. This time the League was harsher in its condemnation, and it applied partial commercial sanctions, but again it proved unable to affect the course of events. Then came the Spanish civil war, already considered, which made the paralysis of the western governments and the impotence of the League of Nations glaringly apparent. Further emboldened, late in 1936 Italy and Germany signed a pact establishing the Rome-Berlin Axis, which again divided Europe into two hostile blocs, and very shortly Japan began to move toward the Axis.

There were many reasons why the western powers and the League of Nations did so little to check the aggressive policies of Italy, Japan and Germany. Two great powers did not participate in the League of Nations, the U.S.A. and the U.S.S.R., and without them any burden of enforcement clearly would fall upon France and Britain; but in France and Britain governments were paralyzed by the clash between increasing socialist strength and fearful conservatism, and both countries were reluctant to undertake expensive foreign policies during the depression. France had a special problem in that she had no firm military alliance with Britain, and the first world war had broken her morale to such an extent that she could not contemplate facing Germany alone; in Britain a considerable sympathy for Germany had grown up with a more sophisticated understanding of the world war for which Germany had been the scapegoat, and also there was a tendency to regard a revived Germany as a bulwark against the westward spread of Bolshevism. All in all, during the 1930s the post-war peace settlements had few supporters against moderate revisionism, and those few supporters were handicapped seriously by the effects of the depression.

By the middle of the 1930s the combination of Stalinist nationalism and the menace of Nazi Germany had led to some regularization of the Soviet Union's international position, but this came too late and was too uncertain to exercise any restraining influence upon Hitler. In 1932 France and a number of east European states with which she had close ties signed non-aggression pacts with the Stalin government; in 1933 the United States extended formal recognition; in the autumn of 1934 the Soviet Union joined the League of Nations; and in the spring of 1935 a Franco-Soviet alliance provided for joint action if either were the victim of unprovoked aggression. But underlying all of these developments was continued hostility. The Soviet government had not forgiven the other powers their counter-revolutionary interventions in Russia's domestic affairs in 1918–1920, and the westerners tended to regard international communist activity, which the Soviet Union supported, as a threat at least as dangerous as a rearmed Germany.

The lack of any fundamental agreement between the Soviet Union and the western powers was demonstrated clearly during negotiations aimed at an international agreement to oppose German aggression. The British and French governments were eager for Russian participation, but they were unwilling to make any territorial concessions at Poland's expense, while Russia desired to reclaim territory lost by the Treaty of Brest-Litovsk. Soviet demands were received more cordially by the Germans, and in the summer of 1939 first a trade treaty and then a non-aggression pact were concluded between the Soviet and German governments.

Growing bolder as they met no opposition, Japan and Germany intensified their aggressive revisionism. Still endeavoring to win recognition of her special position in Asia, Japan launched an undeclared war upon China in the summer of 1937, and in a little over a year she conquered a large part of the Chinese coast. The League of Nations condemned the action but did nothing more. Meanwhile Hitler was developing a propaganda campaign based upon aggressive German nationalism, aimed at the Austrians and at the German minorities that existed in several countries. Austria was a Germanic state in an unrealistic economic position because of the peace settlements; and given the virulence of nationalism at the time, it is undeniable that German minorities often were the victims of discrimination, as Hitler claimed. But Hitler's government was not concerned primarily with the welfare of these Germanic peoples outside of Germany; rather, the propaganda campaign sought to develop support for aggressive Nazi intervention in the affairs of neighboring states and for German expansion through annexations.

There is no doubt that union with Germany was attractive to Austrians and to German minorities in other countries, for the national mobilization and remilitarization undertaken by Hitler had a tremendous economic impact. By 1938, when most countries still faced serious problems of idle industry and high unemployment, both agriculture and industry in Germany were operating at levels of peak production, and there actually was a shortage of labor. Much of this was an artificial prosperity, for a large proportion of the production was directed to military purposes and paid for by high taxation, so there was no general improvement of standards of living, but in the 1930s full production and full employment anywhere were impressive to the uncritical observer.

Early in 1938 Hitler precipitated a governmental crisis in Austria through a speech promising protection to Germans outside of Germany, and unable to control the agitation of the Austrian Nazi Party without provoking German intervention, the Vienna government resigned. Then the Austrian Nazis took office demanding annexation to Germany, German troops poured across the border and Hitler proceeded to Vienna to proclaim the union of the two countries, another successful violation of the Versailles Peace.

Having achieved the incorporation of Austria, Hitler turned his attention to the Sudeten Germans in Czechoslovakia, three million people in a population of fifteen million. Nazi influence spread rapidly, and there were outbreaks of violence against the Czech government; then in September of 1938, Hitler demanded that the Sudeten Germans be given the right of national self-determination, a clear threat of German intervention if the Czechs tried to move forcefully to control public disorder in the Sudetenland. As this situation clearly was dangerous to international peace, Britain's Prime Minister Chamberlain travelled to Germany for personal discussions with Hitler in mid-September, and a larger international conference was held in Munich later in the month. On the basis of Hitler's assurances that his ambitions did not extend beyond the Sudetenland, Britain and France abandoned the Prague government, and the Czechs then had no choice but to surrender to Hitler's demands, losing a third of their territory and population and giving up their defensible frontiers.

The Munich agreements of 1938 have been damned as cowardly surrender, but it is difficult to conceive what alternatives the western powers might have adopted at that point. Germany was rearmed, and Hitler made it clear that he was willing to risk war. In both Britain and France pacifism was widespread, economies were just beginning to recover from the depression and there was great political confusion in the wake of the Spanish civil war and of growing socialist strength. Britain's armed forces were ill-equipped and under strength, and though French forces appeared in better condition, they were trained and equipped wholly for defensive action. Hitler may have been bluffing, but neither Britain nor France was in any position to call his bluff, and they had to seek accommodation. That his assurances were totally unreliable was demonstrated a few months later, in March of 1939, when German troops occupied the rest of Czechoslovakia, but the Czech crisis had stimulated rearmament in Britain and France, and the western powers hoped to negotiate from strength in any future clashes.

Hardly was the dismemberment of Czechoslovakia completed when Hitler launched a comparable campaign based upon the German minorities in Poland. Understandably, he believed on the basis of past record that Britain and France would object but would acquiesce, and when the matter developed into a crisis, he did not hesitate to invade Poland on September 1, 1939. This time, however, Britain and France did not acquiesce, and two days later they declared war on Germany.

Polish resistance to the German attack was crushed in eighteen days as Hitler's armies employed a new type of campaign called the *blitzkrieg* (lightning war), a combination of air strikes at vital communication centers and deep penetration through enemy lines by armored columns; most strategists still thought in terms of the static operations of World War I, but the Germans had developed fast-moving mobile warfare. Under the terms of the nonaggression pact, Germany and the Soviet Union divided Poland between them, but otherwise nothing much happened during the winter of 1939–1940;

probably Hitler hoped that confronted with his rapid victory in Poland and denied Russian support, Britain and France would negotiate. But no accommodation was achieved during the winter, and in April of 1940 Hitler's forces occupied Denmark and Norway, an important move that protected Germany's northern flank and assured access to Scandinavian iron ores. Then, in May, German armies crossed into Belgium, the Netherlands and Luxemburg and began the invasion of France.

In the face of German successes, Prime Minister Chamberlain resigned, and a British war cabinet was formed by Winston Churchill, while French resistance crumpled. German mechanized units slashed to the sea, dividing French forces and almost trapping the British expeditionary force at Dunkirk. Italy joined the war against France and Britain, and in late June, France surrendered. For all practical purposes, by mid-1940 fascist governments controlled the European continent from Russia to the English Channel and from Scandinavia to the Mediterranean. Given the acquiescence of Russia, based upon the nonaggression pact, and the nonintervention of the United States, based upon strong American isolationist sentiment, Britain was left to face the German onslaught alone. In the late summer the Battle of Britain began, a fierce struggle for control of the air on which hinged the feasibility of a German invasion, but the British air force maintained its superiority, and Britain survived.

The new hostilities in Europe were paralleled by rising tensions in east Asia and the Pacific. Fearing Japanese aggression, in the summer of 1940 the American government undertook a considerable expansion of naval strength aimed at creating a two ocean navy, and a few months later it inaugurated military conscription. Confirming the American concern, in September Japan occupied French Indo-China and concluded a Three Power Pact with Germany and Italy. Although the government of the United States still was not prepared to intervene militarily, its sympathies were obvious, and in March of 1941 it passed a Lend Lease Act that provided for the supply of arms and war materiel to Britain on credit. Japan's desire to be free for action in the Pacific and Stalin's concern that his agreements with Hitler would not endure resulted in a Russo-Japanese neutrality treaty in April, and by the summer of 1941 the stage was set for a vast expansion of hostilities.

Having failed to crush Britain, Hitler was eager for a successful campaign, and he distrusted Stalin; at the same time, Japan was controlled by a military government and was aggressively resentful of years of discrimination and humiliation by the west. The war exploded to a global scale when the Germans invaded Russia on June 22, the Japanese attacked American and British positions in southeast Asia and the Pacific on December 7, and Germany and Italy declared war upon the United States on December 8. The fury of the onslaught, combined with growing evidence of German atrocities against captured westerners and German genocidal policies against the Poles, Russians and especially Jews, added an ugly racist note to the struggle, and popular commitment to total war developed rapidly.

In early 1942 the British-French-American-Russian position was grim. German armies had penetrated deeply into Russia and were threatening to take her most important western cities, while another German force had slashed through north Africa and seemed about to overrun the British position in Egypt, which would open the way to the middle eastern oil fields. The Japanese had swept into southeast Asia, taking the Philippines, Indonesia, Malaya and Burma, and they appeared to threaten Australia and India, while at the same time their seizure of Pacific islands caused concern for Hawaii. During 1942, however, the allied position stabilized. Two American fleet actions in May and June, the Battle of the Coral Sea and the Battle of Midway, halted the Japanese advances toward Australia and Hawaii; in late summer the British stopped the German drive in north Africa at El Alamein and began a counteroffensive; and in the winter Russian defenses stiffened, and the Germans were held before Stalingrad. From early 1943 onward, the allied position continued to improve as the enormous productive capacities of the allies, particularly the United States, began to outstrip the capabilities of the Axis countries. The Russians launched a winter counteroffensive that pushed the Germans back on all fronts, and in the first three months of 1943 the Germans lost a half million men. In February of the same year the Battle of Guadalcanal broke Japanese naval air power, securing allied possession of the Solomon Islands and beginning the Japanese retreat. In May Axis resistance in north Africa ended, and in July allied forces invaded Sicily. The direction of the war was becoming clear, though there were still two years of hard fighting ahead before the Germans surrendered in May of 1945 and the Japanese followed suit in August.

The nature of the peace settlement intended by the allied powers, assuming they were victorious, was outlined at several wartime conferences. As early as August of 1941, before the United States was even in the war officially, President Roosevelt and Prime Minister Churchill had conferred and had issued a statement of peace aims called the Atlantic Charter, essentially a repudiation of territorial ambitions by the great powers, an endorsement of freely chosen self-government everywhere and an expression of hope for international cooperation. Early in 1943 at another meeting in Casablanca, they determined to prosecute the war until their enemies were forced to unconditional surrender. Then, through 1943 and 1944 representatives of the allied powers created a Relief and Rehabilitation Administration, an Organization for Educational and Cultural Reconstruction, an International Monetary Fund and an International Bank for Reconstruction and Development, all agencies intended to promote postwar recovery. The Big Three—Churchill, Roosevelt and Stalin—met at Tehran in the winter of 1943–1944, at Yalta early in 1945 and at Potsdam in July of 1945 (at the latter conference President Truman replaced Roosevelt who had died in April); at these meetings they coordinated their military operations, endorsed the idea of a new postwar international organization to maintain the peace and determined upon occupation and close control of their enemies to assure demilitarization, denazification and trial of war criminals. A formal organization to achieve these aims was founded officially in October of 1945, when a draft charter for a United Nations Organization was accepted by more than two dozen participating nations.

To some extent these peace aims represented an understanding of basic weaknesses in the treaties of 1919, and to some extent they were reactions to immediate problems. The principles of the Atlantic Charter illustrated a desire to avoid repetition of the imperial ambitions and the minority problems that the Versailles Peace had left unresolved. The decision to demand unconditional surrender probably reflected reaction to the stab in the back legend as much as contemporary wartime hatreds. The intention to try war criminals likely was a response to mounting evidence of shocking atrocities, but provisions for occupation, reeducation and restructuring of social institutions showed some understanding of the contradictory nature of the 1919 treaties which had removed weapons from the defeated but left them the kind of leadership and economic organization that made remilitarization relatively easy. Finally, the creation of agencies to aid reconstruction indicated recognition of the fact that political stability depended in large part upon economic recovery.

On the other hand the victors of 1945 proved no more successful than their predecessors of 1815 or 1918 in grappling with significant new problems resulting from the war, and they showed equal reluctance to accept the fact that serious issues could divide the coalition quickly once the common goal of victory had been attained. Among the many problems of the postwar world, three in particular were difficult for the peacemakers to recognize and accept: the diminished importance of the European great powers due to the military maturation of the two superpowers, the U.S. and the U.S.S.R.; the development of non-European peoples to a point where they no longer would accept peacefully European imperial domination; and rapid emergence of fundamental conflicts of interest between the U.S.S.R. and the west.

The French armies had been crushed early in the war, and the only thing that saved France from depending totally upon the allies for liberation was that two groups of Frenchmen refused to accept defeat, a resistance movement within France largely led by the Communist Party and a determined band of exiles called the Free French led by General Charles De Gaulle. At the end of the war, France's economy was chaotic, her industry and communications had been damaged badly by military operations and these two rival groups struggled for political control, each claiming to have been the major French element in the allied victory. In such condition, France was unable to resume her former international role smoothly.

Britain had escaped defeat and occupation, but she had suffered German bombing, her economy was staggering under the load of wartime expenditure and her domestic politics were rather turbulent as postwar elections swept the Labour Party to power and it embarked upon rapid nationalization of industry. Germany was a defeated and bombed-out ruin, divided into allied occupation zones; and though Italy had escaped harsh terms by repudiating Mussolini in the summer of 1943, it was war-torn, economically ruined and politically impotent. Behind the facade of the wartime alliance and the United Nations Organization, the old global preponderance of Europe had been broken, and at the end of the war there were two great powers economically and militarily, the U.S. and the U.S.S.R.

Moreover, the war had transformed fundamentally the nature of Europe's relationship to non-European peoples. Hard-pressed by the Axis, the western Europeans had appealed for support and help from their colonial peoples as never before, making them active partners rather than subject populations. The Free French in particular had relied upon France's African colonies, though to a greater or lesser degree the British, Dutch, Belgians and Americans had done the same thing. In Africa, the Pacific and southeast Asia the colonial powers had proved unable to defend their colonies during the early years of the war, undercutting their former prestige. Perhaps most significant of all, the Japanese had demonstrated the capacity of an Asian people to defeat westerners, and while they were unable to rally other Asian peoples to their own war aims, they had stimulated enormous national pride and confidence among non-European populations all over the world through the spectacle of western armies in retreat and western soldiers as prisoners. For both of these reasons, when the war ended many colonial peoples were unwilling to accept passively the reestablishment of their former colonial status.

Finally, the attempt to work out the details of the peace settlements outlined at wartime conferences quickly illustrated that the distrust and latent hostility between the U.S.S.R. and the west had not disappeared during the war. Even while they were fighting as allies there had been serious misunderstandings between them, as when Stalin wanted the westerners to open a second front in Europe long before the actual invasion of Normandy, to draw some of the pressure off Russia's armies, but the western governments felt that the estimated casualties would be higher than they could bear; and if the westerners underestimated the severity of Russia's suffering, so also the Russians, working in a different social and political context, misunderstood western hesitation and thought the western powers wanted the U.S.S.R. to be exhausted before the ultimate victory. Thus, the specter of the old struggle between socialist and capitalist never disappeared entirely, even when they were fighting in a common cause, and after the war it became more pronounced.

The Soviets, like their imperial predecessors, were very conscious of their long and indefensible frontiers and were eager to maintain a buffer of friendly or subservient states along them. Consequently, after the collapse of Germany, a divisive issue arose quickly between Russia and her western allies concerning the governments to be recognized in Poland, Czechoslovakia, Hungary and other east European areas liberated by the repulse of Axis forces. On the one hand, there were governments in exile in London, generally procapitalist and prowestern, claiming authority over liberated areas; on the other, people's governments, generally communist dominated and pro-Russian, arose out of resistance movements. Where Russian armies were responsible for the German retreat, the Russians tended to hand authority to people's governments, while in areas liberated by the west, governments in exile were restored. Since Russia had declared war on Japan in August of 1945, a comparable situation existed in east Asia with regard to Manchuria. And where the surrender agreements provided for joint occupation, as in Germany, Austria and Korea, or left an unstable political situation with the competing influence of the victorious powers undetermined, as in Greece, Turkey, China and the colonial areas of southeast Asia, conflict arose almost immediately. Despite wartime conferences and the establishment of the United Nations, allied cooperation broke down, and a new polarization quickly became apparent, a polarization in which the once dominant European powers played only a secondary role.

Rulers and Regimes of the Leading States
of Europe since 1815

AUSTRIA

Francis I, 1792–1835
Ferdinand I, 1835–1848
Francis Joseph, 1848–1916
Charles I, 1916–1918
Republican Regime, 1918–1938
Union with Germany, 1938–1945
Republican Regime, since 1945

ENGLAND

George III, 1760–1820
George IV, 1820–1830
William IV, 1830–1837
Victoria, 1837–1901
Edward VII, 1901–1910
George V, 1910–1936
Edward VIII, 1936
George VI, 1936–1952
Elizabeth II, since 1952

FRANCE

Louis XVIII, 1814–1824
Charles X, 1824–1830
Louis Philippe, 1830–1848
 (Orléanist Monarchy)
The Second Republic, 1848–1852
Napoleon III, 1852–1870
 (the Second Empire)
The Third Republic, 1870–1940
Pétain Regime, 1940–1944
Provisional Government, 1944–1946
The Fourth Republic, 1946–1958
The Fifth Republic, since 1958

GERMANY

William I, 1871–1888
Frederick III, 1888
William II, 1888–1918
The Weimar Republic, 1918–1933
The Third Reich, 1933–1945
Military Government, 1945–1949
The Federal Republic (West) and the
 Democratic Republic (East),
 since 1949

ITALY

Victor Emmanuel II, 1861–1878
Humbert I, 1878–1900
Victor Emmanuel III, 1900–1946
 (Mussolini Regime, 1922–1943)
Humbert II, 1946
Republican Regime, since 1946

PRUSSIA

Frederick William III, 1797–1840
Frederick William IV, 1840–1861
William I, 1861–1888
Part of United Germany, since 1871

RUSSIA

Alexander I, 1801–1825
Nicholas I, 1825–1855
Alexander II, 1855–1881
Alexander III, 1881–1894
Nicholas II, 1894–1917
Provisional Government, 1917
Communist Regime, since 1917

SARDINIA

Victor Emmanuel I, 1802–1821
Charles Felix, 1821–1831
Charles Albert, 1831–1849
Victor Emmanuel II, 1849–1878
Part of United Italy, since 1861

CENTRAL and EASTERN
EUROPE in 1947

0	200	400

MILES

Petsamo

NORWAY

SWEDEN

FINLAND

**Porkkala
(Leased to USSR)**

Oslo

Stockholm

Helsinki

L. Ladoga

U. S. S. R.

25°

55°

Estonia

Latvia

Lithuania

ANNEXED
BY USSR

Moscow

DENMARK

Copenhagen

Baltic Sea

**East
Prussia**

Berlin

**Occupied
by
Poland**

GERMANY

POLAND

Warsaw

**Eastern
Poland**

Prague

CZECHOSLOVAKIA

Carpathian Ruthenia

Northern Bucovina

Vienna

SWITZ.

AUSTRIA

Budapest

HUNGARY

Bessarabia

ROMANIA

Belgrade

YUGOSLAVIA

Bucharest

ITALY

Adriatic Sea

Rome

Sofia

DOBRUDJA

Black Sea

BULGARIA

Istanbul

ALBANIA

Ankara

GREECE

TURKEY

Athens

Epilogue

Brave New Worlds

The superpower rivalry that emerged from World War II soon divided the world into armed camps again, and when civil wars broke out in Greece and Turkey in 1947, the United States supported conservative postwar governments while the U.S.S.R. supported communist insurgents. To organize this support several western governments·agreed to a European Recovery Program financed by the U.S. (the Marshall Plan), and the Soviet Union and a number of east European states set up the Communist Information Bureau (Cominform). Generally the western powers made some progress: the communist rebellions were crushed in Greece and Turkey; nationalist and anti-Russian elements were so encouraged in Yugoslavia that in 1948 that country was expelled from the Cominform, though its government remained nominally communist; and in Italy and France liberal-democratic governments were reinforced against the threat of communist electoral victories.

In subsequent years the dichotomy between east and west was institutionalized further. In April of 1949 the North Atlantic Treaty was signed, a defensive arrangement within the Atlantic community (later extended) which provided for mutual assistance, especially American support against aggression, and for military integration in an American dominated alliance; on the other side of the earth a comparable arrangement was attempted in 1954 by a Southeast Asia

Treaty. Most Asian nations refused to participate, however, so the treaty's chief effect was to rally colonial powers around the United States. At the same time, the Soviet Union was tightening its ties with supporters and client states; in 1950 it signed an alliance with the new communist government of China, and in 1955 the Warsaw Pact provided for military bases and the integration of east European forces under the U.S.S.R. in much the same manner as the North Atlantic Treaty had integrated western European forces under the U.S. Thus, the Soviet Union and the United States divided over the shaping of the postwar world, and each rapidly developed a galaxy of satellite states.

The dispute between the superpowers slowly intruded itself upon the independence struggle of colonial peoples. Agitation in the Indian subcontinent, mostly in the guise of nonviolent demonstrations led by Mahatma Ghandi, resulted in a British concession of independence to both India and Pakistan so quickly (August of 1947) that the movement did not then become an issue in the superpower rivalry, though much blood was shed between Hindus and Moslems. Burma followed the same course and was granted independence in January of 1948, but in this case a communist rebellion contested the authority of the newly established government, and fighting on a large scale continued into 1950, never dying out altogether. By contrast, when Indonesian leaders proclaimed a republic two days after Japan's surrender in August of 1945, the Dutch government refused to accept this declaration of independence, and with British support soon found itself engaged in open hostilities against a people's army. A full-scale civil war ensued until the end of 1949, despite U.N. efforts at mediation, and the Netherlands finally had to accept Indonesian independence. During the course of the war the independence movement showed more and more communist influence while the western powers showed themselves committed to the colonial status quo.

By 1948 a comparable situation had developed in Malaya where the communists had espoused the nationalist cause, and the British found themselves in the unfortunate position of apparently defending continued colonial domination; in this instance, however, effective British military action combined with political concessions and astute manipulation of local racial tensions managed to achieve compromise leading to eventual friendly independence rather than surrender of the country to pro-communist insurgents.

In Indochina another nationalist movement proclaimed independence immediately after the Japanese surrender in 1945, and again there was conflict. The French were willing to grant the new government limited autonomy, but fighting broke out as the Indochinese sought more extensive independence, and again the communists adopted the nationalist cause while the west rallied to France. In 1950 the west recognized the pro-French states of Vietnam, Laos and Cambodia, while communist states recognized the insurgent Viet Minh, and with foreign aid the fighting intensified. The Viet Minh's capture of the French position at Dien Bien Phu in 1954 finally forced the French to admit defeat in Vietnam; the north was surrendered to the Viet Minh while a prowestern independent government was established in the south of the divided country.

Indisputably, however, the great event in Asia was the revolution in China. As far back as the 1920s the Chinese Communists had made a serious bid to dominate the government, and though Chiang Kai-shek had defeated them, they had not been destroyed. During World War II they won considerable prestige in China for their vigorous resistance to the Japanese, and after the war they were strengthened when the Russians made certain that large supplies of captured Japanese weapons fell to them rather than to the Nationalist government. Chiang Kai-shek and his Kuomintang Party were in a difficult position. Nationalist forces had achieved no great success in the struggle with the Japanese; the Nationalist government had become riddled with corruption, and, confined to inland areas where it was dependent upon the conservative country gentry, it had found no solution to China's single most pressing problem, land reform. Thus, in the postwar era the communists made rapid progress, for they enjoyed a good war record, were well armed with captured Japanese equipment and were willing to tackle the land redistribution problem by shooting landlords. In the latter part of 1949 surviving Nationalists withdrew from the mainland to the island of

Taiwan, and in the now clearly established division between Soviet and American blocs, China passed under the control of a government sympathetic to the Soviet bloc.

By the end of 1949 the Soviet Union was surrounded by a band of satellite or sympathetic states on most of its frontiers, and it had caused serious problems for the westerners elsewhere. Ironically, the U.S.S.R. proclaimed itself anti-imperialist while building a more extensive empire than ever the czars had managed. On the other hand, the western powers had checked the growth of Soviet influence in western Europe and had defeated Soviet-supported Communist uprisings in the Balkans and in parts of southeast Asia, though the west had shown itself curiously ineffective in the propaganda war. Both superpowers practiced the same policies, and both experienced limited successes and some failures, but in the non-European world the Soviet Union managed to present itself as opposing colonialism and favoring national independence while the United States appeared as the supporter of colonialism and the defender of dictators.

In this growing superpower rivalry there had been many small clashes as the U.S. and the U.S.S.R. supported opposing forces in revolutions and colonial wars, and finally a major confrontation occurred in Korea in 1950. Since the end of the nineteenth century Korea had been dominated by Japan, so that at the end of World War II it was regarded as a liberated nation; in 1945 the allies arranged that the U.S. should occupy the south and the U.S.S.R. should occupy the north until elections could be held to establish a unified democratic government. Deteriorating relations between the superpowers in the late 1940s precluded agreement on the conditions for such elections, and two separate regimes developed on a *de facto* basis, each committed to the policy of its superpower patron.

After the Japanese surrender in 1945 the U.S. army had been demobilized so quickly that American military potential practically was destroyed except for the massive retaliation implicit in the possession of the atom bomb, but extensive American economic aid had proved effective in countering Soviet probes except in China, where special conditions prevailed. By 1950, however, the U.S. bloc clearly was on the defensive all around the world, with the U.S.S.R. probing for weaknesses in the defense; in midyear, seeking to exploit this initiative and American military weakness, the Soviets' North Korean client state attacked South Korea. The

U.S. promptly committed troops to the defense of its client, and since the occupation zones were part of a United Nations arrangement, the U.N. Security Council endorsed this action and called for support from member states.

After serious reverses early in the war, by October the U.N. forces were approaching the Manchurian border, and at this point occurred one of the most significant developments of the early post-World War II period. Whether because the Russians were unwilling to risk further commitment or because the Chinese felt their security jeopardized is unknown, but for whatever reasons, Chinese forces intervened, indicating the emergence of a second force within the communist world. Chinese intervention forced a retreat of U.N. forces, and by late November the conflict had stabilized along the old line of demarcation between north and south, where the war finally ended after another two and a half years of desultory fighting.

The Korean War showed that the U.S. was willing to undertake military as well as economic action to defend its sphere of influence and enforce its policy of containment of the Soviet Union. It also showed that the U.S.S.R. set limits to its expansive ambitions and would stop short of superpower war that might involve atomic weapons. Also, it demonstrated that China was not willing to accept Russian tutelage but intended to assert a great power role herself, a position China has continued to maintain and reinforce.

The 1950s and 1960s showed three main themes. First, colonial independence movements, such as had broken out in south Asia in the 1940s, intensified and spread, and comparable racial conflict developed beyond colonial areas as nonwhite peoples became more self-conscious. Second, while the U.S. and the U.S.S.R. remained the prime movers of international affairs, schismatic movements appeared within both blocs and many new nations refused alignment with either of the superpowers. Finally, while the U.S. and the U.S.S.R. continued to support opposing sides in many conflicts, peaceful coexistence became the keynote of their direct competition, channeling some of their rivalry into nonmilitary ventures.

In the Middle East as well as in south Asia, World War II diminished the stature of the colonial powers and stimulated nationalistic aspirations. One of the most bitter problems of the postwar world arose in Palestine, where Jewish nationalists were seeking to reestablish a Jewish homeland in an area claimed by Arab nationalists. The British, who had held the area in trust since the first world war, were regarded with intense hostility by extremists on both sides and were subjected to terrorist attacks, with the result that in 1948 they withdrew from Palestine, leaving the Jews and Arabs to fight it out. The Jews maintained themselves and succeeded in establishing the small state of Israel, while Arab forces tended to consolidate behind Egypt, the foremost exponent of surging Arab nationalism. No compromise could be achieved, and irregular skirmishing has continued ever since, occasionally erupting into full-scale military operations which the Israelis generally have dominated. Inevitably such a quarrel, casting a shadow over the whole eastern Mediterranean and the Middle Eastern oil fields, has attracted superpower interest, and while both the U.S. and the U.S.S.R. have seemed eager to prevent the conflict from spreading, both have supplied economic aid and military equipment to the belligerents while proclaiming their support for a "permanent" peace.

In Africa anticolonial and nationalist sentiment showed itself at first in the formation of secret societies and in outbreaks of terrorism, but it was not until the mid-1950s that nationalist forces became strong enough to force the colonial powers to withdraw. Then in a decade almost all of the continent was freed. The experience of these newly independent states has not been tranquil, for frequently the withdrawal of European authority has been followed by economic chaos and tribal warfare, but former colonial peoples appear willing to pay this price for independence. At the southern end of the continent, the new black nationalism created special problems. South Africa was independent and Rhodesia was moving toward independence, but both states were dominated by long-settled white minorities. Generally the reaction of these white governments has been varying degrees of repression, and while explosive tensions build, no solutions have appeared.

After the French withdrawal from Indochina in the mid-1950s, the government of South Vietnam continued to be insecure as it was threatened by the expansionist ambitions of its northern neighbor and was unable to win broad popular support within its own borders, while at the same time insurgent activities intensified in Laos and Cambodia. To counter the potent combination of nationalist aspirations and communist promises of radical social and economic reform, in the early 1960s the United States and its Southeast Asia Treaty allies began to give more and more military aid to the noncommunist governments of the area, finally making the fateful decision to commit American ground forces—a decision which eventually proved very difficult to reverse. An unfortunate pattern was developing in which nationalist independence movements could find support among the communist powers, while the western nations appeared willing to support any anticommunist element, however authoritarian and unpopular.

Anticolonial agitation had strong repercussions in the western hemisphere, too, for many Latin Americans felt that though nominally independent, their governments really were only clients of the United States; and, in any case, obvious American domination of economies in which the gulf between rich and poor was enormous encouraged anti-Americanism. A whole series of coups and insurgent movements developed, forcing some autocratic governments to programs of social reform, toppling others, and producing one short-lived Marxist regime in Chile. But the only one of these movements that actually accomplished a far-reaching revolution was that of Fidel Castro in Cuba. Shortly after he succeeded in establishing a revolutionary government in the late 1950s, Castro confiscated foreign investments, inaugurated confiscatory taxation of Cuban fortunes and appealed to the communist bloc for support. As in the African anticolonial experience, the price was high in economic recession and extralegal repression of opposition, but Castro's anti-Americanism and his support of nationalism seem to have found broad popular support. This restiveness in the western hemisphere has been terribly disturbing to the United States, which has considered the Americas its special preserve since the promulgation of the Monroe Doctrine in 1823, the more so as most of the insurgent movements are strongly anti-American and some are avowedly communist, hoping to fight American influence through close ties with Russia or China as did Castro.

While worldwide patterns of economic exploitation and white domination have been breaking before the strength of anticolonial-ism, comparable quarrels between dominant and dominated peoples, often including virulent racial animosities, have disrupted the domestic tranquility of many nations old and new. Thus, there are riots against economically dominant minorities, such as East Indians in Africa and Chinese in Indonesia; and the United States experiences ever more militant protest movements by economically dominated minorities seeking the elimination of poverty and the establishment of black and American Indian equality, protests which challenge the traditional domination of the American white Protestant middle class so forcefully that they sometimes threaten to shred the very fabric of American society.

But if the 1950s and 1960s witnessed a grim parade of colonial wars and racial violence, these two decades also saw an encouraging redevelopment of pluralism on the international scene, agitation for greater independence on the part of nations within the superpower blocs and the growth of a "third world," mostly new nations, which have refused commitment in the superpower rivalry. Where the grasp for greater independence is too radical and causes superpower concern for basic defense, the result sometimes has been military intervention, such as the Soviet Union practiced in Hungary in 1956 and in Czechoslovakia in 1968 and the United States attempted in Cuba in the famous Bay of Pigs incident in 1961. But that the world no longer can be described in terms of two monolithic blocs is attested not only by the startlingly virulent Sino-Soviet dispute but also by the increasingly independent policies of Rumania and Albania within the communist orbit and of France and Japan within the American orbit, while the growing strength of former colonial nations offers grounds for hope that an increasingly pluralistic international society will continue to ameliorate the dangerous rivalry of the superpowers.

It is in this frame of reference that Europe's role seems to be cast for the immediate future. In 1945 a shattered western Europe was almost totally dependent upon the United States for military guarantees against Russian expansionism and for economic aid for reconstruction. After three decades of recovery, however, Europe appears unwilling to continue docilely to allow the U.S. to direct western policy and is demanding more equal partnership. Germany is dominated by aspirations for reunification; Britain, though beset by continuing economic crises, has moved significantly toward European integration; and France, which quickly recovered economic stability and national assertiveness, has rejected American domination quite forcefully. All of these developments encourage a diffusion of leadership and a reduction of the dangers implicit in domination of international affairs by only two intensely competitive superpowers.

Finally, there appears to be an encouraging tendency for the superpowers to subsume their rivalry into economic, scientific and diplomatic competition designed to win prestige and attract the support of the uncommitted nations. Thus in Africa, in India and in many other parts of the world the United States, the Soviet Union, and more recently China offer economic and technical aid, each eager to demonstrate the superiority of her own sociopolitical system in meeting the rising levels of expectancy in developing nations. In space technology, the exploration of the moon and unmanned probes to Venus, Mars and Jupiter replace military confrontations. And in diplomacy the attempt to win popular support has made the U.N., whatever its shortcomings as a supranational government, a forum of international debate, the focus of a war of words that is infinitely preferable to a war of atomic weapons.

No one can afford to be too optimistic, for the fearsome arsenals of the superpowers continue to grow, despite efforts at arms limitations; and nuclear technology, including weaponry, is spreading. Constant hunger, and even starvation, continue to be daily experiences for millions of people, brutal wars continue in many parts of the world, and cities burn when confrontation politics turns into violence. But in the past man has shown an encouraging capacity to survive his own follies. Whatever may be the future, however, it is certain that the European political hegemony has ended; and while European ideas such as nationalism, capitalism and communism continue to exercise global influence, the future rests largely in the hands of non-European peoples.

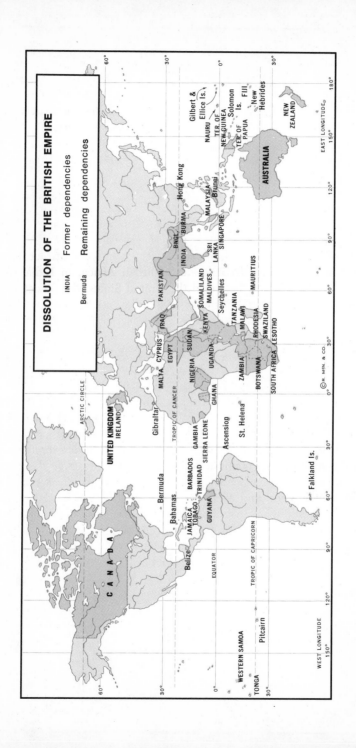

DISSOLUTION OF THE BRITISH EMPIRE

INDIA — Former dependencies

Bermuda — Remaining dependencies

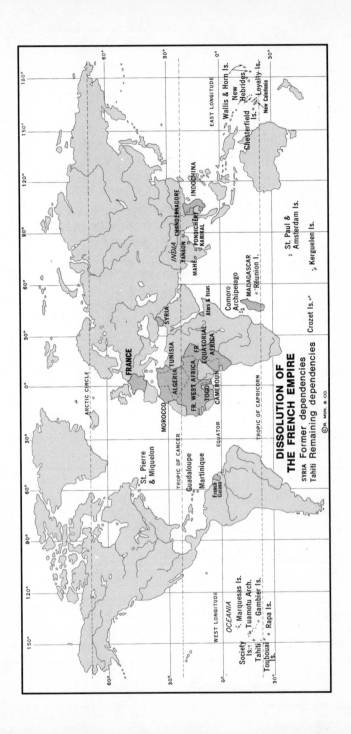

DISSOLUTION OF
THE FRENCH EMPIRE
SYRIA Former dependencies
Tahiti Remaining dependencies

©R. MCN. & CO.

Suggestions for Further Reading

The following lists include books of considerable variety—source material, monographs, and interpretive essays. Some are new studies, others classics in their fields. Obviously, so short a list cannot be exhaustive, but it is hoped that this one at least will provide some introduction to the varieties of history and of historical writing. Naturally some works are applicable to more than one chapter, but they have been listed only once, with the chapters to which they seem most appropriate.

The student seeking more detail of subjects touched here only briefly also would be well advised to consult the great compendia published by Cambridge University, as they treat an enormous range of topics. Examples are *The Cambridge Medieval History,* 8 vols.; *The Cambridge Modern History,* 14 vols., and *The New Cambridge Modern History,* 14 vols.; *The Cambridge History of the British Empire,* 8 vols.; and *The Cambridge History of Islam,* 2 vols.

Introduction

Cahnman, W., and Baskoff, A., eds. *Sociology and History: Theory and Research.* New York, 1964.

Collingwood, R. G. *The Idea of History.* Oxford, 1946.

Dray, W. H. *Philosophy of History.* Englewood Cliffs, N.J., 1964.

Gardiner, P. *The Nature of Historical Explanation.* London, 1961.

Gooch, G. P. *History and Historians in the Nineteenth Century.* Boston, 1959.

Gottshalk, L. *Understanding History.* New York, 1963.

Jones, T. B. *Paths to the Ancient Past.* New York, 1967.

Meyerhoff, H., ed. *The Philosophy of History in Our Time.* New York, 1959.

Muller, H. *The Uses of the Past.* New York, 1954.

Thompson, J. W. *A History of Historical Writing,* 2 vols., New York, 1942.

Chapter 1.   The Renaissance

Ady, C. M. *Lorenzo de' Medici and Renaissance Italy.* London, 1955.

Burckhardt, J. *The Civilization of the Renaissance in Italy.* New York, 1958.

Ferguson, W. K., et al. *The Renaissance, Six Essays.* New York, 1953.

Hay, D. *The Italian Renaissance in Its Historical Background.* Cambridge, England, 1961.

Helton, T., ed. *The Renaissance: A Reconsideration of the Theories and Interpretations of the Age.* Madison, 1961.

Kristeller, P. *Renaissance Thought.* New York, 1961.

Mattingly, G. *Renaissance Diplomacy.* Boston, 1955.

Schevill, F. *The Medici.* New York, 1949.

Sypher, W. *Four Stages of Renaissance Style.* Garden City, 1955.

Von Martin, A. *Sociology of the Renaissance.* New York, 1945.

Chapter 2.   Religious Reaction and Reform

Bainton, R. *Here I Stand: a Life of Martin Luther.* New York, 1955.

Bindoff, S. T. *Tudor England.* Harmondsworth, 1950.

Brandi, K. *Emperor Charles V.* New York, 1940.

Dickens, A. G. *Reformation and Society in Sixteenth Century Europe*. London, 1966.

Elton, G. R. *Reformation Europe, 1517–1559*. Cleveland, 1963.

Hillerbrand, H. J. *Men and Ideas in the Sixteenth Century*. Chicago, 1969.

Hughes, P. *A Popular History of the Reformation*. Garden City, 1957.

Mattingly, G. *Catherine of Aragon*. Boston, 1941.

Tawney, R. H. *Religion and the Rise of Capitalism*. New York, 1955.

Weber, M. *The Protestant Ethic and the Spirit of Capitalism*. New York, 1948.

Chapter 3. Habsburg Hegemony

Elliott, J. H. *Europe Divided, 1559–1598*. New York, 1969.

————. *Imperial Spain, 1469–1716*. London, 1963.

Franklin, J. H., ed. *Constitutionalism and Resistance in the Sixteenth Century: Three Treatises by Hotman, Beza and Mornay*. New York, 1969.

Lewis, M. *The Spanish Armada*. London, 1966.

Mattingly, G. *The Armada*. Boston, 1959.

Neale, J. E. *The Age of Catherine de Medici*. London, 1943.

————. *Queen Elizabeth I*. London, 1957.

Oman, Sir C. *A History of the Art of War in the Sixteenth Century*. New York, 1937.

Roth, C. *The Spanish Inquisition*. New York, 1964.

Trevor-Davies, R. *The Golden Century of Spain, 1501–1621*. London, 1937.

Chapter 4. The Scientific Revolution

Andrade, E. N. *Isaac Newton*. London, 1954.

Butterfield, H. *The Origins of Modern Science*, rev. ed. New York, 1957.

Caspar, M. *Kepler*. London, 1959.

Farrington, B. *Francis Bacon: Philosopher of the New Science*. New York, 1961.

Fermi, L. *Galileo and the Scientific Revolution*. New York, 1961.

Hall, A. R. *From Galileo to Newton, 1630–1730*. New York, 1963.

————. *The Scientific Revolution, 1500–1800.* 2nd ed. Boston, 1962.

Koyré, A. *From the Closed World to the Infinite Universe.* New York, 1957.

Kuhn, T. S. *The Copernican Revolution.* Cambridge, Mass., 1956.

Tillyard, E. M. W. *The Elizabethan World Picture.* London, 1961.

Chapter 5.   The Rise of the National State

Aston, T., ed. *Crisis in Europe, 1560–1660.* London, 1965.

Barbour, V. *Capitalism in Amsterdam in the Seventeenth Century.* Baltimore, 1950.

Cronin, V. *Louis XIV.* London, 1969.

Geyl, P. *The Netherlands in the Seventeenth Century.* London, 1961.

Nussbaum, F. L. *The Triumph of Science and Reason, 1660–1685.* New York, 1953.

Steinberg, S. H. *The Thirty Years' War.* London, 1966.

Wedgwood, C. V. *Richelieu and the French Monarchy.* New York, 1949.

————. *The Thirty Years' War.* London, 1933.

Willson, D. H. *King James VI and I.* London, 1956.

Wolf, J. B. *Louis XIV.* New York, 1967.

Chapter 6.   The Birth of the Balance of Power

Bruford, W. H. *Germany in the Eighteenth Century.* Cambridge, England, 1935.

Cobban, A. *A History of Modern France,* 2nd ed., vol. 1. Baltimore, 1962.

Dorn, W. L. *Competition for Empire, 1740–1763.* New York, 1940.

Fay, S. B., and Epstein, K. *The Rise of Brandenburg-Prussia to 1786.* New York, 1964.

Goubert, P. *Louis XIV and Twenty Million Frenchmen.* New York, 1970.

Klyuchevsky, V. *Peter the Great.* New York, 1959.

Moote, A. L. *The Seventeenth Century.* Lexington, Mass., 1970.

Plumb, J. H. *England in the Eighteenth Century.* Harmondsworth, 1950.

Roberts, P. *The Quest for Security, 1715–1740.* New York, 1947.
Wolf, J. B. *The Emergence of the Great Powers, 1685–1715.* New York, 1951.

Chapter 7. Man, God, and Reason

Barber, E. *The Bourgeoisie in Eighteenth Century France.* Princeton, 1955.
Becker, C. *The Heavenly City of the Eighteenth Century Philosophers.* New Haven, 1932.
Cassirer, E. *The Philosophy of the Enlightenment.* Boston, 1951.
Cobban, A. *Rousseau and the Modern State.* London, 1964.
Ford, F. *Robe and Sword: the Regrouping of the French Aristocracy after Louis XIV.* Cambridge, Mass., 1953.
Hazard, P. *The European Mind, 1680–1715.* London, 1953.
————. *European Thought in the Eighteenth Century.* New Haven, 1954.
Lanson, G. *Voltaire.* New York, 1966.
Martin, K. *French Liberal Thought in the Eighteenth Century,* 2nd ed. London, 1954.
Talmon, J. L. *The Origins of Totalitarian Democracy.* New York, 1961.

Chapter 8. A Harvest of Violence

Beik, P. H., ed. *The French Revolution.* New York, 1970.
Brinton, C. *A Decade of Revolution, 1789–1799.* New York, 1934.
Brunn, G. *Europe and the French Imperium, 1799–1814.* New York, 1938.
Gershoy, L. *From Despotism to Revolution, 1763–1789.* New York, 1944.
Geyl, P. *Napoleon: For and Against.* New Haven, 1949.
Lefebvre, G. *The Coming of the French Revolution, 1789.* Princeton, 1947.
Palmer, R. R. *Twelve Who Ruled.* Princeton, 1941.
Rudé, G. *The Crowd in History, 1730–1848.* New York, 1964.
————. *Revolutionary Europe, 1783–1815.* Cleveland, 1964.
Tocqueville, A. de. *The Old Regime and the French Revolution.* Garden City, 1955.

Chapter 9.   Restoration and Reaction

Artz, F. B. *Reaction and Revolution, 1815–1832*. New York, 1932.

Bertier de Sauvigny, G. *The Bourbon Restoration*. Philadelphia, 1966.

De Ruggiero, G. *The History of European Liberalism*. New York, 1927.

Jelavich, B. *The Habsburg Empire in European Affairs, 1814–1918*. Chicago, 1969.

Kissinger, H. *A World Restored: Metternich, Castlereagh and the Problem of Peace, 1812–1822*. London, 1957.

May, A. J. *The Age of Metternich, 1814–1848*. New York, 1966.

Mazour, A. G. *The First Russian Revolution, 1825*. Berkeley, 1937.

Nicolson, H. *The Congress of Vienna: a Study in Allied Unity*. New York, 1946.

Webster, C. K. *The Congress of Vienna, 1814–1815*. London, 1950.

Wolf, J. B. *France, 1815–1919*. New York, 1940.

Chapter 10.   Industrialization and Its Consequences

Ashton, T. S. *The Industrial Revolution, 1760–1830*. London, 1948.

Berlin, I. *Karl Marx*. New York, 1948.

Clapham, J. J. *The Economic Development of France and Germany, 1815–1914*. Cambridge, England, 1936.

Fasel, G. *Europe in Upheaval: the Revolutions of 1848*. Chicago, 1969.

George, M. D. *London Life in the Eighteenth Century*. New York, 1964.

Langer, W. L. *Political and Social Upheaval, 1832–1852*. New York, 1969.

Marcuse, H. *Reason and Revolution: Hegel and the Rise of Social Theory*. New York, 1941.

Mayo, E. *The Human Problems of an Industrial Civilization*. New York, 1933.

Robertson, P. *The Revolutions of 1848*. Princeton, 1952.

Young, G. M. *Victorian England*. Garden City, 1954.

Chapter 11.   The Nation Deified

Blake, R. *Disraeli*. London, 1969.

Delzell, C., ed. *The Unification of Italy, 1859–1861.* New York, 1964.

Mosse, W. E. *Alexander II and the Modernization of Russia.* New York, 1958.

Shafer, B. C. *Nationalism: Myth and Reality.* New York, 1955.

Strachey, L. *Eminent Victorians.* Cape Town, 1947.

————. *Queen Victoria.* New York, 1921.

Taylor, A. J. P. *Bismarck: the Man and the Statesman.* New York, 1955.

Thompson, J. M. *Louis Napoleon and the Second Empire.* Oxford, 1954.

Williams, R. *Gaslight and Shadow: the World of Napoleon III.* New York, 1957.

Chapter 12. The New Europe

Barzun, J. *Darwin, Marx, Wagner.* Garden City, 1958.

Gay, P. *The Dilemma of Democratic Socialism: Eduard Bernstein's Challenge to Marx.* New York, 1952.

Hayes, C. J. H. *A Generation of Materialism, 1871–1900.* New York, 1941.

Himmelfarb, G. *Victorian Minds.* New York, 1970.

Irwin, W. *Apes, Angels and Victorians.* New York, 1955.

Schorske, C. E. *German Social Democracy, 1905–1917.* Cambridge, Mass., 1955.

Seton-Watson, H. *The Decline of Imperial Russia, 1855–1914.* London, 1952.

Thompson, D. *Democracy in France Since 1870.* New York, 1952.

Tuchman, B. W. *The Proud Tower.* New York, 1966.

Williams, R., ed. *The Commune of Paris, 1871.* New York, 1969.

Chapter 13. Competition and Collapse

Fay, S. B. *The Origins of the World War,* 2 vols. New York, 1928.

Langer, W. L. *European Alliances and Alignments, 1871–1890.* New York, 1950.

Lenin, V. I. *Imperialism: the Highest Stage of Capitalism.* New York, 1939.

Massie, R. K. *Nicholas and Alexandra.* New York, 1967.

Northrop, F. S. C. *The Meeting of East and West.* New York, 1946.

Remak, J. *The Origins of World War I, 1871–1914.* New York, 1967.

Schumpeter, J. A. *Imperialism and Social Classes.* New York, 1955.

Tuchman, B. W. *The Guns of August.* New York, 1962.

Winks, R. W. *British Imperialism.* New York, 1963.

Wolfe, B. D. *Three Who Made a Revolution.* Boston, 1955.

Chapter 14. The Retreat of Liberal Democracy

Abel, T. F. *Why Hitler Came into Power.* New York, 1938.

Chamberlain, W. H. *The Russian Revolution, 1917–1921,* 2 vols. New York, 1935.

Deutscher, I. *Stalin.* New York, 1949.

Fischer, L. *The Life of Lenin.* New York, 1964.

Graves, R. and Hodge, A. *The Long Weekend: a Social History of Great Britain, 1918–1939.* New York, 1941.

Jaszi, O. *The Dissolution of the Habsburg Monarchy.* Chicago, 1929.

Seton-Watson, H. *Eastern Europe Between the Wars, 1918–1941.* New York, 1945.

Thomas, H. *The Spanish Civil War.* New York, 1961.

Wheeler-Bennett, J. W. *Brest-Litovsk, the Forgotten Peace, March 1918.* London, 1939.

Wolfers, A. *Britain and France between Two Wars.* New York, 1940.

Chapter 15. The End of European Hegemony

Bullock, A. L. C. *Hitler, a Study in Tyranny.* New York, 1958.

Carr, E. H. *The Twenty Years' Crisis, 1919–1939.* London, 1939.

Churchill, Sir W. S. *The Second World War,* 6 vols. Boston, 1948–53.

Gilbert, F., and Craig, G. A., eds. *The Diplomats, 1919–1938.* Princeton, 1953.

Shirer, W. L. *The Rise and Fall of the Third Reich.* New York, 1959.

Snell, J. L. *Illusion and Necessity: the Diplomacy of Global War, 1939–1945.* Boston, 1963.

Taylor, A. J. P. *The Origins of the Second World War.* New York, 1961.

Waite, R. G. L., ed. *Hitler and Naxi Germany.* New York, 1965.

Wheeler-Bennett, J. W. *Munich: Prologue to Tragedy.* New York, 1948.

Wilmot, C. *The Struggle for Europe.* New York, 1952.

Epilogue. Brave New Worlds

Feis, H. *The China Tangle.* Princeton, 1953.

————. *From Trust to Terror: the Onset of the Cold War, 1945–1950.* New York, 1970.

Gatzke, H. *The Present in Perspective,* 2nd ed. Chicago, 1965.

Kennan, G. F. *Realities of American Foreign Policy.* Princeton, 1954.

Roberts, H. L. *Russia and America.* New York, 1956.

Seton-Watson, H. *The East European Revolution.* London, 1956.

Snell, J. L., ed. *The Meaning of Yalta.* Baton Rouge, 1956.

Spear, T. G. P. *India, Pakistan and the West.* New York, 1952.

Staley, E. *The Future of Underdeveloped Countries.* London, 1954.

Werth, A. *France, 1940–1955.* New York, 1956.

Index

Absolutism: early modern, 62, 63, 67, 68, 71, 72, 105; Napoleon, 112; Stalin, 197

Act of Settlement (1714), 79

Act of Supremacy (1534), 25

Afghanistan, 181, 187

Africa: colonial rivalries, 166, 176–181, 183, 186; independence struggles, 193, 225

Agricultural revolution, 133

Aix-la-Chapelle: Treaty of (1748), 82; conference at (1818), 127, 128

Albania, 175, 188, 227

Alberti, Leone Battista (1404–1472), 6

Alexander I, czar of Russia (1801–1825), 113–114, 117–118, 218

Alexander II, czar of Russia (1855–1881), 150, 171, 218

Alexander III, czar of Russia (1881–1894), 171, 172, 218

Algeria, 146, 176, 179

Alsace, 65, 75, 76; and French nationalism, 164, 180, 183; to Germany (1871), 162

Alva, duke of (1508–1582), 39

American Civil War (1861–1865), 145

American War of Independence (1775–1783), 85, 87, 110

Amiens, Treaty of (1802), 112

Anabaptists, 24, 33, 58

Anglicanism, 58, 157, 158. See also Act of Supremacy; Church of England; Henry VIII

Anglo-French Entente (1904), 159, 187

Anglo-Russian Entente (1907), 159, 187

Anjou, duke of (1554–1584), 43

Anne, queen of England (1702–1714), 79

Anne of Austria (1601–1666), 68

Anti-Semitism: in Dreyfus Affair, 165; and Nazis, 202, 203, 213

Anti-Socialist Law (Germany, 1878), 168

Arabs, 51, 225. See also Islam; Moslems

Aragon, 33

Ariosto, Ludovico (1474–1533), 8

Aristotelianism, 47–49; challenged, 48–54

Aristotle (384–321 B.C.), 14; scientific theories, 45–47, 49, 50, 53

Armada of Spain, 37, 38, 60

Articles of Confederation (1777), 86

Artois, count of. See Charles X, king of France

Asiento (1713), 81

Assembly of Notables (1787), 104, 105

Astronomy, Aristotelian, 46–54

Athens: British blockade (1850), 145

Atlantic Charter (1941), 214, 215

Aüerstadt, Battle of (1806), 112

Augsburg: Confession of (1530), 20; League of (1688–1697), 76, 77; Peace of (1555), 21, 32, 33, 64

Augustine, Saint (354–430), 2, 21

Austerlitz, Battle of (1805), 112
Australia, 176, 177, 213
Austria, 61, 63, 70; allied occupation, 217; annexation by Nazi Germany, 210; in Balkans, 183–185; Congress of Vienna, 117, 118; in eighteenth century, 77–85; French Revolutionary Wars, 107–114; German unification, 124, 125, 150–153; Italian unification, 141, 147, 149, 152; postwar, 192, 195, 203; Quadruple Alliance, 119, 128
Austria-Hungary, Dual Monarchy: formed (1867), 150, subject nationalities, 158, 170, 171, 188. *See also* Austria; Hungary
Austrian Netherlands. *See* Netherlands
Austrian Succession, War of the (1740–1748), 81, 82
Austro-Prussian War (1866), 148, 151, 152, 193

Bacon, Francis (1561–1626), 55, 56
Bacon, Roger (c. 1214–1294), 14, 48
Balance of Power (early modern), 74–85
Balkans: Communist states, 223; crises, 175, 183–185, 187–189; revolts against Turks, 150; Russian ambitions, 113, 183, 187, 188; after World War I, 192, 193, 195. *See also* Albania; Bulgaria; Czechoslovakia; Hungary; Rumania; Yugoslavia
Baroque, 13
Bastille, 106
Batavian Republic, 109, 112
Bavaria: electorate, 62, 65; Hitler in, 202
Bayle, Pierre (1647–1706), 89
Bede, "the Venerable" (673–735), 2
Belgium, 118, 128, 139, 192, 212. *See also* Netherlands
Bellini family, 7
Bentham, Jeremy (1748–1832), 119, 120, 137, 144
Berlin: Conference (1884–1885), 180; Congress of (1878), 183; to Baghdad railway, 186
Bernard, Saint (1116–1153), 18
Berri, Charles, duke of (1778–1820), 122
Bethlen Gabor, prince of Transylvania (1580–1629), 63

Bismarck, Otto von (1815–1898): foreign policy, 181, 183–185; internal consolidation, 167, 168; unification of Germany, 150–153
Black Death, 6
Blanc, Louis (1811–1882), 138, 140
Blitzkrieg, 211
Bloody June Days (1848), 140, 154
Boccaccio, Giovani (1313–1375), 6
Boer War (1899–1902), 178, 179, 186
Bohemia: in Dual Monarchy, 170; revolution (1848), 141, 142; Thirty Years War, 61, 63
Boleyn, Anne (1507–1536), 36
Bologna: Concordat of (1516), 22
Bolshevism, 196, 197, 203, 208
Bonaparte dynasty, 119. *See also* Napoleon, Louis Napoleon
Bonapartism, 140, 141, 164, 165
Bordeaux: National Assembly (1871), 162, 163
Borgia, Caesar (1475–1507), 9
Borodino, Battle of (1812), 113
Bosnia-Herzegovina, 175, 188
Botticelli, Sandro (1444–1510), 6
Boulanger Affair (1889), 164, 165
Bourbon, House of, 59; gains French crown, 42–44; restored after Napoleon, 117, 118, 121–124. *See also* Henry IV; Louis XIII; Louis XIV; Louis XV; Louis XVI; Louis XVIII; Charles X (kings of France) *and* Philip V; Ferdinand VII (kings of Spain)
Boyle, Robert (1627–1691), 55
Brahe, Tycho (1546–1601), 52
Brandenburg, 70, 71, 78
Brest-Litovsk, Treaty of (1918), 196, 197, 209
Britain: Labour Party, 203; foreign policy, 184, 187; imperialism, 166, 176–183; mid-nineteenth century, 143–145, 147, 160, 162; post-war foreign policy, 193, 204, 205–211; post-war, 216, 221–222, 225, 228; World War I, 191; World War II, 211–215. *See also* England, Scotland
British East India Company, 177
British South Africa Company, 178, 179
Brunelleschi, Filippo (1377–1446), 6
Buffon, Georges (1707–1788), 55
Bulgaria, 175, 184
Burgundian Circle, 38
Burgundian inheritance, 38

Burma, 181, 182, 213, 221
Burns, Robert (1759–1796), 121
Byzantine empire: artistic influences, 7–10

Cajetan, cardinal (1469–1534), 18
Calvin, John (1509–1564), 12, 21, 23
Calvinism: early spread of, 23–25, 27, 29, 36, 58; in France, 42–44, 67, 69, 70; in the Netherlands, 39, 40; in Peace of Westphalia, 65; compared with Jansenism, 99; Thirty Years War, 62
Cambodia, 222, 226
Canada, 84, 177, 193
Canning, George (1770–1827), 128
Cape Colony, 178–180
Capitalism, 119, 137, 139
Carlsbad Decrees (1819), 125
Carnot, Lazare (1753–1823), 109, 110
Casablanca, conference at (1943), 214
Castiglione, count Baldassare (1478–1529), 8
Castile, 33
Castlereagh, Robert Stewart, viscount (1769–1822), 127, 128
Castro, Fidel (b. 1927), 226
Catalonia, 66
Cateau-Cambrésis, Peace of (1559), 42
Cathedral schools, 2
Catherine of Aragon (1485–1536), 24, 33, 36
Catherine "the Great," czarina of Russia (1762–1796), 98
Catholic Center Party (Germany), 167
Catholic Emancipation Bill (1829), 127
Catholic League (French), 43, 44
Catholic League (German, 1609), 61–63
Catholic Reformation, 26, 27, 99
Catholic Union (German), 20, 21
Cavaignac, General Louis-Eugène (1802–1857), 140
Cavendish, Henry (1731–1810), 55
Cavour, count Camillo di (1810–1861), 149, 169
Cervantes, Miguel de (1547–1616), 11
Chamberlain, Neville (1869–1940), 210, 212
Chambers of Reunion, 75
Charles VIII, king of France (1483–1498), 2
Charles IX, king of France (1560–1574), 42, 43
Charles X, king of France (1824–1830),

59, 121, 122, 124, 128, 146, 176, 218
Charles V, Holy Roman emperor (1519–1556), 32; in Netherlands, 38; wars with France, 42; religious wars, 18–21; sacks Rome, 24; in Spain, 33
Charles VI, Holy Roman emperor (1711–1740), 81, 82
Charles XI, king of Sweden (1660–1697), 71
Charles XII, king of Sweden (1697–1718), 71, 78, 79
Charles I, king of England (1625–1649), 72
Charles II, king of England (1660–1685), 72, 73
Chartist Movement, 138, 179
Chaucer, Geoffrey (c.1340–1400), 6
Chiang Kai-shek (b. 1887), 198, 222
Child Labor, 135
China: Communist government, 221–223; European imperialism, 182, 183, 193; missionaries in, 27; Opium War, 144; revolution (1911), 194, 197, 198, 199; Korean War, 224; dispute with Soviet Union, 227, 228; war with Japan, 209
Christian IV, king of Denmark (1588–1648), 63
Christianity, challenged by Enlightenment, 90; reinforces Aristotelianism, 47; Renaissance, 3–5, 11–13. *See also* Church; Papacy
Christina, queen of Sweden (1632–1654), 71
Church: early modern, 42, 50, 63, 64, 80, 101, 102; medieval, 2; nineteenth century, 111, 112, 121, 144, 166, 167, 169, 170; Peace of Augsburg, 21, 33, 64; sixteenth century reform, 15–17. *See also* Christianity; Papacy; *names of popes and monastic orders*
Church of England, 25, 27, 58. *See also* Anglicanism
Churchill, Sir Winston (1874–1965), 212, 214
Class warfare, 140, 154, 155
Classical heritage: natural sciences, 14, 50, 51; Renaissance, 5–8
Cleves-Jülich, 61
Clovis, king of the Franks (481–511), 43
Colbert, Jean-Baptiste (1619–1683), 68
Cold War, 216–226
Colonies: eighteenth century rivalries,

81, 82, 84; independence struggles after World War II, 216, 221, 222, 224–227; industrial revolution, 133, 134; nineteenth century imperialism, 176–183

Columbus, Christopher (c.1451–1506), 46

Committee of Public Safety (French Revolution), 107, 109

Common Market, European, 228

Commonwealth (England, 1649–1660), 72

Commune of Paris: French Revolution, 107; in 1871, 163, 193

Communist Information Bureau (Cominform), 220

Communist Party: China, 198, 222; French Resistance, 215; Germany, 202; Russian Revolution, 196, 197

Conciliar movement, 20

Concordat of Bologna (1516), 22

Condottiere, 8, 9

Confederation of Bar (Poland), 84

Confederation of the Rhine, 112

Congo, Independent State of the, 180

Congress of Vienna (1815), 117, 118; Act of the, 118, 124, 129

Conservative Party (Britain), 135

Constantinople, 7

Constitutional Democratic Party (Russia), 172

Constitutional monarchy: in Britain, 144; in France, 121, 123, 139; in Piedmont-Sardinia, 141, 149; in Prussia, 141

Consulate (France, 1799–1804), 111, 112

Continental Blockade, 112, 113

Copernicus, Nicolas (1473–1543), 49–54

Coral Sea, Battle of the (1942), 213

Corn Laws (1815), 126, 127, 138, 139

Cottagers, 133

Council of Blood (Netherlands), 39

Counter-Reformation, 26, 34, 35, 62, 65

Crimean War (1854–1856), 147, 148, 161, 193

Croats, 195

Cromwell, Oliver (1599–1658), 72, 110

Cuba, 84, 226, 227

Czechoslovakia, 192, 195, 210, 211, 217, 227

Czechs, 158

Dante Alighieri (1265–1321), 3, 4, 6

Darwin, Charles (1809–1882), 55, 137

Dawes Plan (1924), 205

Declaration of Independence, 85, 95

Deism, 93, 99

De Kalb, baron Johann, 86

della Rovere popes, 7

Denmark: Great Northern War, 78; war of 1864, 151; and Hitler, 212; Thirty Years War, 63, 198

Depression (1930s), 194, 195, 199, 202, 203, 206, 207, 211

Descartes, René (1596–1650), 53–56, 88

Devolution, War of (1667–1668), 75

Dialectical materialism, 154, 155

Dickens, Charles (1812–1870), 135

Diderot, Denis (1713–1784), 96–98

Diem Bien Phu, 222

Directory (France, 1795–1799), 108–111

Disraeli, Benjamin (1804–1881), 144, 161, 177

Divine right of kings, 71, 72

Domestic system, 132, 135

Don Juan of Austria (1545–1578), 34, 35, 39

Donatello, Donato (1386–1466), 6

Drake, Sir Francis (c.1540–1596), 37

Dreadnought, 187

Dreyfus Affair, 165–167

Dual Alliance (1879), 159, 184

Duma (Russia), 172, 173, 194, 196

Dunes, Battle of the (1658), 66

Dutch, in East Indies, 41, 181, 221. *See also* Netherlands

Dutch War (1672–1678), 75

Eck, Johann Mayer von (1486–1543), 18

Edict of Nantes (1598), 44, 67; revocation, 69, 76

Edict of Restitution (1629), 64, 65

Education Act (1902), 162

Edward VI, king of England (1547–1553), 25

Edward VII, king of England (1901–1910), 162, 218

Egypt, 111, 134, 177, 178, 193, 225

Einstein, Albert (1879–1955), 54

El Alamein, Battle of (1942), 213

Elba, Island of, 114, 116, 117

Elizabeth, czarina of Russia (1741–1762), 83

Elizabeth I, queen of England (1558–1603), 25, 27, 33, 35–37, 71
Emigré nobility, 108, 109
Enabling Act (1933), 202
Enclosures (England), 133
Engels, Friedrich (1820–1895), 154
England: American colonies, 81–85; early modern, 41, 69–73, 75–78; economic problems, and reform, 125–127; Enlightenment, 90, 91; French Revolution and Napoleon, 105, 108–114; Hanoverian succession, 79; industrialization, 130–134; Methodists, 99; nineteenth century foreign policy, 117–119, 128; Reformation, 24–25; Renaissance, 9–11; socialism in, 138, 139; and Spain, 33, 35, 37, 38. *See also* Britain; Parliament
Enlightened Despotism, 97, 98
Enlightenment: 88–98; political influence, 95, 97, 98, 101, 105, 106; reaction against, 98–100, 119–121
Entente Cordiale, 159. *See also* Anglo-French Entente
Erasmus, Desiderius (c.1466–1536), 15, 16, 18; and Catholic Reformation, 26
Estates General (in 1788), 105, 106
d'Etaples, Lefebvre (c.1450–1537), 12, 21
Ethiopia, 169, 180, 208
Evolution, 55, 137
Excommunication: Luther, 18; Henry VIII, 24; Napoleon, 113
Exploration, 132

Factories: in industrial revolution, 131–135; in Russia, 195
Falkland Islands, Battle of the (1914), 191
Farnese, Alexander, duke of Parma (1545–1592), 37, 40, 41
Fascist Party (Italy), 200, 202
Fashoda crisis (1898), 179, 186
Fénélon, François de (1651–1715), 90
Ferdinand of Styria. *See* Ferdinand II
Ferdinand I, Holy Roman emperor (1556–1564), 31, 32
Ferdinand II, Holy Roman emperor (1619–1637), 31, 62–65
Ferdinand VII, king of Spain (1814–1833), 123, 124, 128, 142
Feudalism, in Japan, 182

Flanders, 11
Fleury, cardinal (1726–1743), 80
Florence: Renaissance, 3–8
Fourier, Charles (1772–1837), 138
Fra Angelico (1387–1455), 6
France: Bourbon Restoration, 117–122, 128; Calvinism, 23, 27; civil wars, 42–44; Consulate and Empire, 111–114; Dreyfus Affair, 165–167; eighteenth century foreign affairs, 80–87; eighteenth century social order, 101–105; Enlightenment, 92, 95–97, 98, 99; foreign policy, 185–189; and Habsburg hegemony, 34, 38, 42–44; Indochina, 222, 229; Louis Philippe and 1848 Revolution, 123, 139, 140; nineteenth century imperialism, 176, 177, 181, 183; post-war foreign policy, 192, 193, 201, 204, 205, 208, 209; radical left, 203; reconsolidation, 60; rejection of American domination, 227, 228; religious dissent, 20–22; Renaissance, 10–12; Revolution of 1830, 122, 123, 127, 139; the Revolution of 1789, 105–111; Second Empire, 146, 147, 153; Second Republic, 140, 141; seventeenth century, 66–69, 73; Third Republic, 160, 161, 163–167; Thirty Years War, 64–66; war debts, 206, 207; World War I, 190, 191; World War II, 211–215; wars of Louis XIV, 74–78
Franche-Comté, 32, 75
Francis I, king of France (1515–1547), 12, 21, 22, 29
Francis II, king of France (1559–1560), 29, 35, 36, 42, 43
Francis II, Holy Roman emperor (1792–1806), then emperor of Austria (1806–1835), 31, 108, 218
Francis Ferdinand, archduke of Austria (1863–1914), 188, 189
Francis Joseph, Emperor of Austria (1848–1916), 142, 192, 218
Franco, General Francisco (b.1892), 203, 204
Franco-Prussian War (1870–1871), 148, 149, 153; effects, 161, 162, 164, 183
Franco-Russian Entente (1894), 159, 185, 189, 190
Frankfort, Assembly at (1848–1849), 141

Frederick V, Elector count Palatine (1596–1632), 62, 65
Frederick, Elector of Brandenburg (1688–1701), then Frederick I, King of Prussia (1701–1713), 70
Frederick II "the Great," king of Prussia (1740–1786), 82, 83, 85, 96, 98
Frederick William "the Great Elector" of Brandenburg (1640–1688), 70
Frederick William I, king of Prussia (1713–1740), 80
Free French, 215, 216
Free Imperial Knights, 19, 20
Free trade, 144, 147
French Revolution: (1789), background, 101–105; course of, 105–108; wars, 108–111; (1830), 122, 123; (1848), 123, 139, 140
Friedland, Battle of (1807), 112
Fronde (1648–1652), 68

Gabelle (French salt tax), 104
Galen (c.130–c.210), 49, 50
Galileo Galilei (1564–1642), 26, 52, 53
Galvani, Luigi (1737–1798), 55
Gandhi, "Mahatma" (1869–1948), 221
Garibaldi, Guiseppe (1807–1882), 149
Geneva, 22, 23, 27
George I, king of England (1714–1727), 79
George II, king of England (1727–1760), 79, 83
George III, king of England (1760–1820), 83, 108, 143, 218
German Confederation, 118, 124, 125, 150–152
German Renaissance, 1, 2
Germany: divided, 217, 227, 228; economic collapse and rise of Hitler, 195, 201–203, 205-210; foreign policy, 179–181, 183–189; French hostility, 160–166; internal development, 167, 168; revolutions of 1848, 141–142; revolution of 1918, 192; Treaty of Brest-Litovsk, 196, 197; Treaty of Versailles, 192, 193; unification, 124, 125, 150–153, 157; World War I, 190, 191; World War II, 211–215. *See also* Holy Roman Empire, Prussia
Ghiberti, Lorenzo (1378–1455), 6
Gibraltar, 78
Giotto di Bondone (1266–1337), 6
Gladstone, William (1809–1898), 161, 177

Glorious Revolution (1688), 73, 91
Goethe, Johann Wolfgang von (1749–1832), 99
Gothic style, 7, 10
Grand Alliance (1688, 1701), 76, 77
Grand Army (Napoleonic), 113, 114
Gray, Thomas (1716–1771), 100
Great Encyclopedia, 96, 97, 100
Great Northern War (1700–1721), 79, 80
Great Protestation (1621), 72
Greece, 128, 144, 145, 220
Gregory of Tours (538–594), 2
Guadalcanal, Battle of (1943), 213
Guicciardini, Francesco (1483–1540), 8
Guilds, 3, 132, 135
Guise, House of, 42, 43
Guizot, François (1787–1874), 139, 140
Gustavus II Adolphus, king of Sweden (1611–1632), 64, 65, 71
Gutenberg, Johann (c.1400–1468), 19

Habsburg, House of, 29; decline, 112, 141, 142, 150, 192; sixteenth century hegemony, 32–44, 60, 75, 76; Thirty Years War, 61–66, 73. *See also* Maximilian I; Charles V; Ferdinand I; Ferdinand II; Joseph II; Leopold II; Francis II; Francis Joseph (Holy Roman Emperors); Philip II, Philip III, Philip IV (Kings of Spain); Holy Roman Empire; Austria; Spain
Hanover, 78, 79, 83, 157; House of, 79
Hansa (league of towns), 19
Harvey, William (1578–1657), 54
Hegel, Georg W. F. (1770–1831), 154
Henry Tudor. *See* Henry VII
Henry VIII, king of England (1509–1547), 21, 24, 25, 30, 36
Henry II, king of France (1547–1559), 12, 23, 29, 42, 49
Henry III, king of France (1574–1589), 29, 43, 44
Henry IV, king of France (1589–1610), 29, 43, 44, 60, 66
Herder, Johann G. von (1744–1803), 99
Hindenburg, Marshal Paul von (1847–1934), 202
Hitler, Adolph (1889–1945), 201–203, 207–213
Hobbes, Thomas (1588–1679), 90, 91
Hobereaux, 237
Hohenzollern, 70
Holland, 6. *See also* Netherlands

Holstein, 63, 151, 152
Holy Alliance (1815), 119
Holy Roman emperors: French Revolutionary wars, 3; failure, 70, 74; Thirty Years War, 60–66
Holy Roman Empire, xx, 112, 118. *See also* Holy Roman emperors; *names of emperors* and *names of imperial families*
Hoover, Herbert (1874–1964), 207
Hubertusburg, Treaty of (1763), 84
Hudson's Bay Territory, 77
Huguenots, 43, 44, 64, 67, 69, 70, 76
Humanism: and Erasmus, 15, 16, 18; in Italian Renaissance, 3, 4, 7, 11, 12
Hume, David (1711–1766), 93, 99, 100
Hundred Days, 118, 119, 121
Hungary, 20, 63, 70, 158; autonomous government, 150; communist government, 217; revolt of 1848, 141, 142; republic, 192; Soviet intervention, 227; subject nationalities, 170, 195
Hus, John (c.1369–1415), 18
Hussites, 18, 62
Hutton, James (1726–1797), 55

Ignatius Loyola, saint (1491–1556), 26
Imperialism: *pre-nineteenth century,* see Colonialism: 176–188; Japanese in 1930s, 198, 199; Fascist Italy, 200
Independent Labour Party, 162, 203, 216
Index of Banned Books, 26
India, 51, 84, 108, 177, 181, 193, 213, 221, 228
Indochina: French defeat, 222; French in, 181–183; Japanese occupation, 212
Indonesia, 181, 213, 221
Indulgences, 6, 7
Industrial Revolution, 130, 134
Industrialization: in eighteenth and nineteenth centuries, 123, 130, 134, 160, 168, 184; and imperialism, 176; in Russia, 172, 196, 197; in Japan, 181, 182; and protectionism, 206; and socialism, 137, 140, 154; and urbanization, 130, 134, 135
Inquisition, 16, 39
Intendents, 68
International Association for the Exploration and Civilization of Central Africa, 180

Ireland, 108, 127, 161, 162
Iron law of wages, 136, 154
Irredentism: Italian, 169, 171, 187; Rumanian, 171
Isabella II, queen of Spain (1833–1868), 153
Italy: depression, 207; Enlightenment, 98; foreign policy, 184, Habsburg domination, 33, 34, 70, 77, 118; imperialism, 179, 180, 208; irredentism, 161, 169, 171; post-war, 216; problems with church, 169, 170; Renaissance, 2, 14; Revolutionary Wars in, 111; revolutions (1820s and 1830s), 123, 124; revolutions of 1848, 141; rise of Mussolini, 199–201; unification, 147, 149, 152, 153; World War I, 191, 192; World War II, 212, 213

Jacobins, 107, 108, 123, 163
Jacobites, 79
James I, king of England (1603–1625), 30, 36, 62, 63
James II, king of England (1685–1688), 30, 73, 79
Jameson Raid (1895), 179, 186
Jansenists, 99
Japan, 69, 181, 182, 194; imperialism of, 183, 198, 199, 203, 209; Russo-Japanese War, 172, 187; World War II, 212–214
Jena, Battle of (1806), 112
Jenkins' Ear, War of (1739–1748), 81
Jesuits, 26, 27, 167
Jews: anti-Semitism, 213; founding of Israel, 225
Joffre, Marshal Joseph (1852–1931), 82
Joseph II, Holy Roman emperor (1780–1790), 31, 98
Jutland, Battle of (1916), 191

Kaunitz, Wenzel Anton von (1711–1794), 83
Kellogg-Briand Pact (1928), 206
Kepler, Johannes (1571–1630), 52, 53, 54
Kitchener, General Lord Horatio H., (1850–1916), 177
Knox, John (1505–1572), 23, 36
Korea, 182, 183, 217; Korean War (1950–1953), 223, 224
Kruger, Paul (1825–1904), 178, 179, 186
Kulturkampf, 167, 168

Kuomintang Party, 197, 198, 222

Labor laws (England, 1883), 127
Lafayette, Marquis de (1757–1834), 86, 123, 139
Laibach, conference at (1821), 128
Laissez-faire doctrines, 136, 137
Lamarck, Chevalier de (1744–1829), 55
Laos, 222, 226
La Rochelle, siege of (1627–1628), 67
Lassalle, Ferdinand (1825–1864), 168
Lavoisier, Antoine-Laurent de (1743–1794), 55
Law of Guarantees (1871), 169
League of Nations (1920–1946), 192, 206–209
LeBreton, André-François (1708–1779), 97
Legislative Assembly (France, 1791–1792), 107
Leibnitz, Gottfried von (1646–1716), 53, 93
Leipzig, Battle of (1813), 114
Lend-Lease Act (1941), 212
Lenin, Nikolai (1870–1924), 155, 196, 197
Leopold II, Holy Roman emperor (1790–1792), 31, 98
Leopold II, king of the Belgians (1865–1909), 180
Lepanto, Battle of (1571), 34, 35
Liberal Party (Britain), 135
Liberalism, 119–128; in Belgian Revolution, 139; "classical", 137; in Habsburg Empire, 139, 141, 142; in Russia, 171, 172
Linnaeus, Carolus (1707–1778), 55
Locarno Treaties (1925), 205
Locke, John (1632–1704), 56, 90, 91, 100
Lombardy, 141
Lorraine, 164, 183, 190; House of, 42
Louis XIII, king of France (1610–1643), 41, 59, 64–68
Louis XIV, king of France (1643–1715), 59, 66–67, 74–77, 80
Louis XV, king of France (1715–1774), 59, 80
Louis XVI, king of France (1774–1792), 59, 85, 86, 98, 105–109
Louis XVIII, king of France (1814–1824), 121, 123
Louis Napoleon Bonaparte (1808–

1873), 140, 141, 145, 146; Napoleon III, 134, 146–148, 150–153, 162, 176
Louis Philippe, king of the French (1830–1848), 123, 139, 140, 176
Louvois, Michel Le Tellier, marquis de (1641–1691), 68
Lübeck, Treaty of (1629), 63
Ludendorff, General Erich von (1865–1937), 201, 202
Ludovico "the Moor" (1425–1508), 7
Lunéville, Treaty of (1801), 111
Lusitania, 191
Luther, Martin (1483–1546), 15–19, 23, 24, 51, 125
Lutheranism, 17–22, 24–33, 42, 58, 62, 64, 65
Lütter am Barenberge, Battle of (1626), 63
Lutzen, Battle of (1632), 64
Luxemburg, 118, 189, 212
Lyons: revolts (1848), 123

Mabilon, Jean (1632–1707), 89
Machiavelli, Niccolo (1469–1527), 7–9
MacMahon, Marshal Patrice de (1808–1893), 163, 164
Madagascar, 179, 180
Magyars: nationalism, 170, 171, 188; raids, 2; revolts, (1848, 1849), 141, 142
Malaya, 181, 213, 221, 222
Malebranche, Nicolas de (1638–1715), 56, 90
Malpighi, Marcello (1628–1694), 54
Manchuria, 182, 183, 198, 208, 217
Maria Theresa, empress of Austria (1740–1780), 31, 82, 83, 98
Marlborough, John Churchill, first duke of (1650–1722), 77
Marne, Battle of the (1914), 190, 191
Marshall Plan, 220
Marxism, 154, 155, 168
Mary I, queen of England (1552–1558), 24, 25, 30, 33
Mary II, queen of England (1689–1694), 30, 73, 79
Mary Stuart, queen of Scots (1542–1587), 30, 35–37
Mathematics, development of, 51, 52, 56
Matthias, king of Bohemia and Holy Roman emperor (1612–1619), 61, 62
Maximilian I, Holy Roman Emperor (1493–1519), 29, 38

Maximilian, emperor of Mexico (1864–1867), 148

Maximilian I, duke of Bavaria (1573–1651), 62

Mazarin, cardinal (1602–1661), 68, 74

Medici: House of, 6, 7; Catherine de (1519–1589), 42; Cosimo di (1434–1464), 6, 7; Lorenzo "the Magnificent" (1449–1492), 6

Medicine, in scientific revolution, 47–51, 54, 57

Mediterranean Agreements (1880s), 185, 186

Mediterranean basin, 34; Sea, 34, 184, 185, 187

Meiji Restoration, 182

Mennonites, 24

Mercantilism, 133, 134, 137

Mercenaries: in Renaissance Italy, 9

Methodism, 99, 120

Metternich, Prince Klemens von, 124, 125, 128, 141

Mexico, 147, 148

Michelangelo Buonarroti (1475–1564), 13

Midway, Battle of (1942), 213

Milan, 7, 10, 32

Ministerial responsibility, 164

Modena, 147, 149

Monarchists (French Third Republic), 163–167

Monroe Doctrine (1823), 128, 226

Montaigne, Michel de (1533–1592), 12

Montesquieu, Charles de Secondat, baron de (1689–1755), 95, 96

Montmorency, House of, 42, 43, 67

Moors, 33. *See also* Moslems

Moravian brethren, 99

Morocco, 179, 180, 187

Moscow, 113, 195, 197

Moslems: war with Spain, 11, 34, 35. *See also* Moors

Munich: revolt in (1918), 192; Agreements (1938), 211

Mussolini, Benito (1883–1945), 169, 200, 201, 204, 216

Nantes, Edict of, *see* Edict of Nantes

Naples, 10, 32, 66, 112, 113; Kingdom of, 124, 128, 129, 149

Napoleon Bonaparte: General, 108, 110, 111; Emperor Napoleon I (1804–1814), 112–114, 119, 140, 195; First Consul (1799–1804), 111, 112

Napoleon III. *See* Louis Napoleon Bonaparte

National Assembly (France, 1789–1791), 106, 107

National consciousness: English, 73; Sweden, 71

National consolidations: religion in, 21, 23, 58; in seventeenth century, 66–71, 73

National Convention (France, 1792–1795), 107–109

National Insurance Act (1911), 162

National Socialist German Workers Party. *See* Nazis

National workshops (France), 140

Nationalism, 120, 124, 125, 128, 139–146, 149–151, 153, 161, 169, 176; in colonial independence movements, 222, 224–226; division in Austria-Hungary, 158, 161, 170, 171; French anti-German expression, 164–167; Slavic, 185, 187, 188; in 1920s and 1930s, 197, 200, 202, 203, 206, 209, 210

Nations, Battle of the (1813), 114

Natural Law, 91, 92, 94, 136

Natural philosophy, 45–48

Natural religion, 93

Natural rights, 94, 95, 98

Nazis, 195, 201, 203, 207, 210

Necker, Jacques (1732–1804), 106

Netherlands, 23, 27, 38, 52, 212; Austrian, 77, 109, 111; Dutch, 39–41, 60, 61, 65, 69, 70, 73, 75–78, 109, 110; Kingdom of the (1815), 118, 119; and Spain, 23, 32, 33, 35, 38–41; Spanish, 62, 66, 70, 75–77

Neuilly, Treaty of (1919), 192

New Economic Policy (Russia, 1921), 197

New Socialist Offensive (Russia), 197

Newcomen, Thomas (1663–1729), 131

Newton, Sir Isaac (1642–1727), 52–54, 56, 88, 90, 91

Nicholas I, czar of Russia (1825–1855), 59, 150, 218

Nicholas II, czar of Russia (1894–1917), 59, 172, 173, 196, 218

Nicholas V, pope (1447–1455), 7

Nimwegen, Peace of (1678), 75

Ninety-five Theses (Luther, 1517), 18

Nobility: in early modern France, 67,

68, 102, 103; exodus in French Revolution, 106, 108, 109
Nördlingen, Battle of (1634), 65
North Atlantic Treaty (1949), 220
North German Confederation, 152, 153
Northmen. See Vikings
Norway, 212
Nystadt, Treaty of (1721), 79

October Manifesto (Russia, 1905), 172
Old Age Pension Law (Britain, 1909), 162
Olivarez, Gaspar de Guzman, count-duke (1587–1645), 66, 67
Opium War (1840), 144, 182
Optimism (Enlightenment), 93, 94
Orange, House of, 69
Orange Free State, 174, 178, 179
Orléanist monarchy. See Louis Philippe
Orléans: duke Philippe III (1674–1723), regent of France, 80
Ottoman Turks. See Turks
Owen, Robert (1771–1858), 138

Pacification of Ghent (1576), 39, 40
Pacifico, Don (fl. 1850), 144
Pacifism, 211
Pakistan, 221
Palatinate (in Thirty Years War), 62, 65
Palestine, 225
Palladio, Andrea (1508–1580), 13
Palmerston, Henry Temple, Lord (1784–1865), 145
Panama Canal, 165
Pan-Slavism: 1848 Congress in Prague, 141; in Russia, 171, 187
Papacy: Conciliar Movement, 20; dogma of papal infallibility, 167; and Habsburgs, 34; sixteenth century reformation, 18, 22, 26; in unified Italy, 169, 170, 201. See also Church: Christianity; names of popes
Papal States, XXII, 10, 111, 113; unification of Italy, 147, 149, 156
Paris: Commune (1871), 163; early modern, 21, 22, 44, 68; Enlightenment, 92, 100; peace conference at (1919), 192; Revolution (1789), 106, 107; Revolution (1830), 122, 139; Revolution (1848), 123, 139, 140
Paris, Treaty of: American War of Independence (1783), 86; Napoleonic Wars (1814, 1815), 117, 119; Seven Years War (1763), 84
Parlement of Paris, 105
Parliament (English): development, 71–73; establishes Church of England, 25; nineteenth century reform laws, 127, 144, 145
Parma, 147, 149; Duke of, see Alexander Farnese
Pascal, Blaise (1623–1662), 53
Pays d'élection, Pays d'états, 104
Peasants: eighteenth century French, 103, 104, 106; nineteenth century Irish, 127, 161, 162; Russian, 171, 172, 195
Peel, Sir Robert (1788–1850), 127, 144
People's Charter, 138
Perry, Commodore Matthew C. (1794–1858), 182
Persia, 187
Peter I "the Great," czar of Russia (1689–1725), 59, 78–80
Peter III, czar of Russia (1762), 59, 83, 84
Peterloo massacre (1819), 126, 138
Petition of Right (1628), 72
Petrarch, Francesco (1304–1374), 6
Philip II, king of Spain (1556–1598), 25, 27, 31, 32–44
Philip III, king of Spain (1598–1621), 31, 41, 60
Philip IV, king of Spain (1621–1665), 31, 66
Philip V, king of Spain (1700–1746), 31, 77, 80
Philippines, 27, 181, 213
Philosophes, 95, 97, 100, 105
Piedmont-Sardinia: constitutional monarchy, 141; revolt (1821), 124, 139; unification of Italy, 147, 149, 156
Pietism, 12, 17, 18, 99, 120
Pillnitz, Declaration of (1791), 108
Pitt, William (1708–1778), 84
Pius X, pope (1903–1914), 169
Poincaré, Raymond (1860–1934), 188, 189
Poland: communist government, 217; early modern, 71, 81, 84, 85; German invasion (1939), 211, 212; independence, 192, 195; nineteenth century, 117, 118, 149, 150, 158; World War I, 191, 197
Polignac, Jules Armand, prince de (1780–1847), 122

Polish Succession, War of the (1733–1735), 81
Politiques, 44
Pompadour, Jeanne Antoinette Poisson, marquise de (1721–1764), 83
Pope, popes. *See* Papacy; *names of popes*
Popular piety: eighteenth century, 98, 99, 120
Populist movement (Russia), 171, 172
Portugal, 37, 40, 66, 98, 113, 114
Potsdam conference (1945), 214
Power of the Keys, 17
Pragmatic Sanction (Austrian), 82
Prague: Pan-Slav Congress (1848), 141; Peace of (1635), 65
Predestination, 22
Printing press, 13, 19, 51
Proletariat: growth, 130, 134–136, 161; in Germany, 168; in Russia, 172, 196, 197; socialist development and revolts, 138–140, 154, 155
Protestant Reformation. *See* Reformation of the sixteenth century
Protestant Union (1608), 61, 62
Prussia: Congress of Vienna and Quadruple Alliance, 117–119; eighteenth century, 78–85; Revolutionary and Napoleonic Wars, 107, 109, 112, 114; revolutions of 1848, 141, 142; royal crown acquired, 70, 71, 78; and unification of Germany, 124, 125, 148–153, 157
Ptolemy, 14, 48–50
Public Schools (Britain), 161
Purgatory, 17
Puritans, 72
Pyrenees, Peace of the (1659), 66, 74

Quadruple Alliance (1815), 119, 128
Québec, Battle of (1759), 84
Quietists, 99

Rabelais, François (c.1494–1553), 11, 12
Radicalism, 137, 140, 141, 163, 171–173
Railway construction, 134, 146, 172, 182, 186
Rastatt, Treaty of (1714), 77, 78, 80
Rationalism, 90–93, 97
Reformation, Sixteenth century. *See* Anabaptists; Anglicanism; Calvin; Calvinism; Catholic Reformation; Charles V; Council of Trent; Edward V; Elizabeth I; Henry IV; Henry VIII; Jesuits; Knox; Luther; Lutheranism; Mary I; Mary Stuart; Philip II; Zwingli
Reign of Terror, 107, 109, 163
Reinsurance Treaty (1887), 185
Religious Wars: France, 43, 44, 64, 67; Germany, 19–21: Thirty Years War, 61–65
Renaissance, 18, 19, 50, 51; Carolingian, 2; Italian, 2–9; northern, 9–14, 19
Reparations, 192, 201, 205–207
Republicanism: in France, 107, 122, 123, 139, 140, 146, 163, 164; in pre-Victorian England, 137
Requesens, Luis de Zuñiga y (1528–1576), 39
Restoration (post-Napoleonic), 120–124
Revolts: in China, 182; in sixteenth century Germany, 20
Revolutions: after World War I, 192; Belgium, 128, 139; China, 194, 222, 223; France, 101–111, 122, 123, 139, 140; Germany, 124, 125; Greece, 128, 193; Hungary, 142, 143, 167; in Marxism, 153, 154; Naples, 128; Piedmont-Sardinia, 124, 139; Poland, 123, 149, 150; repercussions in England, 127; rioting in Germany and Italy, 141; Russia, 172, 173, 191, 195–197, 203; Spain, 123, 128, 153
Rhineland, 192, 208
Rhodes, Cecil (1853–1902), 178, 179
Rhodesia, 178, 225
Richelieu, Armand Jean du Plesis, cardinal de (1585–1642), 65–68
Robespierre, Maximilien de (1758–1794), 107
Rochambeau, J. B. Donatien, comte de (1725–1807), 86
Rocroy, Battle of (1643), 66
Roman Inquisition, 26
Roman Republic (1849), 142, 145, 147, 149
Romanesque style, 10
Romanticism, 120, 121
Rome, 24; capital of Italy, 149, 169; Renaissance, 7; Republic (1849), 142, 145–147
Rome-Berlin Axis (1936–1944), 208

Ronsard, Pierre de (1524–1585), 12
Roosevelt, Franklin Delano (1882–1945), 214
Rousseau, Jean-Jacques (1712–1778), 100, 121
Ruhr (French occupation, 1923–1925), 201, 205
Rumania, 171, 219, 227
Russia, 78–81, 83–85, 111–114; internal development, 150, 171–173; nineteenth century foreign policy, 117–119, 128, 147, 148, 161, 181–189; World War I, 190, 191; Revolution (1917), 195–197, 201; in Spanish Civil War, 204. *See also* Union of Soviet Socialist Republics
Russification, 171
Russo-Japanese War (1904–1905), 172, 187, 198
Ruthenians, 195, 219
Ryswick, Peace of (1697), 76

Saar, 192
St. Germain, Treaty of (1919), 192
St. Helena, Island of, 118
St. Petersburg, 172, 195, 197
Saint Simon, Claude Henri, comte de (1760–1825), 138
Salic Law, 43
Saratoga, Battle of (1777), 86
Sardinia, 78, 81, 118, 119, 124
Savoy: ceded to France (1860), 147; duke of, 76, 78
Saxony, 18, 78, 83, 117, 118, 157
Scandinavia, 21, 27. *See also* Denmark; Sweden
Schleswig-Holstein, 151, 152, 157
Schlieffen Plan (1905), 190
Schmalkaldic League, 20
Scientific method, 45, 55, 56
Scientific Revolution, 45, 47–57, 88, 90
Scotland, 23, 27, 35, 36, 79, 82
Scripture, 18; in Enlightenment, 89, 90; Methodists, 99
Sedan, Battle of (1870), 148
Serbia, 158, 184, 187–189
Seven Years War (1756–1763), 83–85
Sforza, House of, 7, 10
Shakespeare, William (1564–1616), 11
Shogun (Japan), 182
Siam, 181
Sicily, XXII, 81, 149, 156, 214
Silesia, 82, 84
Simon, Richard (1638–1712), 89, 90
Sino-Japanese War (1894–1895), 182

Six Acts (England, 1819), 126
Slave trade, 81, 117, 127, 178, 180
Slavs, 170, 171; Pan-Slav movement, 171, 185–188, 195
Smith, Adam (1723–1790), 119, 136
Smoot-Hawley Tariff Act (1929), 206, 207
Social Contract, 90, 91, 95
Social Darwinism, 137
Social Democratic Party (Russia), 172
Social Revolutionary Party (Russia), 172
Socialism, 123, 137–141, 146, 154, 155, 162, 164, 168, 171–173, 192, 195–197, 199, 200, 211
Socialist Workingman's Party (Germany), 168
Society of Jesus. *See* Jesuits
South America, 128, 226
South East Asia Treaty (1954), 220, 221, 226
Spain: eighteenth century, 80, 81, 84; end of hegemony, 60, 68, 70, 74–77; French Revolutionary and Napoleonic Wars, 109, 113, 114; Philip II, 32, 35, 37–42, 44; Renaissance, 9–11; restoration, 118, 123, 124, 128, 129, 153; Mediterranean Agreements (1887), 185; Civil War (1936–1939), 203, 204, 208
Spanish Armada. *See* Armada of Spain
Spanish Inquisition, 26, 39
Spanish Netherlands. *See* Netherlands
Spanish Succession, War of the (1701–1714), 77
Spencer, Herbert (1820–1903), 136, 137
Speyer, Diets of (1526, 1529), 20
Spinoza, Baruch (1632–1677), 56
Stalin, Josef (1879–1953), 197, 209, 212–214, 217
Stalingrad, Siege of (1942), 213
Steam power, 130–132, 134
Steamship, 134, 177
Stockholm, Treaty of (1720–1721), 79
Strasbourg, 76
Stuart, House of, 30, 35, 36, 72, 73; Charles Edward, 82; James Edward, 79. *See also* James I, Charles I, Charles II, James II
Submarine warfare, 191
Sudan, 177, 179
Sudeten Germans, 195, 210, 211
Suez Canal, 134, 177
Sun Yat-sen (1866–1925), 197

Sweden, 21; eighteenth century, 71, 73, 78, 79; Napoleonic Wars, 112; Thirty Years War, 64, 65. *See also* Gustavus Adolphus; Charles XI; Charles XII; Christina
Switzerland, 22–24, 60, 65, 111, 118

Taille (French tax), 104
T'ai P'ing Rebellion (1850), 182
Taiwan, 222, 223
Talleyrand, Charles-Maurice de (1754–1838), 118
Tax-farmers, 104
Tehran Conference (1943–1944), 214
Tetzel, Johannes (1465–1519), 17, 18
Thiers, Adolphe (1797–1877), 163
Thirty Years War, 41, 61–65, 69, 70
Three Emperors League (1881), 184, 185
Three Power Pact (1940), 212
Tilsit, Treaties of (1807), 112
Tintoretto, Jacopo Robusti (1518–1594), 7
Titian, Tiziano Vecellio (1477–1576), 7
Tokyo, 199
Tories, 73, 79, 125–127, 139, 144
Tory democracy, 144, 161
Towns: Church as center, 18; medieval, 3, 4
Trade Disputes Bill (1906), 162
Trade unionism, 138, 155, 161
Trafalgar, Battle of (1805), 112
Transvaal, 178, 179, 186
Transylvania, 63, 171
Trent, Council of (1545–1563), 26
Triple Alliance: seventeenth century, 75; (1882), 185–187, 191
Triple Entente (1907), 187
Tripoli, 179
Troppau, Conference at (1820), 128
Truman, Harry S (1884–1972), 214
Tudor, House of, 30. *See also* Elizabeth I; Henry VIII; Mary I
Tunis, 179, 180
Turgot, Anne Robert (1727–1781), 98
Turkestan, 181
Turkey, civil war (1947), 220
Turks: Ottoman, 20, 32, 34, 61, 70, 78, 84, 108, 128, 183, 184, 187
Tuscany, 3, 141, 147, 149
Twelve Years' Truce (1609–1621), 41, 60

Ukrainians, 195, 196

Ultraroyalists (Ultras, France), 121, 122
Union of Liberation (Russia), 172
Union of Soviet Socialist Republics: foreign policy, 208, 209, 211, 214, 216–217, 220–222, 224–227; organized (1922), 197
Union of South Africa, 179, 193
Union of Utrecht (1579), 41
Unions (trade), 127, 162, 164
United Nations, 214, 216, 217, 224, 228
United Netherlands. *See* Netherlands
United States of America: Civil War, 145; Cold War, 216, 220, 221, 223–226; founded (1777), 86; French in Mexico, 148; internal problems, 227; and Japan, 181, 182; Monroe Doctrine, 128; Philippines, 181; postwar, 192, 193, 206–209; World War I, 191; World War II, 212–215
Universal manhood suffrage, 107, 137, 138, 140, 146, 164, 170
Universities: medieval, 2; and renaissance, 11; and scientific revolution, 50
Uomo universale, 8
Urbanization, 130, 133–136
Utopian socialists, 138
Utrecht, Treaty of (1713), 77–81

Valmy, Battle of (1792), 109
Valois, House of, 42, 44. *See also* Charles VIII; Francis I
Vasa, House of, 41
Vatican, 169, 201; Library, 7; State, 169
Venetia, 147, 149, 151, 152, 169
Venice: Habsburgs in, 34; Renaissance, 7; revolution of 1848, 141
Verona, conference at (1822), 128
Versailles, 68, 69, 163; and Hitler, 207, 208, 210; Treaty of (1919), 192, 193, 205
Vesalius, Andreas (1514–1564), 49–52, 54
Victor Emmanuel II, king of Piedmont-Sardinia (1849–1861), then king of Italy (1861–1878), 149, 218
Victoria, queen of England (1837–1901), 137, 143, 144, 162
Vienna, 20, 64, 141, 142; Congress of. *See* Congress of Vienna
Viet Nam, 222, 225, 228
Vikings, 2

Vinci, Leonardo da (1452–1519), 6, 7
Volta, count Alessandro (1745–1827), 55
Voltaire, François-Marie Arouet (1694–1778), 22, 92, 94, 96, 98

Wagram, Battle of (1809), 113
Wallenstein, Albrecht von (1583–1634), 63–65, 67
Walpole, Sir Robert (1726–1742), 79, 81, 82
War debts, 206, 207
Wars of the Roses (1455–1485), 24
Warsaw Pact (1955), 221
Washington, George (1732–1799), 86
Waterloo, Battle of (1815), 118, 121
Watt, James (1736–1819), 131
Wellington, Arthur Wellesley, duke of (1769–1852), 114, 118, 121, 127
Wesley, John (1703–1791), 99
Westphalia: kingdom of, 113; Peace of (1648), 66, 75
Whigs, 73, 79, 81, 127, 144
White Mountain, Battle of (1620), 62
White Terror (France), 121, 122
Whitefield, George (1714–1770), 99
Will of the People (Russia), 171
William I of Nassau-Orange, "the Silent" (1533–1584), 40
William III of Orange (1650–1702), Stadtholder of Dutch Netherlands, then king of England (1689–1702), 30, 69, 73, 75, 76, 79, 91
William I, king of Prussia (1861–1871), then German emperor (1871–1888), 150, 153, 218
William II, German emperor (1888–1918), 185, 186, 192, 218
Wilson, Woodrow (1856–1924), 192, 193
Witt, John de (1625–1672), 69
Wolff, Christian (1679–1754), 94
Workmen's Compensation Act (1906), 162
World War I (1914–1918), 188–194; results, 199–201, 211
World War II (1939–1945), 211–215
Worms, Diet of (1521), 18

Yalta Conference (1945), 214
Yorktown, Battle of (1781), 86
Young Czechs, 170
Young Plan (1929), 206
Yugoslavia, 192, 195, 219, 220

Zero, mathematical concept, 51
Zola, Emile (1840–1902), 135, 165
Zollverein, 125
Zwinglians, 23, 24